WORKSHOPS IN COMPUTING
Series edited by C. J. van Rijsbergen

Also in this series

AI and Cognitive Science '89, Dublin City University, Eire,
14–15 September 1989
A. F. Smeaton and G. McDermott (Eds.)

Specification and Verification of Concurrent Systems, University of
Stirling, Scotland, 6–8 July 1988
C. Rattray (Ed.)

Semantics for Concurrency, Proceedings of the International
BCS-FACS Workshop, Sponsored by Logic for IT (S.E.R.C.), University
of Leicester, UK, 23–25 July 1990
M. Z. Kwiatkowska, M. W. Shields and R. M. Thomas (Eds.)

Functional Programming, Proceedings of the 1989 Glasgow
Workshop, Fraserburgh, Scotland, 21–23 August 1989
K. Davis and J. Hughes (Eds.)

Persistent Object Systems, Proceedings of the Third International
Workshop, Newcastle, Australia, 10–13 January 1989
J. Rosenberg and D. Koch (Eds.)

Z User Workshop, Proceedings of the Fourth Annual Z User Meeting,
Oxford, 15 December 1989
J. E. Nicholls (Ed.)

Dan Craigen (Editor) and
Karen Summerskill (Assistant Editor)

Formal Methods for Trustworthy Computer Systems (FM89)

Report from FM89: A Workshop on the
Assessment of Formal Methods for
Trustworthy Computer Systems

23–27 July 1989, Halifax, Canada

Published in collaboration with the
British Computer Society

Springer-Verlag Berlin Heidelberg GmbH

Dan Craigen, MSc
Odyssey Research Associates
265 Carling Avenue, Suite 506
Ottawa, Ontario K1S 2E1, Canada

Karen Summerskill, BA
Odyssey Research Associates
265 Carling Avenue, Suite 506
Ottawa, Ontario K1S 2E1, Canada

ISBN 978-3-540-19635-8

British Library Cataloguing in Publication Data
Workshop on the Assessment of Formal Methods for Trustworthy Computer Systems
(1989, Halifax, N. S.)
Formal Methods for Trustworthy Computer Systems (FM89): A Workshop on the
Assessment of Formal Methods for Trustworthy Computer Systems, 23–27 July 1989,
Nova Scotia, Canada. – (Workshops in Computing).
1. Computer systems.   I. Title II. Craigen, Dan *1953–*   III. Summerskill, Karen
1958– IV. Series 004
ISBN 978-3-540-19635-8   ISBN 978-1-4471-3532-6 (eBook)
DOI 10.1007/978-1-4471-3532-6
Library of Congress Cataloging-in-Publication Data
Workshop on the Assessment of Formal Methods for Trustworthy Computer Systems
(1989:Halifax, N.S.)
Formal methods for trustworthy computer systems (FM89):report from FM89 – a
Workshop on the Assessment of Formal Methods for Trustworthy Computer Systems,
23–27 July 1989, Nova Scotia, Canada/Dan Craigen, editor, and Karen Summerskill,
assistant editor.
    p.cm. – (Workshops in computing)
"Published in collaboration with the British Computer Society."
ISBN 978-3-540-19635-8

1. Computer software – Validation – Congresses.   2. Computer software –
Verification – Congresses.   3. Computer software – Testing – Congresses.
I. Craigen, Dan, 1953–   .   II. Summerskill, Karen, 1958–   .   III. Title.   IV. Series.
QA76.76.V47W67   1989
005.1'4 – dc20   90–10317
                                                                            CIP

2128/3916–543210   Printed on acid-free paper

Prologue

Computer controlled systems are penetrating almost every aspect of our society. The diversity of application is staggering and includes accounting packages, banking systems, financial markets, flight control systems, medical systems, nuclear reactor shutdown systems, and switching systems.

Yet, it is generally recognized that much of the development of computer controlled systems, and especially of the software, is still in a craft stage. The behaviours of the resulting systems are often unpredictable. The mathematical and scientific foundations for the development of such systems and for the predictability of their behaviours are still rather limited, and those which exist have been applied only to a limited extent.

The software crisis is ongoing and no end is in sight. Systems continue to be delivered late, over budget, and without meeting client requirements. The poor state of affairs is further manifested by a software industry which, to a great extent, does not provide warranties for the products it develops. It would seem that the quality of systems is so poor that not only are warranties not provided, but the customer must pay (through maintenance agreements) to have the systems fixed. Professional accreditation of individuals developing critical systems is not required and, furthermore, the standards for such accreditation have not been defined.

With computer technology increasingly controlling critical systems, it is crucial that our methods for developing and understanding systems be substantially improved. When lives are at stake (as, for example, with nuclear reactor shutdown systems and heart pacemakers) it is exceedingly dangerous to depend upon unscientific processes. Systems must be developed in such a way that assurance can be measured and decisions can be made on a scientific basis to determine whether the benefits of fielding the system outweigh the risks.

Technology has brought many benefits to society, but there are also risks. A list of illustrative risks in the use of computer systems and related technology is appended to these proceedings. The extent of this list makes it clear that the concerns are not solely intellectual curiosities. People *have* died. Systems *have* been lost. Confidential data *has* been illicitly acquired. Money *has* been lost.

If we are unable to improve the quality of the systems we develop, if we are unable to improve our understanding of how they will behave, if we are unable to measure the risks entailed from the fielding of systems, then there is the danger of a backlash and the possibility that the beneficial applications of the technology will be disallowed because of fears of the potential failures. No technology is perfect; but we must be able to identify the boundaries of the technology and the risks entailed.

It was with this backdrop that the 1989 *Workshop on the Assessment of Formal Methods for Trustworthy Computer Systems (FM89)* was held.

28 November 1989   Dan Craigen
                                                          Ottawa, Ontario

Acknowledgements

The organizing committee for the 1989 *Workshop on the Assessment of Formal Methods for Trustworthy Computer Systems (FM89)* consisted of Dan Craigen, Susan Gerhart, Norm Glick, Larry Hatch, Milan Kuchta, Peter Ryan and Jim Woodcock.

Particular acknowledgement is due to Karen Summerskill for organizing the Halifax facilities for *FM89*. Ms. Summerskill also copy-edited and typeset this report.

Sections of this report were written by members of the organizing committee. Carl Landwehr, John Rushby, Martyn Thomas and Jeannette Wing chaired the working group sessions and helped prepare the reports on their sessions.

Our thanks go to Peter Neumann for his permission to include his list of "Illustrative risks to the public in the use of computer systems and related technologies" in this document.

Summary reports of *FM89* appear in the following:

"Formal methodists warn of software disasters" (1 page news item)
Susan Gerhart, *IEEE Software*, November 1989.

"Preliminary Summary: FM89 Assessment of Formal Methods for Trustworthy Computer Systems"
Susan Gerhart, In: Proceedings of the *ACM SIGSOFT'89 Third Symposium on Software, Testing, Analysis, and Verification (TAV3)*, in *Software Engineering Notes* 14(8):152–155, December 1989, ACM Press.

"FM89: Assessment of Formal Methods for Trustworthy Computer Systems"
Dan Craigen, In: Proceedings of the *12th International Conference on Software Engineering*, Nice, France, March 1990, pp. 233–235.

Of course, this report would not have been possible without the active involvement of those who attended the workshop. A list of participants and their affiliations is presented in Appendix A.

Contents

1   Introduction

The 1989 *Workshop on the Assessment of Formal Methods for Trustworthy Computer Systems (FM89)* was an invitational workshop that brought together representatives from the research, commercial and governmental spheres of Canada, the United Kingdom, and the United States. The workshop was held in Halifax, Nova Scotia, Canada, from July 23 through July 27, 1989. This document reports the activities, observations, recommendations and conclusions resulting from *FM89*.

1.1   Purpose of Workshop

The primary purpose for holding *FM89* was to assess the role of formal methods in the development and fielding of trustworthy critical systems. The need for this assessment was predicated upon four observations:

1. Critical systems are increasingly being controlled by computer systems;
2. Existing techniques for developing, assuring and certifying computer-based critical systems are inadequate;
3. Formal methods have the potential for playing the same role in the development of computer-based systems as applied mathematics does for other engineering disciplines; and
4. Formal methods have had limited impact on the development of computer-based systems and supporting technologies.

The goal of the workshop was to complete the following tasks:

1. Assess the problems retarding the development of trustworthy critical systems;
2. Determine the (potential) impact of applying formal methods techniques to the development of trustworthy critical systems;
3. Determine the research and development required to facilitate a broader application of formal methods techniques;
4. Identify "example systems" that would be useful in measuring the effectiveness of formal methods; and
5. Identify how to improve international coordination and communication of formal methods research.

As discussed in Section 2, the workshop organizers attempted to achieve these goals by dividing the workshop into three sessions: a session on critical systems and governmental concerns, a session on formal methods, and four parallel working groups that focused on various topics of interest.

The first two sessions assessed existing technology (by presenting snapshots of current efforts) and defined a common framework within which the workshop participants could discuss the areas of concern. The four parallel working groups investigated selected issues in greater depth.

1.2   Intended Readership

This report should be of interest to individuals considering pursuing research in the areas of formal methods or critical systems technologies (e.g., graduate students, researchers); to organizations considering or actively pursuing the development of critical systems (e.g., nuclear regulatory bodies, NASA); to organizations contemplating the potential roles of formal methods techniques in enhancing the trustworthiness of critical systems (e.g., nuclear regulatory bodies, defence departments, organizations developing railway switching systems); and to organizations involved in funding research and development of technologies that are of (potential) fundamental importance to the well-being of society (e.g., Science and Engineering Research Council, U.K.; National Science and Engineering Research Council, Canada; and the National Science Foundation, U.S.). Finally, the report should be of interest to members of the general public who are interested in the concerns posed by the fielding of critical systems and the potential roles of formal methods in alleviating some of those concerns.

1.3   Caveat

A major part of the proceedings is reportorial. For each of the formal presentations a "reporter" from the organizing committee was assigned the task of describing the presentation and subsequent discussion. Consequently, it is important that the reader recognize that it is the reporter's perspective that is presented.

1.4   Contents of Report

The next section discusses the general workshop organization. Section 3 focuses on the first day's discussions (on critical systems). Section 4 focuses on the second day's discussions (on formal methods). Section 5 focuses on the activities of the four working groups. The report from Working Group 4 includes a report on the major debate of the workshop, the technology transfer of formal methods to industry. Section 6 is a report of Dave Parnas' concluding remarks to the workshop. Section 7 consists of the conclusions and recommendations arising from the workshop.

Appendix A lists the participants and their affiliations. A list of proposed projects that have significant formal methods components is presented in Appendix B. Appendix C consists of papers by John Rushby and Peter Neumann, which expand upon their comments during the Monday respondents session. Appendix D is a recent version of Peter Neumann's "Illustrative risks to the public in the use of computer systems and related technology." The *FM89* survey of formal methods constitutes Appendix E. A number of acronyms have been defined in Appendix F. The report concludes with References and an Index.

2 Workshop Organization

The organizing committee of *FM89* invited individuals from Canada, the United Kingdom, and the United States, with a concerted effort to have a reasonable distribution of professional backgrounds. There were many difficult decisions as to whom to invite; consequently, a number of meritorious individuals were not invited. As this was a workshop, and not a conference, the organizing committee aimed to have a total of fifty individuals. In fact, fifty-three individuals participated.

The backgrounds of the participants ranged from developers and practitioners of formal methods or critical systems technologies, government representatives interested in, or considering the application of, formal methods or critical systems, and various participants whose professional backgrounds were viewed as assets to achieving the goals of the workshop. If any criticisms were to be levelled at the distribution of those participating, the organizing committee did not invite enough individuals who were directly involved in developing critical systems.

The workshop was held at the Chateau Halifax, Halifax, Nova Scotia. All workshop activities occurred within the hotel. Excluding the reception on July 23, the workshop spanned the four days of July 24 to 27, 1989. Each day had a specific focus topic, as summarized in the agenda in Figure 1.

To simplify the writing of this report, the sessions were recorded (as approved by the participants). Only summaries of the presentations and discussions are included.

During the first two days, a common framework was developed within which the working group sessions (of the third day) could proceed. These days were also used for purposes of problem definition and clarification of concepts and terminology.

Explicit efforts were made to support free-wheeling discussions between the participants. In particular, after each presentation at least fifteen minutes were allotted for discussions pertaining to the presentation.

2.1 Critical Systems (Monday, July 24th)

The focus of the first day of the workshop was the current practice and concerns arising from the development of critical systems and how one proceeds in acquiring trust in the system developed. Section 3 will discuss these presentations and subsequent discussions in greater detail. Table 1 lists the presentations on critical systems.

The first four presentations focused on various technical approaches being used to develop critical systems or identified significant concerns arising from the fielding

Figure 1: FM 89 Agenda

Halifax Formal Methods Workshop — FM '89

SUNDAY July 23	MONDAY July 24	TUESDAY July 25	WEDNESDAY July 26	THURSDAY July 27
	Chair: Dan Craigen (ORA)	Chair: Jim Woodcock (Oxford)	9:00—17:00 Discussion sessions:	9:00—12:30
	8:15 Welcome	30 minute presentations followed by 15 minutes of discussion	What is the applicability of formal methods in systems engineering? Session leader: John Rushby	Chair: Dan Craigen
	8:30 Dave Parnas (Queen's): Making formal methods practical			Reports from sessions (max. 1/4 hour each)
	9:30 Kurt Asmis (AECB): Nuclear plant software	8:30 Jeannette Wing (CMU): What is a formal method?	What are the theoretical and practical limits of formal methods? Session leader: Jeannette Wing	Discussion on reports
	9:45 Paul Joannou (Ontario Hydro): Nuclear plant software	9:15 Carroll Morgan (Oxford): What is a specification?	What example applications should we attempt using formal methods? Session leader: Carl Landwehr	
	10:00 Discussion			
	BREAK	BREAK		BREAK
	11:00 Ricky Butler (NASA): Flight critical systems	10:30 Richard Platek (ORA): What is a proof?	What should be the R & D strategy for formal methods? Session leader: Martyn Thomas	Workshop summary and discussion
	11:45 Steve Sadler (Rolls Royce): Issues in the development of nuclear reactor protection software	11:15 Bill Scherlis (DARPA/CMU): What is the role of automated tools in formal methods?		Dave Parnas Concluding comments 1/2 hour
	LUNCH	LUNCH	LUNCH	LUNCH
	14:00 Martyn Thomas (Praxis): Defence standard 00-55 and other standards: What is proposed and why	Chair: Susan Gerhart (MCC)	Sessions continued	Attendees leave
		13:30 Don Good (CLI): A proven hardware/software system		
	14:45 Chair: Dan Craigen Respondents: J. Rushby, P. Neumann & N. Leveson	14:15 Mack Alford (Ascent Logic): Reasoning about large systems		
		15:00 Jesse Poore (Tennessee): Cleanroom software dvlpmt process		
Attendees arrive	BREAK	BREAK	BREAK	
17:00—19:00 Reception	16:30 Chair: Norm Glick Government forum: P. Ryan, K. Speierman & M. Kuchta	16:00 Mike Gordon (Cambridge): HOL	Sessions concluded	
		16:45 Jim Woodcock (Oxford): Z		
		19:00—?? Banquet		

Table 1: Critical Systems Presentations

Making formal methods practical
   Dave Parnas, Queen's University, Canada

Nuclear plant software
   Kurt Asmis, Atomic Energy Control Board, Canada

Nuclear plant software
   Paul Joannou, Ontario Hydro, Canada

Flight critical systems
   Ricky Butler, NASA, USA

Issues in the development of nuclear reactor protection software
   Steve Sadler, Rolls-Royce, UK

Defence standard 00-55 and other standards: What is proposed and why
   Martyn Thomas, Praxis, UK

Respondents session:
   John Rushby, SRI International, USA
   Peter Neumann, SRI International, USA
   Nancy Leveson, University of California at Irvine, USA

Government forum:
   Peter Ryan, UK
   Milan Kuchta, Canada
   K. Speierman, USA

---

of critical systems and how one can build trust in the system to be fielded. The presentation by Thomas focused primarily on the recently released British Ministry of Defence Interim Standard 00-55, which mandates certain techniques—including formal methods—in the development of MoD critical systems. The "respondents session" allowed for three individuals, with backgrounds in critical systems, to challenge, expand upon, or add to, the various claims of the preceding presentations. Finally, the intent of the "government forum" was to elicit from government representatives, in an informal manner, their concerns and aims regarding formal methods and critical systems.

2.2   Formal Methods (Tuesday, July 25th)

The second day of the workshop focused on formal methods. Section 4 will discuss these presentations and subsequent discussions in greater detail. Table 2 lists the presentations on formal methods.

Table 2: Formal Methods Presentations

What is a formal method?
  Jeannette Wing, Carnegie-Mellon University, USA

What is a specification?
  Carroll Morgan, Oxford University, UK

What is a proof?
  Richard Platek, Odyssey Research Associates, USA

What is the role of automated tools in formal methods?
  Bill Scherlis, Carnegie-Mellon University & DARPA, USA

A proven hardware/software system
  Don Good, Computational Logic Inc., USA

Reasoning about large systems
  Mack Alford, Ascent Logic, USA

Cleanroom software development process
  Jesse Poore, University of Tennessee, USA

HOL   Mike Gordon, Cambridge University, UK

Z   Jim Woodcock, Oxford University, UK

The first three presentations were intented to define the terminology and to clarify various conceptual matters; much debate pertaining to formal methods revolves around differing definitions for 'formal method,' 'specification' and 'proof.' The presentation by Scherlis focused on the roles of automated tools in formal methods. The last five presentations presented snapshots of state-of-the-art research and development efforts. Due the brevity of time available, other promising efforts were excluded.

2.3 Working Group Sessions (Wednesday, July 26th)

On the third day of the workshop, four working group sessions were held.[1] The working groups each had a specific topic area to discuss and were requested to return with a set of concrete observations, recommendations and conclusions.

Section 5 will discuss the working groups in detail. Table 3 identifies the working groups by title and identifies the chair for each group.

Table 3: Working Groups

Working Group 1:
What is the applicability of formal methods in systems engineering?
Chair: John Rushby

Working Group 2:
What are the theoretical and practical limits of formal methods?
Chair: Jeannette Wing

Working Group 3:
What example applications should we attempt using formal methods?
Chair: Carl Landwehr

Working Group 4:
What should be the R & D strategy and objectives for formal methods?
Chair: Martyn Thomas

Briefly, the first working group focused on incorporating formal methods techniques with systems engineering techniques; the second working group looked at the theoretical and practical limitations of formal methods; the third working group identified specific applications and classes of applications, for advancing both the state of the practice and the state of the art of formal methods and critical systems development; and the fourth working group identified strategies and objectives for formal methods R&D.

2.4 Concluding Session (Thursday, July 27th)

On the final day of the workshop the chairs of the working groups reported on their sessions and there were further discussions within the context of a plenary session. The workshop ended with some remarks from Dave Parnas.

---

[1] *Editor's note:* In hindsight, it would have been preferable to have split the working group sessions over two or three days, so that feedback between the groups would have been possible.

3 Critical Systems

The presentations relating to critical systems were given on the first day of the workshop. Each presentation, and subsequent discussion, is reported individually. The respondents session and the government panel are reported in the final two subsections.

3.1 Making formal methods practical

Speaker: Dave Parnas
Reporter: Susan Gerhart

Why is software assessment important?
Because it is increasingly common to use software in safety critical situations, assessment before deployment is essential. Software provides increased flexibility, a relatively easy way to increase accuracy, ease of change (especially with many installations), resistance to deterioration with age, and better system functions such as information displays. However, software is a special concern for several reasons: it "never works the first time"; beneficial flexibility often leads to unprecedented complexity with no natural boundaries within a system; software is all too sensitive to minor errors and difficult to test because interpolation is not valid; and bugs may be related to events long past in the history of the system [Par 86].

How is software assessed?
See [Par 88] for details.

What qualities should be assessed?
Measuring the quality of software requires a specification accepted as the arbiter of what is "right". The qualities of interest, and when they are of interest, include:

Correctness = always meeting the spec
> when you only want to define an ideal. Correctness is unrealistic to expect and not really the issue because some problems are worse than others.

Reliability = probability of correct behavior
> when certain assumptions help, e.g., when all errors are considered equivalent or when there are no unacceptable failures or when the operating conditions are predictable, or when the objectives are estimating cost or comparing risks.

Trustworthiness = probability of undetected catastrophic flaws
    when unacceptable failures can be identified and when trust is vital for meeting requirements.

Note that we never find systems that are correct and we often accept systems that are unreliable, but we do not use systems that we dare not trust.

How should assessment be performed?

Consider three approaches to safety assessment (using the above ways of measuring quality): testing, inspection and review, and verification of people and process.

Testing is impractical for demonstrating trustworthiness—the failure conditions are simply too complex. However, testing can be used to assess reliability using a number of known models. Testing has limits: it cannot predict (availability), where it often falls down (testers make the same assumptions as programmers), and where it is hard to use (reliability does not carry over from older versions).

Variations on testing often appear attractive. *Self-tests* (tests built into the hardware or software to activate during operational failures) still may miss built-in defects. *Simulation* is just another form of testing involving a model, with its inevitable differences from the world. But simulations can be applied as an early form of testing and are used best when they can be validated by comparing predictions with outcome, or when there is certainty about the controlling variables, or when interpolation is in fact valid.

It's intriguing to look at how *reliability* comes into play. Software is not a random process, but the input data can be treated as random. Software is really the initial data of the hardware/software system viewed as a single component. Testing applies to that single component with software as its initial data. Note that the number of errors per line is meaningless for reliability, as are the time derivatives of error rates. Only failure rate matters for reliability.

There is a simple way to estimate how much testing is required for a given level of reliability. Take

$$M = (1 - 1/h)^N$$

as the probability of passing N properly selected tests, where the probability of failure of the program is $1/h$. This gives a probability that a marginal product would pass the test. Suppose you want to know for various h, at what N, M will be around .1. With h =1000, M for 1000 tests is about .35, reaching .1 between 2000 and 2500 tests, but for h =1,000,000, N must be greater than 4,000,000. Thus selecting tests in a black box strategy will require a random selection process and a large number of runs, plus checking the answers if failure doesn't break the system but only results in invalid results. High numbers of runs are needed to cover some reasonable portion of the vast number of states of most systems, but these figures are just guidelines for tests independent of the program at hand. In real-time systems, a test is a trajectory that gives the input values as continuous functions of time, making reliability testing even more difficult.

Another alternative that might help is *fault tolerance*, which applies well to hardware where major design flaws are not expected to be tolerated and where component failures are assumed to be independent. In software, design flaws are the major concern and the only "components" are human programmers, who have been shown through empirical studies [LK 86] not to fail independently.

So, testing can be seen to provide the means to assess quality expressed as reliability.

Trustworthiness requires a reasoning process about catastrophic failures—what could they be and how could they occur? Only inspection of the software can determine how failures could occur. A baseline is easily established for effective inspection processes; unstructured software simply cannot be reviewed, nor can improperly documented software. Guessing at designer's intentions or other forms of suffering inflicted upon reviewers is sufficient grounds for rejection of the software—does one trust software produced by programmers who cannot produce professional quality technical documentation?

Formal Methods for Documentation

Where do formal methods fit into assessing software quality? Testing probes the appropriateness of the mathematical model used in formal methods. Formal methods provide the structure for systematic inspection: the equations, the definitions, the case structure that permit step-by-step reasoning. The documents produced by formal methods can be used for black-box testing through test cases derived from the spec. Formal methods also provide an additional check on white box tests.

Here is a sketch of a formal model for requirements documents. The environment "supplies" values to be monitored (M) and controlled (C) by the system. The system has inputs (I) and outputs (O). Each M, C, I, and O is a vector, each element of which is a function of time. The requirements documents must describe the environment relationship REQ(M,C), the input relationship IN(M,I), the output relationship CON(O,C) while the implementors produce a system described as REM(I,O). The "correctness" condition is paraphrased as "all monitored variables lead through the relationship chain to controlling variable values satisfying REQ".

Module interfaces are documented in terms of traces (sequences of observable values), which yield output values. Internal module designs define functions between data states and traces and a relation between entry and exit states of each program. Throughout the design, functions and relations are the media of description (see Section 4.7).

To make this approach practical, functions are presented in a tabular form. By convention, the functions are represented in the most natural mathematical way, which could be polynomial expressions, tables, APL-like combinators, whatever. The specification technique emphasizes flexibility in function notation but rigidity in information requirements. Most formal specification languages would be the opposite: freedom of information requirements and rigid representation notation.

The point of using formal documents is to support reviews. Each kind of document has a specific kind of reviewer with specific skills and responsibilities. Software engineers review the functional requirements for cost and feasibility, as well as the module guides and designs. Plant engineers focus on correctness of the functional requirements. Programmers look at the internal designs and algorithms. Language specialists examine the code. When the document's contents are mathematical functions, represented by readable tables, a systematic, reliable review can be performed. Note that military standard documents are unreviewable by these criteria.

Furthermore, people must be "reviewed", which is often called *certification*. But the standards for certification are missing.

Conclusion

In conclusion, software can be used in safety-critical systems but not without rigorous inspection based on precise documentation and not without reliability assessments based on thorough random testing. The formal methods described at the workshop help to verify the "logic" of the functions while planned testing verifies the evaluation of the numerical functions. Establishing criteria for professional engineers and their educational backgrounds [Par 89] is an open problem.

Discussion

Q (McHugh): In your model of formal documentation, you assign responsibility for environmental variables to the requirements team and relating inputs and outputs to the programming team. Doesn't that mean the systems engineers make trade-off decisions without having the software people involved?

A: My model does not take into account these assignments of responsibilities. Yes, the software engineers should be part of the system engineering team. God could write the functions of the model, but at the end (for assessment) we must know what those functions are.

Q (Leveson): How do you keep people from trying to do too much with software?

A: In the AECB/Ontario Hydro situation, they agreed to limit what they would try to do with software to what the old analog system did. They aren't going for more flexibility or more accuracy than is reasonable.

Q (Leveson): Related to the increased functionality problem is information displays. In the Vincennes (US Navy vs. Iranian airplane) incident one problem was that displays didn't provide all the information for the operators because there wasn't enough room on the screen. The general argument for putting software in place of operators is that humans are the ones making all the mistakes. We talk about providing them better information but then don't provide them with enough because they're too mistake prone.

A: There is nothing so right that you can't do something wrong with it.

Q (Goguen): We're talking about informal requirements that exist at a higher level in some social sense than the formal requirements written in mathematical notation. Confidence in the system is determined by some social parameters, sometimes cynically as in keeping environmentalists quiet. Compromises made at a relatively low level have consequences that are very important for decisions made at a much higher level and they must remain informal. It would be very desirable to integrate the informal material with the formal material in some way to have a methodology to detect when compromises were being made and what the consequences were. To pretend that there is some absolute interface after which everything is formal seems to me to be a major mistake. Besides the social issues, there are many technical questions. I think it actually is possible to use formal methods on relatively informal material and to integrate that with things that have a mathematical semantics.

A: That's one reason I emphasized the readability of the specifications. I don't know whether the functional requirements are right or not, but it's very important to me that what we write as functional requirements can be read by somebody like the AECB personnel who are not computer scientists and not computer engineers but are specialists in the application area who understand the plan and working conditions. Back in my A-7 work, we found that pilots were able to read our documents and find errors, plus they were right too when they found those errors. I wasn't happy there were errors, but I was happy that pilots were able to read it. One thing we found in the Ontario Hydro and AECL modelling work based on the A-7 work is that engineers in other fields who understand the, let's say, "physics of the situation" can systematically verify. I don't know how we could do any better. The problems have nothing to do with software and they're true in any engineering area.

3.2 Safety critical software in nuclear power plants

Speaker: Kurt Asmis
Reporter: Norm Glick

Asmis is a regulator who verifies that certain procedures have been met in Canadian nuclear power plants. Computers have been used successfully for process control of the CANDU power reactors. They are backed up by hardwired special safety systems, plus containment, plus emergency core injection systems. The special safety systems can intercede to shut down the plant.

Asmis needs to deal with the question of software integrity from a regulatory point of view. The question first arose with a proposal for fully software-controlled shutdown systems in the Darlington reactors (where traditional analog systems were to be replaced by many microcomputers). The Atomic Energy Control Board (AECB) staff investigated the use and avoidance of computers for safety-critical applications within the nuclear and related industries.

They found the following difficulties:

- Software failures, particularly on first use, were common.

- No detailed code of practice existed.

- Exhaustive testing was not enough.

They concluded that a "review" strategy was warranted based on recent advances in software research. This AECB strategy is based on the following requirements:

- Application-specific software must be subjected to formal analysis techniques, which compare code to requirements specifications.

- Two types of verification testing are essential:

  1. Systematic, deterministic testing.
  2. Statistically valid random testing based on plausible plant properties.

- Successful track record, supported by documentation.

3.3 Nuclear plant software

Speaker: Paul Joannou
Reporter: Dan Craigen

Joannou focused on a portion of a methodology that Ontario Hydro is using in the development of the software for the Darlington nuclear power plant shutdown system. Specifically, he focused on Ontario Hydro's method for showing that the implemented software captures completely the intentions of the requirements specification.

Basically, Ontario Hydro uses condition and event tables in a style proposed by David Parnas. Existing source code is translated into a program function table and there is a table for each subprogram. Joannou observed that two sets of programs were written for the shutdown system: one program using FORTRAN and assembler; the other using Pascal and assembler. A function table describes the output of a subprogram as a function of its inputs. The Ontario Hydro methodology then isolates each output (as a function of inputs), identifies the equivalent term in the specification for the output variable, and then compares the relevant terms. The code, with respect to the chosen output variable, satisfies the requirements if the table entries are equivalent.

The application of the above methodology has been labour intensive. Experience has shown that for each line of code a page of documentation has been produced. As a consequence, the lack of tool support has been felt strongly.

From the technical perspective, Ontario Hydro has found that programs written in assembler are very challenging. It is unclear where one should define the boundaries for inputs and outputs. Further, a single assembler instruction can result in a lot of activity. Handling indirect addressing, parameter passing, stack manipulation and interrupts have all been arduous. In addition, Ontario Hydro is having problems with programs that contain loops. For such programs, it is difficult to determine the output of a subprogram as a function of its inputs.

At the time of this lecture, the inspection process of the Darlington shutdown system was still in progress and the methodology was still evolving.

The application of the methodology has been expensive: $2 million as of this lecture. However, Ontario Hydro does have confidence that the code does implement its specifications. The methodology has also resulted in a good audit trail as to why one believes that the code implements the specifications; this is important for the regulatory agencies. The methodology has also been good at finding dead code, poorly structure code and complex programs: it has resulted in another good review of the code.

Unfortunately, with respect to the Darlington software, this methodology is being applied too late in the life cycle. By the time they started applying the techniques reported here, all testing of the software had been performed. The effort should have been a part of the development process.

As to future work, Ontario Hydro intends to develop appropriate tool support, and to incorporate the methodology into the software life cycle. They expect to refine the methodology further. They also feel that the methodology is good for automatic test case generation.

3.4 Flight critical systems (Perspectives for formal verification)

Speaker: Ricky Butler
Reporter: Milan Kuchta

Ricky Butler, NASA, Langley Research Center, presented his perspectives for formal verification as applied to flight control systems.

Mr. Butler described the evolution of aeronautical control systems, which have moved towards architectures for integrated/automated operation. Such evolution has produced performance that would be otherwise unattainable with contemporary technology and with reduced costs for equivalent or improved performance. These systems have evolved from simple mechanical systems, to analog systems, and finally to the current digital fly-by-wire systems.

The control system architecture for these systems can be viewed as hierarchical with the following layers:

Aerodynamic Properties
Functional Diagram of Control System
Control Law Block Diagram
Application Code
Operating System
Redundant Hardware

These architectures have two goals:

Demonstrable ultra-reliability: The reliability analysis must be sound and the parameters of the reliability model must be measurable. The complexity and number of parameters that must be measured should be minimized.

Verifiable design: The scheduling system must be safe, the redundancy management must be sound and the assumptions used during the design must be minimized and carefully enumerated.

The application programmer often has several requirements that must be met by the design and must be supported by the resident operating system:

Hard-deadlines (e.g., there must be an acceptable limit on the delay between reading a sensor and actuation of a control unit);

Multi-Rate Cyclic Scheduling (e.g., functions must be dispatched at various repetition rates);

Minimal Jitter (e.g., there must be an acceptable limit on the variation in the specified time between tasks);

Precedence Constraints (e.g., functional and/or timing sequences must be maintained); and

Mode-switching Constraints (e.g., a set of tasks to be scheduled changes from one flight mode to another, but must be constant within one mode).

Mr. Butler described the design decisions that were involved in ultra-reliable systems. The requirements necessitate fault-tolerance, which is usually achieved through redundancy. Redundant solutions require voting circuitry. Voting is dependent upon two additional system activities: (1) the redundant processing sites must be synchronized and (2) single source input data must be distributed to the redundant sites using interactive consistency algorithms.

Voting can take place at a number of locations in the system. Associated with each choice are various issues:

1. Voting at the actuators, This approach does not offer recovery from transient faults, which can corrupt the state of a good processor;

2. Voting the entire state (e.g., all memory). This approach deals with transients but requires a large cpu overhead; and

3. Voting only the state which is not recoverable from sensor input. This approach also deals with transients but involves increased complexity.

Voting can also take place at various levels:

1. at the instruction level where synchronization must be very tight; and

2. at the task level (i.e., vote outputs of tasks after completed) where loose synchronization is possible.

Mr. Butler stated that there are both technical and political obstacles to the acceptance of formal methods and that their acceptance will require more examples of realistic systems in which the use of formal methods was demonstrably successful, and less overselling of simple examples and partial proofs. The technology must be demonstrated on real systems even if the initial costs are relatively high. The tools supporting formal methods must be improved but demonstration of the utility of formal methods must be a priority.

The validation of ultra-reliable systems requires quantifying the probability of system failure due to physical failure and establishing that design errors are not present. Establishing that design errors are not present is not considered to be a quantifiable problem.

Three approaches to achieving ultra-reliable software were mentioned: testing, software fault-tolerance, and formal verification. Testing is not feasible for very low failure rate requirements since a 1 in 1,000,000,000 probability of failure estimate for a one hour mission requires at least 1,000,000,000 hours (or approximately 114,000 years) of testing.

Software fault-tolerance (i.e., N-version programming, recovery blocks, etc.) techniques often implicitly assume independence of multiple versions of software to generate ultra-high estimates of reliability. Testing for independence or measuring interactions between versions of software requires as much time as life-testing a whole system directly and is also not a feasible option. In addition, experiments have shown that the lack of independence in versions of software is often so serious that it exhibits itself in a "nominal" reliability region. The only thing that enables quantification of ultra-reliability for hardware is the independence assumption and this assumption can not be generally justified for multi-version software.

As long as industry and certification agencies believe that software fault-tolerance will solve the problem, formal verification will not be vigorously pursued.

Mr. Butler concluded that it is possible to quantify the probability of system failure with respect to component failure but that ultra-reliable quantification of design flaws is infeasible. As a result, mathematical proof-of-correctness is the only sound option for achieving ultra-reliable systems.[2]

---

[2]*Editor's note:* For background information, please refer to [But 88], [FKR 79], [KMU 79], [Lala 86], [MMS 87], and [PB 86].

3.5 Issues in the development of nuclear reactor protection software

Speaker: Steve Sadler
Reporter: J.C.P. Woodcock

Report on Talk

Rolls-Royce & Associates was established thirty years ago, primarily to design and supply nuclear reactor plants.

The rôle of the design authority requires that the Company prepare a safety case for examination by independent assessors. The use of formal methods in the development of the software for such safety-critical systems has a significant effect, both on the justification of the safety of the system and on its assessment. It is useful to consider the safety case in terms of a Design Justification (DJ) and a Probabilistic Risk Assessment (PRA).

First, consider the software contribution to the Design Justification. The evidence of early design studies in the Company confirmed that the software component posed a significant threat to successful implementation. Modifications to the software design were examined, showing that 80% of required changes were due to errors and ambiguities at the specification stage. Subsequent studies showed that 75% of these specification problems could have been solved by the use of a formal method such as VDM.

Software also poses problems for PRA studies. Here, the task is to quantify "risk" in terms of the frequency of occurrence of a sequence of hazardous events and the associated consequences. Typically, a risk model would be developed as a sequence of event trees and fault trees; from a set of initiating events, the risk model provides for evaluation of frequency and consequences. A *fault tree* quantifies the contribution from a particular system, by the logical combination of those possible faults that are perceived to be random in nature. There is no statistical basis for applying this model to design flaws in small and critical software systems.

For safety-critical software such as are found in reactor protection systems, we cannot rely solely upon schemes for the "measurement" of software reliability. Instead, the aim is to provide sufficient evidence of good design that software can be accepted as an insignificant contributor to system unreliability.

So, how would one proceed to justify the software design?

The first step is to assess the possible consequences of software failure: a Hazard Analysis is performed using techniques such as Fault-Tree or Failure Modes and Effect Analysis (see, e.g., [MoD 89b]). Where the software component is identified as *safety critical* then a formal development route is required. In practice, the formal approach has also been applied, to great effect, on non-critical systems.

It is important to note that safety-critical systems are required to be simple, defensive, and fault-tolerant. Formal methods are not a cure-all, and software function is restricted to that which can be modelled within the limitations of the selected methods.

Report on Discussion

Question: Formal methods is firstly a tool for exploring requirements and analyzing consequences of requirements prior to building a system, and secondly is a tool for the construction of verified systems. I believe that within the British community formal methods is advocated as a tool for sorting out what you are doing very early in the process. It is a tool for thinking about problems. It is only as a secondary consideration within the British community that it is thought of as a verification tool. What is your experience?

Answer: Formal specification provides a very useful way of communicating between different people: operators, maintainers, designers, and so on. By getting these people to understand the system early on, we were able to eliminate 90% of the errors to that stage. As for the benefits of formal methods, we implemented a number of non-critical systems using formal methods to see how things worked out. We found extremely few, if any, errors when we came to integrating the software with the hardware. There was a staggering reduction in the number of hardware integration errors. Similarly, when we performed dynamic testing of critical systems developed using formal methods, we have still to find any errors. We can go back to our managers and show them the cost and safety arguments, and show them the gains, I claim.

Question: This is a general argument that I would like to direct to all those who have spoken about the application of these methods. Conventional wisdom tells us that our major costs, engineering costs, come not in the development cycle of software, but in that software modification cycle that is known as maintenance. Have any of you carried your projects far enough to be able to get a feel for the relative cost of responding to software changes with formal methods, as against the costs with traditional methods?

Answer: (Sadler) We haven't got far enough to be able to say, but we are starting to see an improvement.

Answer: (Joannou) Our system hasn't entered the maintenance phase yet, but with the simplicity of the system we are hoping that the number of changes are going to be very, very small. We are not looking forward to going through the verification process again.

Question: In the systems that you are building, are you starting from scratch or are you incorporating software components? How does the formal modelling allow you to get the interface to existing products?

Answer: We've applied these methods to a variety of systems that would fall into either category. It is much simpler when you can start from scratch and get the formal boundaries laid down correctly. When we implement a software system, we have been given the hardware and the state of voting in the system as a whole. We have taken the line that we should keep the software as simple as possible, and put relatively little reliance upon it.

Question: What are you doing about quantifying the reliability of the system once you have developed it?

Answer: I think that we have failed miserably in terms of quantifying the reliability of the software. The rest of the system has been quantified in the fashion that I have described here. We claimed that we would not significantly degrade the reliability of the system by including the software, on the grounds of simplicity, fault tolerance, and the formal approach used.

Question: What are the numerical reliability targets for the software components that you have to assert you are achieving in order not to be degrading the system reliability targets?

Answer: I cannot give you a number; it is very much a design argument. The approach has been to design the system such that it excludes reliance on that software.

Question: What do you believe is the lowest probability of failure that you could claim realistically for a small number of thousands of lines of code?

Answer: I think that if you have so few lines of code, I would realistically claim that you could get down to no errors in terms of logic. You may have errors in capturing the requirements though.

Question: Parnas says you can claim anything you want.

Answer: I don't have the numbers; that is the problem.

Question: I am not sure that the numbers mean anything anyway. We need only one error in the software to degrade the whole system, and the mean time between failures for that error is meaningless. Chernobyl had a mean time between failures of one in ten thousand years. Most of these models are based on assumptions that aren't true when you start using the system. Also, you can always violate these assumptions by having the operators do whatever they did at Chernobyl.

Question: My interest in the numbers is that people quote them widely, and in particular it is what the assessors want us to achieve. In the flight software that we were hearing about earlier, the assessors were looking for 10^{-9} failures per flight hour. I think that we all have a responsibility whenever we hear numbers like that quoted, and hear people standing up and claiming that they are achieving them, to pour ridicule upon them. I think that such claims do considerable damage to our industry, to the techniques that we use, and to the whole credibility of this area. We should not allow people to get away with claiming that they are building ultra-reliable systems out of digital computers. It has to stop.

Answer: I would be rather disturbed if you thought that I was trying to extract numbers of that sort. I hope that I have not left the wrong impression.

3.6 Defence standard 00-55 and other standards: What is proposed and why

Speaker: Martyn Thomas
Reporter: Peter Ryan

Defence Standard 00-55 [MoD 89a] lays down standards for the production of safety-related software for MoD procurement. A number of factors motivated the decision to produce such a standard:

1. concern about the rapid increase in the amount and complexity of software in weapon systems;

2. experience that formal methods could improve the quality of software; and

3. a desire to stimulate the defence supply industry to use and develop better software engineering techniques.

It has been observed that software failures tend to be systematic, whereas hardware failures tend to be "random". The philosophy, therefore, is to try to minimize software errors whilst seeking to detect and tolerate hardware errors.

Standard 00-55 lays down requirements for good software engineering practice. Principally, these include the appointment of an independent safety advisor and V&V (Validation and Verification) assessors. The development must be well-documented throughout. Configuration management must be enforced and supported by automated tools. Staff should have appropriate qualifications and experience. Work is in progress to establish standards of training, leading to safety-related software engineering qualifications.

The accompanying standard 00-56 [MoD 89b] lays down procedures for hazard analysis. It thus serves, in effect, to define the scope of 00-55 by defining what software is deemed to be safety-critical, i.e., whose failure could endanger human life. The underlying principal of this document is that all software is deemed to be critical until hazard analysis shows otherwise.

Documentation must include a specification written in English as well as a specification written in formal, mathematical language. Correspondence between these should be demonstrated, for example, via animation. Further design steps must also be fully documented and their validity shown by either rigorous argument or formal proof. Which is appropriate would be subject to negotiation. Allowable development techniques are given in an appendix of the standard.

The compiled language is to be high-level and strongly typed, should have a well-defined syntax and, as far as possible, should have a full semantics.

Several coding practices are forbidden in the current version of the standard (for example, recursion, interrupts, multi-processing on a single processor). It is probable that in due course this index of practices will be replaced by a "principle of analysability". That is, various coding practices will be admitted if and only if they are amenable to full analysis.

Safety-critical code is to be subjected to static analysis, supported by automated tools. This will perform information flow, control flow analysis, and so forth. Coding anomalies, such as unreachable code, will not be allowed.

Testing should simulate all hazardous conditions. Back-to-back testing against existing implementations is not considered admissible.

To summarize, Standard 00-55 calls for the use of the following tools:

- Static analysis tools
- Configuration management tools
- Verified compiler
- Target simulator
- Object code converter
- Test coverage monitor

Standard 00-55 also calls for the use of the following practices:

- The production of, and adherence to, a complete project plan for the development of safety-critical software.
- The use of trained, qualified staff.
- Independent assessment and certification of critical software.
- The use of formal, mathematical specification and design techniques.

Status

Standard 00-55 currently has the status of a draft, interim defence standard. That is to say, it is still subject to review and modification. It is not yet mandatory but is already being used for procurement. It will probably assume full defence standard status in 1991.

The existing version applies only to software, not to systems or hardware. This is an acknowledged deficiency and will almost certainly be rectified in future versions.

Significance

As remarked earlier, one of the aims of the standard was to motivate industry to develop and deploy better software engineering practices and technologies. It is, therefore, pitched quite deliberately beyond the current state of the art. Winning a project tender would depend on getting as close as possible to the requirements, or at least closer than rival bidders.

It is anticipated that, although it is nominally a defence standard, it should prove highly influential in the civil area too.

MoD has every intention to try to internationalize the standard. This clearly should serve to reduce overall costs of defence procurement.

Related standards

A number of other related standards and reports were briefly described:

The U.K. Health and Safety Executive Guidelines [UK 87] are fairly technical, but cover only systems architectures and hardware. The software guidelines are not available, although work has been done on a non-technical framework. These latter guidelines are subsumed in the work of the inter-departmental government committee (chaired by DTI), which is now meeting. A framework will be published in the summer of 1990.

Software in Safety Related Systems [IEE 89], produced by the IEE and BCS, is now available.

A further pair of standards are being prepared by working groups 9 and 10 of TC65A of the IEC (International Electrotechnical Commission). These standards ([IEC94] and [IEC96]) are for non-military, non-nuclear civil applications. WG9 is addressing safety critical software whilst W910 is addressing systems. They are now available for review by the national standards bodies.

Overall message

The standard clearly asserts that certification of critical software should be based on sound design and development techniques and not on *post hoc* analysis. Furthermore, there is a move away from any attempts to quantify probabilities of failure.

Discussion

In response to the first question, Thomas listed the allowed formal methods:

VDM	OBJ	Z	HOL
CCS	CSP	LOTOS	Temporal logic

Subsequent discussion clarified the motivation, history and timing of the standard as well as industry reaction. It was the view of both Martyn Thomas and Robin Bloomfield (one of the authors of the standard) that the standard was a codification of what was, in any case, the trend. Thus the timing seemed rather natural and appropriate.

The proscribed practices list came in for considerable criticism, as indeed it had in the U.K. Thomas' response was that, yes the list was probably not ideal and would almost certainly be revised. Indeed, the list should probably be replaced by some more general principle stating that code should be as easily analyzable as feasible. In any event, the list would be open to negotiation in any project bidding process. If good arguments could be presented for the use of a particular coding practice, a waiver from the proscription could doubtless be obtained. The onus of proof would lie clearly with the developer.

On the contractual side, it was stated that bidding for a contract would proceed by a series of fixed-price contracts, each serving to more clearly define and estimate the cost of the next. Interestingly, when pressed, no-one in the audience would admit to having signed a fixed-price contract to develop verified software.

The problem of evaluating formal specifications, and so forth, was raised. The MoD clearly does not command sufficient in-house expertise to perform such evaluations effectively. Consequently, the procedure would be to contract independent companies to perform the evaluation.

It was also agreed that the decision to address only software development was probably a mistake, and a subsequent version would address the full system development issues.

The discussion turned to the desirability of quantifying risks. It was generally agreed that qualitative measures of risk could not be established. However, a survey of software in safety-critical applications would be beneficial, detailing how the product was developed and what faults had occurred.

3.7   Respondents Session

Respondents: John Rushby
                      Peter Neumann
                      Nancy Leveson
Reporter: Larry Hatch

The speakers in this session presented their views of what system developers need from the formal methods community. The following needs were expressed:

- That there be an integration of techniques into a "systems approach."

- That there be widespread education efforts to expose developers to (mature) formal methods techniques.

- That there be completion and expository publication of more good examples of the application of formal methods techniques in the system development process.

- That there be an increase in the accessibility and applicability of formal methods tools and techniques.

Each of the speakers stressed that the engineering of trusted systems, where the application of formal methods has the potential for significant payoff, is going on now and therefore these needs have great immediacy.

Nancy Leveson

Dr. Leveson made a strong appeal for applying formal methods to hazard analysis and other systems engineering problems. She observed that hazard analysis merely involves a proof of a particular system property and is complementary to other applications of formal methods. For example, the analysis starts from a hazard specification (what the software should not do) other than the usual software requirements specification (what the software should do). This enables potential identification of omissions and problems in the requirements specification, and identification of the basic assumptions being made about the behavior of the environment that could lead to accidents if violated. Furthermore, such an analysis of failure behavior provides backup if there are errors in the proof of consistency between specifications of "correct" behavior. Such hazard analyses are usually limited in scope and therefore may provide a practical use for the application of rigorous formal methods.

As further incentive, Dr. Leveson observed that there are standards (for example, [MIL-STD-882B]) that mandate the application of hazard analysis to the development of safety-critical systems and that it is unlikely that these standards can be satisfied without the use of formal or semi-formal methods.

In her concluding remarks, Dr. Leveson noted that hazard analysis, in the form of Software Fault Tree Analysis, is being used in the nuclear power plant project described by Dr. Parnas, has been found to be easy and cheap to apply in that instance (two to three person-months to analyze 2,000–3,000 lines of code), and has resulted in forty-two recommendations for changes in the software to make it safer (including structural and coding changes and the identification of simple checks on critical variables and intermediate states). She suggested that perhaps hazard analysis should be added to the Troika[4] approach since it complements it well. The Troika approach primarily contains techniques to increase reliability, with a few techniques to increase trustworthiness outside of informal reviews of documentation. Hazard analysis is one way of increasing confidence in the trustworthiness of software. She then reiterated that System Safety Engineers already do these things, albeit *ad hoc*, and that they could benefit from the help of the formal methods community.

John Rushby

Dr. Rushby focused his remarks on two themes. The first theme was described as "The Train is Leaving the Station." He emphasized that, in spite of being unable to meet all required mandates for assurance of dependability, systems of a critical nature are being engineered (and used). He believes that formal methods can improve the situation and must hasten to do so.

The second theme of Dr. Rushby's remarks was "integration." He advocates that formal methods be applied in a systems context. It is a practical and economic reality that formal verification (for example) cannot be applied to every part of a large system—nor is it necessarily the best method of assurance for every part and property of a system. He called for more serious study of the relationship between complementary methods of assurance and validation—for example, between verification, fault-tree analysis, testing, run-time checking and fault-tolerance.

Appendix C includes a paper by Dr. Rushby, written subsequent to the workshop. This paper further clarifies Dr. Rushby's commentary during this session.

Peter Neumann

Dr. Neumann, as often happens when three speakers address the same topic, returned to many of the points of the previous speakers. He stressed the importance of taking a systems view when contemplating using formal methods to assist in engineering critical systems. He observed that often a fundamental and difficult problem for the systems engineer is determining "the least common denominator" of what is being asked. It is necessary to do this first, in order to decide how best to proceed with the design and engineering tasks. He referenced several examples of dire outcomes that were a consequence of not using a systems approach. A "very small" error is often revealed to be the real "source" of one's problems.

Dr. Neumann stated that N-version programming was often more of a burden than a help and that, in general, a more effective approach should be found to build "confidence" into one's systems.

Dr. Neumann also expressed conviction, as did the others, that systems engineering should proceed using formal methods in ways that complement existing practice. He contended that there are techniques and tools used in applications to ensure safety, security, reliability and integrity that are not considered formal and need to be examined for possible use as complementary tools. His suggestion implies that some of these techniques might inspire new formal tools or techniques.

Dr. Neumann challenged the group to try to model important aspects of human behavior and analyze the effect of that behavior on safety.

Finally, Dr. Neumann called, as did the other speakers, for a concerted effort to produce documented examples of the application of formal methods and for more

---

[4]*Editor's Note:* Parnas described the Troika approach as the use of random testing; formal methods and planned testing; and professional engineers, for the development of critical systems.

educational efforts directed toward teaching existing formal methods.

Appendix C includes a paper by Dr. Neumann, which was the basis for much of his commentary.

Discussion

The questions after the presentations were all directed to Nancy Leveson. In the early questions, she was asked to expand her descriptions of techniques used by safety engineers. She indicated that there is extensive literature on the subject. Requests were made for copies of [MIL-STD-882B] and reference was made to [MoD 89b]. During the question period, two observations were made by Dr. Parnas:

> "Systems engineers do what comes before the software is written. They write large amounts of documents, they pile them on a government contract monitor's desk, he accepts them, pays for them, they gather dust and all the work starts over again and that's why we never see that stuff. ... They do the system engineering and then somebody sits down and really designs the system ..."

> "I believe in formal methods ... you don't have to keep looking for hazards at every level all over again if you're also doing the proving."

This reporter concludes that Dr. Parnas' remarks reflected (once more) that more integrated and truly complementary work (by the systems engineering and formal methods communities) is needed.

3.8 Government Forum

Panelists: Milan Kuchta
                Peter Ryan
                K. Speierman
Chair: Norm Glick
Reporter: Dan Craigen

The final activity of the day was a panel session that brought together members of the three participating governments. The panelists spoke informally (i.e., no official government policies were stated), the intent being to increase the workshop participants' general awareness of various governmental concerns and the background to these concerns. Each panelist presented his concerns, observations and opinions, and then accepted questions from the floor.

Milan Kuchta

Milan Kuchta's background relates principally to security. Under his current mandate, he needs to have systems developed that satisfy government requirements and public needs. For example, one of the requirements is the privacy of information. Consequently, strong evidence is required that the requirements and policies are met. "Arm waving" is insufficient: the necessary evidence must almost be as strong as that required within legal contexts. Further, for reasons of accountability, he must be able to identify those responsible for the development of such systems.

Kuchta identified the following as areas where he believes that R&D should to be focused:

- Realistic models of system behaviour.

- Techniques that allow for the top level specification of all necessary functionality of a system. Currently, it is not possible to completely specify such functionality.

- A better understanding of the composition and decomposition of systems. Specifically, better formalism of the processes involved are required.

- Practical notations. Current computing science notations are woefully inadequate and are inferior to those of mathematics.

- Models of "certainty." This recommendation is motivated by the many problems with systems that arise because the underlying assumptions are faulty.

- Capabilities that support the testing of specifications.

- Practical, commercial formal methods tools. Such tools would be supported fully by their developers (e.g., through maintenance and courses).

- Methods that integrate formal methods with other techniques so as to obtain adequate coverage. No one method can stand alone; synergistic interaction is necessary.

Kuchta believes that a broad spectrum of techniques must be applied to the development and assessment of critical systems. However, one caveat that Kuchta made during his presentation is that, while research diversity is important, the diversity of tools is counter-productive.

Finally, Kuchta observed that standards (e.g., [MoD 89a]) are extremely helpful for motivating advances in the state of the practice of (critical) systems development. By mandating techniques that are extensions of current practice, such standards strongly motivate industry to improve and enhance their capabilities.

Peter Ryan

The U.K. Government considers formal methods to be an important technology and believes that the application of formal methods will lead to higher assurance levels of system functionality. However, it also recognizes that the goal of very high levels of assurance will increase the development costs.

Ryan observed that there is a problem with the dissemination of formal methods. The lack of dissemination appears to be a consequence of negative perceptions of the technology, including that it is inadequate, impractical, requires highly trained and specialized staff (implying that it is expensive), and that formal methods aims for "total assurance." The latter, in particular, is a myth that Ryan feels needs to be dispelled.

One further problem relating to the dissemination of formal methods is the validation of specifications. A client must be able to grasp intuitively whether the specification stipulates what is actually desired. Embodied within this concern are questions relating to desirable formal notations.

In response to the rhetorical question "Why do we perform machine proofs?" Ryan gave two answers: to take care of the drudgery that many proofs of programs and specifications manifest; and to lead to greater assurance and objectivity of the proof process.

Ryan feels that much can be gained in the absence of machine proofs and by solely using pen and paper (in a manner reminiscent of classical mathematics). He also suggested that there is a distinction between proofs found in mathematics and proofs found in software engineering. An analysis of how formal methods fits into the software engineering development process is required.

Ryan agreed with Kuchta that there are too many tools, but maintained that most existing tools are inadequate. Tools must be incrementally developed to a more satisfactory level. Ryan is in agreement with Kuchta that research diversity is important, but that duplication of effort on tool development is counter-productive.

Ryan believes that the profile of formal methods needs to be raised. The release of 00-55 has certainly helped in this regard.

The perception that formal methods add to the cost of systems must be addressed. Ryan recommends that we must proceed with the application of the technology to various efforts and then publish both the successes and the failures.

Finally, Ryan argued that education is crucial and that more training is required. As well, standards of professionalism and codes of practice are required for those involved in developing critical systems. In summary, he noted that

- formal methods are difficult, but can yield significant benefits;
- progress in formal methods will be incremental;
- the public relations aspects of formal methods need to be improved; and
- formal methods should be a part of a software engineer's tool kit.

Throughout Ryan's presentation was a general theme of the objectives for formal methods: economic and assurance. These objectives are often disjoint, in that one or the other may be the target, which should therefore affect the approach adopted.

K. Speierman

Speierman noted that there is a growing awareness of the difficulties in developing critical systems (though those involved in security have been aware of the problem for sometime). One significant advantage of this growing awareness, especially within the safety critical community, is that there is a greater concern for the problem and it has become embedded within a more general context.

The main target that one seeks in the development of critical systems is that such systems behave predictably, not anomalously. Speierman observed that the systems we are developing are exceedingly complex and that controlling this complexity is one of the more difficult tasks facing us.

Speierman agrees that formal methods are a form of applied mathematics (even when automated tools are used). With such a strong mathematical foundation to formal methods, he showed concern that the mathematical maturity of many US students (especially in comparison with other countries) is poor. If students do not have the proper training, whether at high school or at the undergraduate level, they will be unable to proceed with theoretical work. Unfortunately, students are being lured from fields such as mathematics and science by the significant publicity of the potential financial gains from business-related matters (such as hostile takeovers and leveraged buy-outs).

Speierman brought attention to the comments that John Hopcroft made in his Turing Award Lecture. In particular, there is the assertion that little theory exists to support the development of reliable complex software systems. Speierman quoted Hopcroft:

> "Despite a sizable body of knowledge, tools, and techniques, the science base of computer science is not developing as rapidly as it should. ...
> As we build larger and more complex systems, we must develop the conceptual tools that will allow us to comprehend the essence of a task ..."

Formal methods need this strong science base, with students and researchers that have received adequate training. If we are unable to achieve such a result, then there is a serious barrier to the effective and beneficial use of computers in society.

Discussion

The first area of discussion was whether the panelists believed that there would be sufficient funding to continue research into formal methods. Generally, the responses from the panelists were in the affirmative, though it was underlined that funding would depend on what the formal methods community produces: are new ideas being discovered or are old ideas just being recycled? The formal methods community must speak more clearly and loudly about the benefits of the technology and why it is so important. Two challenges were specifically mentioned. First, there is the challenge of motivating industry to work with the governments in support of the development of formal methods. (00-55 was once again mentioned as being a positive step in this direction.) Secondly, there is the challenge of improving how the research community works together. Where possible, an active and aggressive consensus-building process is necessary.

The discussion then moved to the economics of formal methods. While much of the motivation for formal methods has been based on the achievement of trustworthy critical systems, it was also felt that there is a strong economic motivator: formal methods are a means for developing systems at a lower cost. The major evidence supporting this view is the increasing application of the technology in the hardware area. Those involved in hardware development are not being motivated by safety concerns; it is the potential economic gains that are of interest.

There was also a warning that we should not take too narrow a view of formal methods. "Formal" pertains to form: dictionaries do not refer to correctness proofs and first order logic. It was suggested that, at the different levels of a system hierarchy, different kinds of formality could be applied. Specific examples mentioned were the Jackson and Yourdon methodologies.

4 Formal Methods

In this section we report on the presentations, and subsequent discussions, relating to formal methods that were given on the second day of the workshop.

4.1 What is a formal method?

Speaker: Jeannette Wing
Reporter: Dan Craigen

The purpose of Jeannette Wing's presentation was to describe her definition of a formal method and to define appropriate supporting terminology.

Informally, a formal method consists of a *formal system* and *pragmatics*. Formal systems can be described precisely as can interesting properties about those systems. For example, the properties of consistency, soundness and completeness are well understood and appropriate for most formal systems. Further, within a formal system, one is able to specify and implement programs and precisely characterize notions of correctness.

The pragmatic aspects of a formal system are, in general, imprecise. Pragmatics relate to issues arising from who will be using the formal method, why they are using the method, and how they are using the method. Pragmatics refer, in part, to ergonomic aspects of the formal method.

Wing viewed a formal system as a pair $< L, C_n >$ where L is a language and C_n a consequence relation (i.e., a mapping between strings written in L). A language consists of symbols and a grammar that describes how to write sentences within the language. A consequence relation is determined by a set of inference rules (e.g., modus ponens).

A *theory* in a formal system $< L, C_n >$ is a set of statements S, $S \subseteq L$, such that S is closed under the consequence relation C_n (i.e., $S = C_n(S)$). The notation $S \vdash A$ indicates that A is in the consequence relation of S.

A *structure* $< U, I >$ for a given language L consists of a *universe* U and an *interpretation* I. A universe is a set of values (e.g., integers, real numbers, and boolean values) and an interpretation a mapping from the language L into the universe U. In essence, a structure is used to give meanings to sentences written in L.

A structure M is a *model* of a statement A when A is true in M (denoted by $M \models A$). A statement A that is true in every model of L is said to be *valid*.

Table 4 summarizes the relationship between language and structures (i.e., between syntax and semantics).

Table 4: Syntax and Semantics

Syntax	Semantics
A is deducible from S ($S \vdash A$)	A is a consequence of S ($S \models A$)
A is a theorem, $\vdash A$	A is valid, $\models A$
S is consistent.	S has a model

Wing then discussed specifications. She defined a formal specification S as a set of statements of L. A specification S is *consistent* if and only if
$$\neg \exists A . A \in C_n(S) \text{ and } \neg A \in C_n(S).$$
A specification is *complete* if and only if
$$\forall A . A \in S \text{ or } \neg A \in S.$$
A statement A such that neither $A \in C_n(S)$ nor $\neg A \in C_n(S)$ is said to be *independent* of S.

A formal system for specification F is *sound* with respect to a formal system for implementation F', with $L \subseteq L'$, if and only if
$$\forall S \subseteq L . C_n(S) \subseteq C'_n(S).$$
A formal system for specification F is *complete* with respect to a formal system for implementation F', with $L \subseteq L'$, if and only if
$$\forall S \subseteq L . C'_n(S) \subseteq C_n(S).$$
A specification S' in a formal system F' *implements* a specification S in a formal system F if and only if
$$L \subseteq L' \text{ and } C_n(S) \subset C'_n(S').$$
Wing observed that we are not usually interested in the completeness property as specifications are often intentionally underspecified. In addition, one cannot realistically expect to capture all scenarios within which a system runs.

The above definitions are summarized by the commutative diagram in Figure 2. The above framework may be used to justify various practical activities that we pursue in developing systems. Examples of such are presented in Table 5.

To summarize the first part of her presentation, Wing characterized a method as formal if it has a sound mathematical basis, as given by a formal system.

Wing then discussed the pragmatics of formal methods. This part of the presentation subdivided into four sections: environment, audience (who), purpose (why) and style (how).

The execution of any system is dependent upon, and affects, an environment. It is not possible to "constrain" the environment, only the system. It is possible to make assumptions about the environment and it was strongly recommended that these assumptions be made explicit. In support of these comments, Wing quoted Conte's "Burnt Cookie Principle":

> No matter how perfect your cookie recipe is, if the oven thermostat fails, you may burn the cookies.

Figure 2:

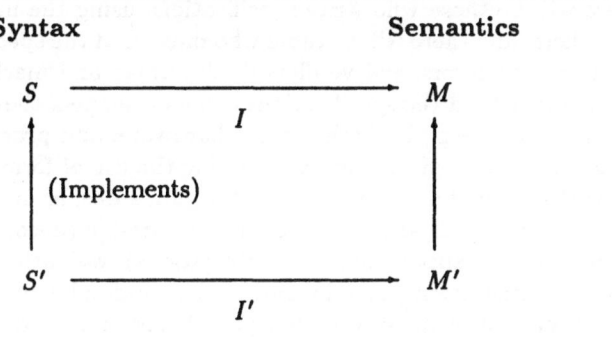

Table 5:

What we do	Formal Justification
Add new symbols, definitions properties	Language extensions, definability composition
Modularize	Conservative extension and composition
Renaming	Translation
Abstraction	Theory interpretation
Parameterization	Genericity
Combination of methods	Composition

With respect to audience, one must consider the intended users of a method. Usually there will be those who write specifications using the notation of the method (i.e., specifiers) and there will be those who must read the specifications (i.e., clients, specifiers, implementors, and verifiers [both human and machine]). For these individuals to understand the specifications being developed, they will need some background knowledge (e.g., in mathematics, hardware, and programming languages).

Wing then discussed the purposes driving the use of formal methods. Her main point was that formal methods are used "to gain a deeper understanding of the system." The formal method then can be used for design (decomposition, modularization), development (abstraction, proof obligations), validation (testing), verification (correctness, satisfaction), and documentation (redundancy).

Formal methods come in various styles. Wing presented Table 6 to suggest the widespread techniques that are available.

Table 6: Styles of formal methods

Kind	Examples	
Model-oriented	VDM, Gist	
Property-oriented	Clear, Act-1, CIP,	(algebraic)
	Iota, Larch, Z, ANNA,	(first-order)
	ML, λ-calculus	(higher-order)
State-machine	Petri nets, I/O automata, Ina Jo	
Visual	Statecharts, Miro	
Executable	OBJ, Paisley, Prolog	
Concurrency	CSP, CCS, Unity, Temporal logic	
Tool-based	Affirm, Special, Gypsy	
AI	Requirements apprentice	

Wing summarized her presentation on pragmatics by reiterating that:

- one should explicitly state the assumptions of the system's environment; that the audience be identified, by stating the intended users of the formal method (clients, specifiers, implementors, verifiers, machines) and by stating what knowledge these individuals require to use the method properly;

- the purpose of the formal method should be identified (by stating the intended users of the formal method and by realizing that the benefit of formal methods is a deeper understanding of a system); and, finally,

- the style of the formal methods should be characterized.

Discussion

The first point was that Wing's presentation suggested that a formal system had to be Hilbertized, i.e., that a formal system must be based on a predicate calculus or some similar such logic. It was felt that there are other formal methods that cannot be characterized within this framework. Wing admitted that for the sake of concreteness, her presentation was biased towards a Hilbert-style system. Her main point, however, is that a formal method must be based on a sound mathematical basis (although sometimes this basis is not explicitly given, *in principle* it could be). It was observed that there are many "methods" circulating under the banner of formal methods that are not so based.

It was observed that many engineering disciplines have existed for a long time and have made extensive use of mathematics, yet have not become involved with the intricacies of formal mathematical logic. Why is it necessary that such an approach be used in computing science? Wing's response to this question was that computing science, as a brand new engineering discipline, has yet to identify a large set of underlying definitions of what is done in practice. This is unlike other engineering disciplines where they can go back to mathematical analysis, physics, etc., to provide a formalism for what they do.

Early in her presentation, Wing stated that she doubted that there is anything available for real-time, safety-critical software. This provoked a question as to what current formal methods techniques are being applied. Wing responded that the various existing techniques are being applied to a subset of the properties of interest. She reiterated that she knew of no formal method that could be used to address all the properties of a real-time, safety-critical, fault-tolerant, reliable system.[5]

---

[5]*Editor's note:* For more discussion, readers are directed to [Win 90].

4.2 What is a specification?

Speaker: Carroll Morgan
Reporter: J.C.P. Woodcock

In answer to the question "What is a specification?" we shall examine those properties of a specification method that may be regarded as essential or desirable.

4.2.1 Essential Properties

The following properties are *essential* in a specification method.

Testing (of implementations)

Given a specification and a purported implementation, it must be possible to test for conformance; only then can we have meaningful acceptance procedures.

Consider the fragment of a Larch specification

$$quad = \textbf{proc}\ (a, b, c : int)\ \textbf{returns}\ x : real$$
$$\textbf{requires}\ b^2 \geq 4ac$$
$$\textbf{modifies nothing}$$
$$\textbf{ensures}\ ax^2 + bx + c = 0$$
$$\textbf{end}$$

Suppose that quad is offered as an implementation of *quad*; we can test for conformance by observing the results that we get for various inputs. For example,

(i)	$quad(1, -3, 2) = 1$	possibly correct
(ii)	$quad(1, -3, 2) = 2$	possibly correct
(iii)	$quad(1, -3, 2) = 0$	definitely incorrect
(iv)	$quad(1, 0, 1) = 17$	possibly correct

because

(i) $(-3)^2 \geq 4 \times 1 \times 2 \Rightarrow 1 \times 1^2 - 3 \times 1 + 2 = 0$

(ii) $(-3)^2 \geq 4 \times 1 \times 2 \Rightarrow 1 \times 2^2 - 3 \times 2 + 2 = 0$

(iii) $(-3)^2 \geq 4 \times 1 \times 2 \not\Rightarrow 1 \times 0^2 - 3 \times 0 + 2 = 0$

(iv) $0^2 \geq 4 \times 1 \times 1 \Rightarrow 1 \times 17^2 + 0 \times 17 + 1 = 0$

As an example of an untestable specification, consider the temporal logic predicate that states that "if a message is sent, eventually it will be received":

$$\Box(send \Rightarrow \Diamond receive)$$

This is untestable, since if a message has been sent, we must be prepared to wait forever to receive it, and that does not constitute a test.

Proof (of properties)

Given a property it must be possible to prove that it is (or is not) a consequence of the specification; only then can requirements analysis be simplified.

In Z, we might specify the operation that moves a file from one directory to another in a file system, by describing the two directories as partial functions from names to contents

$$\begin{array}{|l|}\hline \_Sys _____ \\ \hline dir_1, dir_2 : Name \nrightarrow Data \\ \hline \end{array}$$

and then specifying that the operation *Move* changes the state *Sys*. A file name $f?$ must be supplied which is present in the first directory, but not in the second. The first directory is updated so that it contains everything unchanged, except $f?$; the second directory is updated so that it contains everything unchanged in addition to $f?$

$$\begin{array}{|l|}\hline \_Move_____ \\ \Delta Sys \\ f? : Name \\ \hline f? \in \mathrm{dom}\ dir_1 \\ f? \notin \mathrm{dom}\ dir_2 \\ dir_1' = dir_1 \setminus (\{f?\} \lhd dir_1) \\ dir_2' = dir_2 \oplus (\{f?\} \lhd dir_1) \\ \hline \end{array}$$

Now we can *prove* the theorem that if $f?$ is a file in the directory dir_1, then moving it will result in $f?$ being a file in the directory dir_2, and its contents will be unchanged

$$f? \in \mathrm{dom}\ dir_1 \land Move$$
$$\Rightarrow f? \in \mathrm{dom}\ dir_2' \land dir_2'\ f? = dir_1\ f?$$

Although "obvious", this is not a theorem of the MS-DOS[6] copy command, for example.

In a manual for an operating system, we may see the "specification" of *Move* in Figure 3. There is no way of proving anything about this specification.

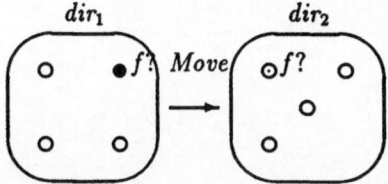

Figure 3: The *Move* Operation.

Development (of code)

It must be possible to develop executable program text from the specification; only then do specifications achieve their full potential.

In JSP (Jackson Structured Programming), a specification of a programming task may be given using a kind of parallel programming combinator. That this is a specification is evident from the fact that most applications of JSP would not have such a combinator available in the intended programming language. As an example, consider the problem of writing a program which must input data and then output it again; the requirement is that the amount of data which must be input each time

---

[6]MS-DOS is a registered trademark of Microsoft Corporation.

is different to that which must be output each time. This program is quite difficult to write using conventional structured programming techniques, since it is not clear whether the major iteration should be governing the input or the output. Michael Jackson calls this a *structure clash*. The solution in JSP is to write two co-routines, one for each task. The input is handled by this program

```
repeat
      read(inblock);
      for i := 1 to IN do
            write(temp, inblock[i])
      end
forever
```

and the output is handled by

```
repeat
      for j := 1 to OUT do
            read(temp, outblock[j])
      end;
      write(outblock)
forever
```

The problem is solved by the parallel composition of these two programs. JSP has a technique known as *program inversion* which is used to eliminate the parallel combinator. The resulting program is

```
j := 1;
repeat
      read(inblock);
      for i := 1 to IN do
          Out(inblock[i])
      end
forever
```

where

```
      procedure Out(x);
            goto γ;
α :   j := 1;
β :   if j > OUT then goto δ;
            goto ε;
γ :   outblock[j] := x;
            j := j + 1;
            goto β;
δ :   write(outblock);
            goto α
ε :   end
```

The important document is the specification with the two co-routines in parallel: it explains very well what the program does. The intricate program, with all its **gotos** and labels, is rather irrelevant. The record of the development of a program is a more important document than the program itself.

A specification language based on English has no development technique.

Desirable Properties

The following properties are *desirable* in a specification method.

Compositionality
Properties of the whole should follow from properties of the parts.

In the specification language LOTOS, we may write a specification for some protocol of the requirement that a connection must be made before sending a message

P_1 : *Connect*; *Send*; *NIL*

We may also write a specification, quite separately, of the requirement that after sending a message, there must be a disconnection

P_2 : *Send*; *Disconnect*; *NIL*

We can now compose these two specifications to obtain both their requirements: $P_1 \parallel P_2$. Here, the parallel combinator in the process algebra corresponds to *conjunction*. This simple idea was not present in LOTOS originally, but was added when its benefits were demonstrated.

Abstraction
It should be possible to specify the key features without at the same time having to describe the realization.

Consider the following description in the refinement calculus of a module which offers the abstract data type *Printers*; users may acquire a printer using the operation *Get*, and release it using the operation *Put*.

> **module** *Printers*
> **var** *ps* : set *P*
> **procedure** *Get*(**result** $p : P$) $\triangleq$
> $\qquad p : [ps \neq \{\}, p \in ps]$;
> $\qquad ps := ps \setminus \{p\}$
> **procedure** *Put*(**value** $p : P$)
> $\qquad ps := ps \cup \{p\}$
> **initially** $ps = \{\}$
> **end**

The description of the operation *Get* has abstracted from the details of how to choose the printer that is to be acquired; the implementation is free to use any appropriate allocation policy. This abstraction is obtained by the ability to mix the notations of programming and specification. The specification statement $p : [ps \neq \{\}, p \in ps]$ has the effect of changing the variable p, such that p denotes a value in ps, providing the set ps is not empty.

Independence of machines
Paper and pencil (and eraser) developments should be allowed.

For example, in the Bird-Meertens formalism a powerful notation gives great economy of expression. The notation captures the behaviour of a functional program as simply as possible. A calculus of functions is then used to *derive* an efficient implementation. The following fragment of the formalism identifies an efficient functional program (which uses an analogy to Horner's rule) with a simple description of what has to be done

$$\oplus \not\rightarrow f* = \oplus \cdot (id, f) \not\rightarrow_e$$

The left-hand side says that the program must compute the result of applying f to every element of a list, and then summing the results using the $\oplus$ operator. The right-hand side gives a cheaper way of computing this. The notation is designed to be manipulated on paper.

Executability

It is well known that executability limits expressiveness (as is shown by the work of Gödel and Church). This matters when the executable language becomes more restrictive than the mathematical system appropriate to the problem. Consider the following if statement

if $(\exists n, a, b, c \bullet n > 2 \wedge a, b, c \geq 1 \wedge a^n + b^n = c^n)$
then $f :=$ false
else $f :=$ true

If our analysis of a problem has determined that this is *what* we must compute, further analysis might show that our system is unimplementable. Compare this with trying to proceed with an executable language that must say *how* the computation is to be made.

Environmental Assumptions

A system cannot be efficient if it checks itself completely; our specification language should allow us to express assumptions under which the system will be guaranteed to work correctly. The following is a fragment of VDM that specifies an operation that sets a state variable f to the factorial of another state variable n

ext rd n : N, wr f : N
pre $n > 0$
post $f = n!$

The definition of the operation tells the implementor that it may be assumed that the variable n is strictly positive. It also tells any potential user of the operation that this assumption is likely to be made. This operation is guaranteed to work correctly only in a context where $n > 0$.

Separation of concerns

Simple behaviours should have simple specifications.

In Hoare's notation CSP (Communicating Sequential Processes) there is a hierarchy of models that deal with different aspects of distributed and concurrent systems, such as determinism, nondeterminism, divergence, timed determinism, timed nondeterminism, and so on. In specifying a system, one can choose precisely where in this hierarchy to work in order to capture the properties of interest. If there were no hierarchy, then one would need the full complexity of the most expressive model: the formidable timed failures-stability model. As an example, the following deterministic recursive process describes this talk

$$Talk1 = (slide \rightarrow Talk1 \square finish \rightarrow STOP)$$

At any time, the environment can choose to *finish* the talk. If we wish to introduce an element of nondeterminism, we can make this choice internal

$$Talk2 = (slide \rightarrow Talk2) \sqcap (finish \rightarrow STOP)$$

Now it is the speaker that decides when the talk will finish, and from the audience's point of view it is nondeterministic. If we wish to add an element of timing, we could say that slides are presented at two minute intervals, and after 45 minutes the speaker's time expires and the talk must *finish*

$$Talk3 = (\mu X \bullet (slide \rightarrow WAIT\ 2 \rightarrow X)\ |||\ WAIT\ 45); (finish \rightarrow STOP)$$

Discussion

Question: Have you addressed the fact that real machines do not implement the ideal integers, reals, etc?
Answer: No.

Question: You presented an example using JSP with a clean specification using parallelism, and then a dirty implementation. How do you address maintenance in such a system?
Answer: To maintain a system using a method like this, you must keep not only the final code, but also the way that you got there. The structure in a program is revealed not by the indentation or comment or names of identifiers, but by the development history that sits above it. People who are worried about maintaining the "dirty" code that results from the application of these methods are perhaps causing the problem by throwing away the very development that would allow them to maintain it.

4.3   What is a proof?

Speaker: Richard Platek
Reporter: Peter Ryan

The talk was an entertaining, brief history of the development of the notion of proof in mathematics. What is accepted as proof has changed greatly over the centuries. These changes reflect changing conceptions of the very nature of mathematical activity and the ontological and epistemological status of mathematical entities. Mathematics education conveys a sense of the contemporary views on these issues but usually neglects the historical perspective which reveals how they came to be and how very different they were in the past. For example, the present "formal" approach to axiomatics aims to identify and make explicit all implicit assumptions. This is done by devising formal logics which transform assumptions into conclusions and themselves encode (near) zero knowledge and thus add no content to the assumptions. This is why the systems are called "formal logics"; they are content free. In this way, one has an assurance that all the content of the conclusions is implicitly contained in the assumptions. In this view, the purpose of proofs is to make explicit what is already implicitly present. This modern view would be fairly unintelligible as recently as 200 years ago and, conversely, eighteenth century proofs leave one wondering what their constructors thought they were doing.

Before the Greeks, mathematics was basically a collection of techniques. The notion of proof seems not even to have been conceived. For example, the Babylonians had procedures to solve the quadratic equation but did not have a language in which to describe the solution. The methods are conveyed by lots of examples.

Consider, for example, the following construction that was known to the Egyptians: Given a line between two points, A and B, construct using a straight-edge and compass, a line perpendicular to AB and intersecting AB at the mid-point between A and B.

As shown in Figure 4, the construction is easy. Construct the arcs of two circles of equal radius centred on A and B. Call the intersection points of these areas C and D. Construct the line joining C and D. This is the required line.

Figure 4: Bisecting a line

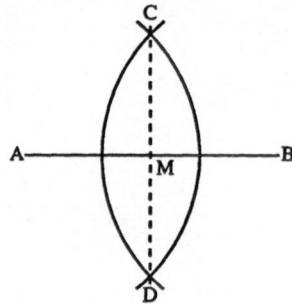

To a certified Egyptian architect, it was obvious that the given construct worked. The notion of "proof" would not have crossed his mind. If pressed, he would probably have invoked some kind of symmetry argument, which in fact would have been a pretty good answer.

Enter Euclid. He is interested in program verification. That is, he is not content just to accept it as obvious that the construct works; he wants to prove it with respect to his axioms for geometry. A proof is duly produced and presented to our Egyptian who exclaims, "Well, I knew it worked, so who needs program verification?"

The validity of the proof has, of course, now been pushed back to that of the Euclidean axioms, whereon hangs another tale.

Consider another illustration: the derivation of the formula for the period of a pendulum:

$$T = 2\pi\sqrt{\tfrac{l}{g}}$$

where l is the length of the pendulum and g the acceleration due to gravity.

The derivation relies on making the approximations:

$$\sin\theta = \theta \qquad \text{"for small } \theta\text{"}$$

In general, what is meant by "small θ" is not made clear but, in fact, the formula is usually used in appropriate situations and serves well.

The moral is that physicists continuously mis-apply mathematics but do it well, which is to say successfully.

Another example of this is the Dirac "delta functions." As originally presented, this little device was very poorly defined. In fact, one can show that there does not exist a function in the "classical" sense that satisfies the properties that Dirac required of it. On the other hand, there do exist functions that satisfy them with arbitrary precision. It was not until the theory of distributions was devised by Laurent Schwartz and others that Dirac's notation was put on a sound foundation.

If one compares the use of mathematics in computer science, one tends to find that where it is sloppily applied it is wrong. It also appears that computer scientists do not create new mathematics.

Nature is generally supposed to be continuous whereas machines are discrete in their opération. This leads to a gap. In particular, most people's intuition tends to be based on the notion of continuity: i.e., small perturbations result in small changes in behaviour. This is often not the case for automata, etc. Does computer science require a non-continuous calculus, for example?

Discussion

During the discussion, it was suggested that in some ways there was too much reinvention of mathematics in computer science, not enough reuse. For example, the idea of pre and post conditions is handled by the notion of function, and probably better. This was accepted but it was pointed out that there did seem to be areas where genuinely new mathematics was needed. For example, a calculus that took account of the fact that one may only have a finite number of integers.

The question was posed: "Well okay, but what *is* a proof?" Richard admitted that he had not answered the question of the title. The answer depended very much on the context. Within a given formalism, one could certainly explain what constituted a proof. The more interesting question of, say, "What is the proof of the equation for the period of a simple pendulum?" has no easy answer.

4.4 The role of automated tools in formal methods

Speaker: William L. Scherlis
Reporter: Norm Glick

The Defense Advanced Research Projects Agency (DARPA) has been considering a restructuring and possible increase of its support of formal methods research in the United States. DARPA's approach is to integrate formal methods into software engineering tools by emphasizing issues related to architecture and engineering for environments and formal methods tools. But this is part of a balanced research program that covers topics ranging from foundations to large-scale experimental systems development. The challenge in this engineering approach is to develop a means for enabling incremental investment by users of the technology to yield incremental improvements in capability. In other computer science communities (e.g., object management or VLSI CAD) there has been some agreement on interfaces and components and enough conventionalization to have at least the beginnings of such an incremental model. The formal methods community does not yet have such agreement, but there are "glimmerings" of it.

In the past, there have been "boom and bust" cycles in formal methods research and investment. Early support for purely *a posteriori* formal methods efforts in the early 1970s spawned the Demillo, Lipton, and Perlis reaction. These early efforts failed because they did not scale up and integrate effectively into software and systems engineering. Similarly, the artificial intelligence based efforts with natural language interfaces kept the community from addressing scaling or integration issues. The DARPA focus is on scalable, hybrid approaches. "Scalable" refers to the size of the target system, the depth of analysis supported, and the extent to which the system is formally (as opposed to informally) analyzed. "Hybrid" refers to mixing informal and formal techniques, and to mixing multiple formal approaches within a single framework.

The formal methods community has been very fragmented. For example, there are distinct groups focused on foundational issues, programming languages (with Ada in its own compartment), safety, program transformation, systems engineering (which does not communicate much with computer science), and testing. The several communities need to pull together and encourage cross-fertilization.

Scherlis suggests that the formal methods community needs to expand the scope of its activity. This expansion should be to an appropriate level of generality. It should not focus just on security but should be expanded to include reliability and other assurance-related issues. Formal methods can enable adaptability and reuse. Formal methods can also facilitate prototyping and requirements engineering.

In various other engineering disciplines there are social mechanisms to achieve agreement on certain conventions to enable a more efficient and structured marketplace. Since nobody owns an interface, motivation to create one must come through consensus in the community involving both producers and consumers. In the operating system area POSIX, OSF, and X/OPEN are examples of conventionalization activities. A negative example is the CASE industry, where growth has been limited by the lack of consensus on architecture and interoperability mechanisms.

There is evidence that sound engineering pays off. The LCF/ML effort at Edinburgh is an example where the theory community has thought carefully about engineering and has had exceptional results. The result is that thousands of people are using the results without necessarily knowing where they came from, and they are spawning several derivatives. A negative example is past efforts in which multiple research groups have built several "syntax munchers" having very similar abstract interfaces, without effectively sharing and coalescing the results.

Scherlis presented Table 7 to summarize the history of formal methods and to contrast this with his "optimistic" characterization of trends.

Table 7: A History of Formal Methods

Early Manifestations	Optimistic Characterization of Trend
A posteriori, a priori	Simultaneously build and prove systems; "small-hop" tools
Purity of formalism	Hybrid formalisms; open architecture formal methods environments
Purity through formalism	Small theorems/big programs; mixed informal/formal (e.g., empirical [testing] / analytical [formal methods])
"Verified"; no software maintenance; small examples	Documentation as key linking element
Uniform target implementation technology	Module Interconnect Formalisms; componentwise systems engineering
No support for requirements engineering	Early validation techniques; advance requirements frontier; iterative ("risk-driven") process models

In the past, the formal methods community ignored maintenance, which is generally considered to be approximately 70% of the overall Department of Defense software effort. Scherlis suggests that documentation support is a key element of a solution. He noted that he has examples of one-line specifications with ten-line implementations that could not be understood because of the absence of design rationale and documentation.

DARPA is encouraging heterogeneous implementation. They will address the problem of mediating interfaces in systems. Several groups are working on module interconnect formalisms. The next major step in programming languages might be interconnect formalisms to support heterogeneous software assemblies. On the subject of standardization, Scherlis noted that much conventionalization activity (work to encourage consensus) is going on in the guise of standardization activity (work to codify consensus). Conventionalization is a social process that requires compromise and is often difficult to accomplish. But some degree of conventionalization is an element of most of the major technology transition successes.

Regarding requirements engineering: Careful attention to the integration of formal methods and software environment could yield major improvements in requirements engineering through the simplification of the codification (formalization) of informal requirements and through the hastening of validation. Right now, late validation of requirements (i.e., conformance of codified requirements with actual need) is a major source of risk in large systems developments.

Regarding reuse: Specifications, because they are unburdened by performance considerations, can be flexible and expressive. Because of the lack of need for concreteness, specifications can be structured to follow natural conceptual structures and they can be organized into conventional components. Both of these create a high potential for reuse at the level of specifications (more so than source code).

Scherlis suggests that areas for possible consensus in the formal methods community are low-level components and interfaces for integrated software engineering/formal methods tools (e.g., workstation/server systems support, persistent object base, theorem prover, syntax support, user interface, documentation support, interpreter, analysis tools). Indeed, these components form the bulk of any implementation of a formal reasoning system.

In summary, Scherlis noted that:

- There is a need to facilitate better interaction of the formal methods community with the software engineering and programming environment communities.

- Systems documentation, including specification, design rationale (formal and informal), code, assertions, test cases, and the like, will be at the core of an advanced environment for applying formal methods in software engineering.

- Formal methods practitioners should attend more directly to issues related to scaling up, including hybrid approaches and systems whose engineering infrastructure is not dependent on specific formal deductive theories.

- With regard to engineering for formal methods tools, building infrastructure "is boring stuff, but we have to participate if we want to have impact."

Discussion

Scherlis was asked to describe his criterion for success. He stated that there was no single criterion. For ML or LCF the criterion was that they survived the social process and became accepted.

Platek called for acceptance in the research community first. His group is pleased with the ML work because they needed a theorem prover that would fit into what they were doing, and ML stopped in the right place to be usable by them. Scherlis noted that the designers of ML and LCF were careful to seek and expose "natural interfaces" in their system.

Good wanted to know the dimensions of scalability. Scherlis mentioned three: scale of the system being managed, level of capability of the environment (e.g., how smart is the theorem prover), and the degree of openness (i.e., ability to incrementally adapt or improve capability).

4.5   A Proven Hardware/Software System

Speaker: Don Good
Reporter: Milan Kuchta

Don Good from Computational Logic Inc. (CLI) provided an overview of one of the few projects in which coordinated efforts are being made to provide a mathematical proof that several layers of a design work together to form a virtual machine on top of a real machine (paper design).

The proofs are not 'pre' and 'post' condition proofs but are interpreter equivalence proofs. The CLI "stack" consists of four layers: (1) a μ-Gypsy machine (High-Level Language machine); (2) a Piton machine (assembler level machine); (3) the machine code level FM8502; and (4) the microcode gate level of FM8502. The bottom level proof considered the visible registers and the internal registers and treated the microprocessor as a bit string interpreter.

A proof has also been done of a separation kernel (not part of the above mentioned stack) which consists of about 750 words of machine language. The kernel was written to operate on a variation of the FM8501 microprocessor design which included some basic memory management features. The machine language is treated as bit strings and multi-tasking is time sliced. Tasks communicate through a 1 byte buffer.

An interpreter equivalence proof of data/program separation has been provided for the Piton compiler.

The stack components include a μ-Gypsy Code Generator which operates on a subset of sequential Gypsy (compiles μ-Gypsy to Piton). The proofs include an equivalence proof to show that the parameter passing in μ-Gypsy is equivalent to Piton. The proofs also deal with a μ-Gypsy condition handling mechanism.

The CLI stack is represented as commuting diagrams (see Figure 5) and each of the arrows in the commuting diagrams represents a function defined in Boyer-Moore Logic. Each commuting diagram represents a theorem that has been proved using either the Boyer-Moore theorem prover, Nqthm, or Kaufmann's interactive proof checker, PC-Nqthm. Kaufmann's proof checker was used for the μ-Gypsy compiler (μ-Gypsy $\rightarrow$ Piton).

Dr. Good presented a number of examples of the programs and specifications associated with each level in the stack and briefly described possibilities for the "stack of the future."

Dr. Good noted that the most difficult problem in the process of verification is obtaining an accurate model of the physical system. The issue is one of being able to model accurately what's in the physical reality of the hardware at the bottom of the stack and being able to model accurately the problem to be solved (i.e., getting good specifications that accurately represent the things that you want to happen).

Dr. Good provided a number of references that give details of the work he described: [Bev 89a], [Bev 89b], [Boy 88], [Hun 89], [Kau 88], [Moo 89], and [You 89].

50

Figure 5: A Proven Hardware/Software System

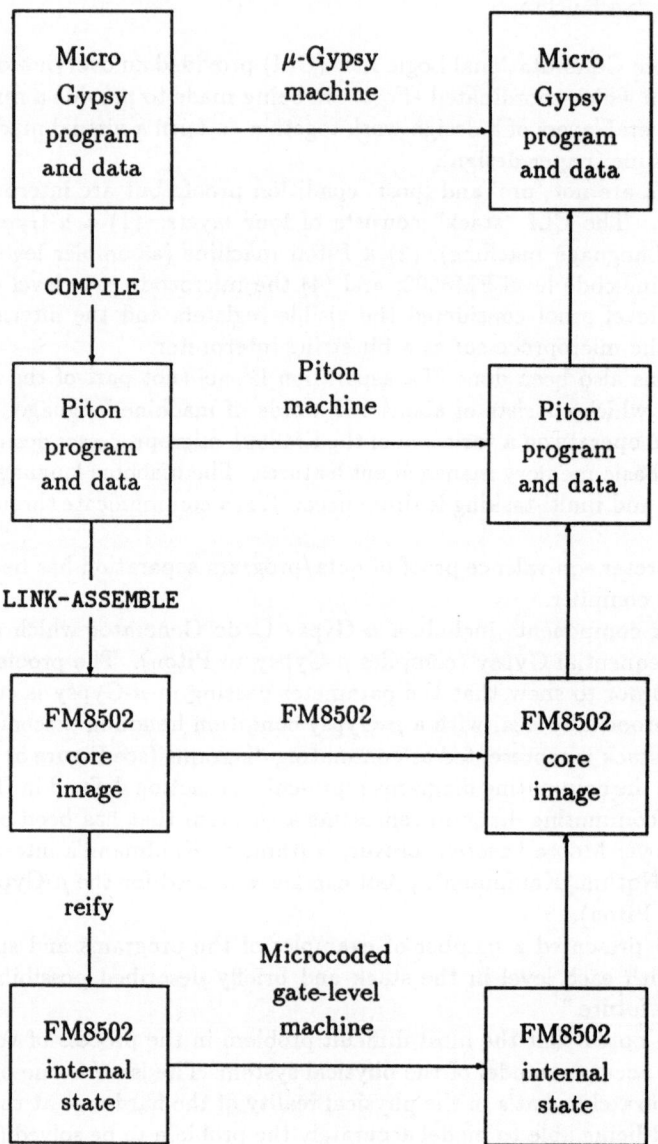

4.6 Reasoning About Large Systems

Speaker: Mack Alford
Reporter: Norm Glick

There are several views that can be taken of the systems engineer's domain of discourse: the system. It can be viewed as a collection of interacting components with a common goal, as a black box which transforms inputs to outputs, as entities interacting with an environment, or even as the product of a systems engineering process. Since systems are often too big to understand as a unit, building blocks are necessary to assist in knowing what the system is supposed to do. Some degree of formality is required to reason about the properties of systems.

Classical systems engineering involves the following steps:

- Define objectives and draw the system boundaries
- Define functions
- Decompose functions and produce component architecture
- Allocate bottom-level functions to components
- Define interfaces
- Evaluate components (e.g., feasibility, cost/schedule, limitations, faults)
- Evaluate constraints (e.g., safety, security, logistics, training)
- Tradeoff and select
- Define a test plan (e.g., normal, exceptions, stress)
- Document

Note that any component can be considered a system.

Alford described his view of the limitations of traditional systems engineering. The Functional Flow Block Diagram (FFBD) notation handles sequence and conditions but not concurrency. The Data Flow Diagram (DFD) and the Integrated Definition Language 0 (IDEF0) notations deal with I/O but do not address performance issues. Interface designs have been heuristic. Decomposition has not been defined. There has been no separation of normal and exceptional behaviors, no replicated concurrency, and no mapping of designs to simulations.

Alford observed that a system is reliable if it performs as the user expects. This implies that the system must capture the user's expected behavior. Normal behavior must be separated from exceptional behavior to define recovery from exceptions. Components fail; functions (being the ideal) do not. A system could be described in terms of hundreds of concurrent interacting state machines, but nobody would understand it in that form. To be accepted by systems engineers, notation and methods cannot change too much from what they already use.

A systems engineer's approach to describe behavior is to start with a choice at the bottom (e.g., pseudocode, specification language, Petri net, state machine). At the first level he aggregates to a discrete function (e.g., the response of the system to a single discrete input, outputs, transition to a new state). Finally, he aggregates sequences of concurrent discrete functions to time functions and repeats. The above approach is sufficient to describe arbitrarily complex behavior in a bottom-up way.

Alford gave examples of his graphical and textual representation for entities of systems (e.g., sequences of items, sequences of functions, item iteration, function iteration with state items, item sequence and selection, function selection, item concurrency, function concurrency, function replication, and function aggregation).

The systems engineering community has several techniques for graphically representing behavior (e.g., the US-Army-preferred FFBD, the US-Air-Force- preferred IDEF0, and others like N^2 Charts, DFD, PDL, and Trace). These are all different views of the same underlying information.

In the top-down approach, the decomposition is not unique. For any time function, there is more than one sequence of lower-level functions that can do the job.

To handle faults the systems engineer does a Failure Mode Effects Analysis (FMEA) which requires a "formal definition" of layers of defense against exceptions.

Alford described his Requirements Driven Development (RDD) method of systems engineering, which clearly separates logical sequences from temporal sequences. The logical sequence involves:

- Defining the system (drawing boundaries and identifying inputs/outputs)
- Identifying components
- Defining "Black Box" behavior
- Decomposing (allocating to components)
- Defining interfaces
- Bottom-up analysis of feasibility, faults, cost, schedule, limitations
- Adding fault detection/recovery
- Defining a test plan
- Documenting

He claimed that this approach permits analysis (at each stage) of the behavioral results, selection of a strategy, and addition of fault detection and recovery. In summary, it is a constructive, reviewable approach to getting the desired system behavior.

The RDD formalisms provide a basis for reasoning about termination (deadlock, livelock, reachability), invariants (e.g., are things delivered in sequence?), performance, synchronization of concurrency, and reliability versus cost.

Alford has a set of tools to support his approach to systems engineering. This includes graphical and text editors and tools to record design decisions, traceability, and issues. There are also tools for checking consistency, generating documents and supporting reviews, and "groupware" to support the efforts of many people working together.

Alford claims his approach is sufficiently close to the classical systems engineering approach to be accepted by systems engineers and sufficiently rigorous to permit the structuring of proofs (e.g., of termination). He stated that he has developed a proof for the low water mark security problem.

In the future, he will continue the development of tools to do simulations and to provide a smooth transition to software requirements and real-time distributed design. He claims that any of his tools will ensure preservation of behavior in decomposition, allocation, interface design, fault detection and recovery—all the way to the "least unit of code."

Discussion

Most of the discussion involved requests for definitions of terms used and interpretations of diagrams presented. Roger Stokes noted that some of the diagrams were reminiscent of Petri nets. Alford commented that both Petri nets and state diagrams were influences in the development of his notation.[6]

---

[6] *Editor's note:* For background information, please refer to [ALC] [Alf 85], [PS 85].

4.7 An Overview of the Cleanroom Software Development Process

Speaker: Dr. Jesse Poore
Reporter: Larry Hatch

Dr. Poore described a process, called "Cleanroom," which he advocates for the development (from specification to code) of software.

Dr. Poore claimed that skilled practitioners of the methodology can attain the goal of producing a finished job in one-half the time, with one-tenth the number of errors, and one-third as many lines of code, as previously accustomed to experiencing. However, data which clearly supports the general claim is not yet available.

The steps in the Cleanroom development of software are:

- Establish meaningful management control over the development process.

- Use the Cleanroom life cycle of executable product increments for specification, design, development and certification.

- Use the box structure techniques for system analysis and design.

- Design statistical tests based on the intended usage environment. Allow insight, gained in defining and constructing the tests, to question the specification and influence the design.

- Use functional verification to determine that the design is ready to code and certify.

- Conduct the statistical tests and use the certification model to calculate the reliability values and to demonstrate that the software meets the contractual requirements.

The aspects of Cleanroom which might be considered formal methods are box structures, functional verification, and statistical testing.

The *box structure* is a hierarchy of black box, state box, and clear box descriptions of the software (the last description is written in what is termed the "box description language" (BDL) and is referred to as pseudo-code). The "boxes" are representations of the results of refinement steps in the development process. At each step, the emerging product (box) is subject to various analyses.

Functional verification seems to be, essentially, human intensive scrutiny (including, perhaps, mathematical proofs that provide some assurance of hierarchical consistency) and is carried out on the BDL description.

Finally, *statistical testing* is based upon an understanding and characterization of the usage environment. Dr. Poore admitted that presently, in many cases, it is difficult to generate an effective characterization of the usage environment.

Dr. Poore reported on some of his experiences of using the Cleanroom methodology and the results are encouraging. However, Dr. Poore stated that more examples of the use of Cleanroom need to be carried out and the results published. He also indicated that research to develop techniques that better characterize the usage environment and to develop tools to assist the transforming of BDL descriptions to target languages are needed.

A novel aspect of Cleanroom is that the certification testing is performed by a group separate from that carrying out previous steps of the development process. If the code fails certification testing, the "product" is returned and the process reiterated in whatever detail the development group deems necessary (and then resubmitted for certification).

Discussion

The questions after the presentation tended to focus on two points that Dr. Poore did not contest at the time. However, upon reviewing an earlier version of this report, Dr. Poore has recommended the inclusion of two points of clarification:[8]

Observation: The present ability to perform effective statistical testing (to assure "good" code) is inadequate.
Response: The ability to perform statistical testing is adequate but may be a difficult job (the individual who asked the question did not think it was adequate for her "safety" interests). It is adequate if your objective is to certify the highest possible mean time to failure for a given testing budget.

Observation: The (functional) verification is not completely rigorous (since design errors have been found by the statistical testing).
Response: Functional verification can be as rigorous as one wishes to make it. In practice, the rigour is relaxed in the interest of completing the task and the remaining errors appear to be superficial rather than deep. As Parnas suggested, "one does not have to be doing axioms and rules of inference in a strange notation to be doing formal methods ..." So, any failings rest with the provers rather than the method.

---

[8] *Editor's note:* For more information about Cleanroom, please refer to [LM 88], [Mil 88], and [CDM 86].

4.8 HOL

Speaker: Mike Gordon
Reporter: Milan Kuchta

Mike Gordon from Cambridge University described the history and motivation behind HOL (Higher Order Logic) and some examples to which HOL has been applied.

HOL is a programming environment for interactively checking and generating formal proofs in higher order logic, and writing secure special purpose theorem proving tools. HOL was originally selected for hardware verification. HOL is based on (the ideas and code of) LCF (Logic of Computable Functions).

The original motivation for HOL came from the need to deal with hardware design errors (erroneous results from arithmetic logic and unpredictable system crashes); the increasing number of safety and security critical systems and subsystems that are microprocessor controlled (e.g., automotive steering and braking, medical systems, aircraft control systems, railway signalling and nuclear power stations); and the significant financial losses that can occur when design errors cause delays in the delivery of products.

Dr. Gordon presented the case that Computer-Aided Formal Reasoning (CAFR) can be "very useful" with "existing tools" but more basic research is needed to maintain the current momentum.

The design of current systems is hard to get right since many of these systems are complicated and have many levels (i.e., circuit, architecture and programming).

Currently, design verification is largely based on "simulation." Unfortunately, simulation is not a comprehensive method for identifying design errors. It is usually not feasible to simulate more than a small fraction of possible situations; as designs get bigger, simulation becomes computationally intractable; and it is difficult to combine the results of simulations at different levels. Verification using CAFR provides an attractive alternative since requirements can be specified in a formal language and achievement of requirements can be demonstrated by formal mathematical proof.

Current research in HOL is directed at organizing multi-level proofs (formal reasoning about abstractions and larger-scale proof experiments); identifying new applications of HOL (protocol analysis, signal processing, and verified synthesis functions such as cell generation for hardware and language translators for software); and proof processing (high level proof accounts and proof deliverables).

HOL has its roots in LCF, which was developed at the University of Edinburgh in the 1970s. It evolved through further work at Edinburgh and Cambridge to HOL88. The work also generated standard ML which was developed at Edinburgh.

HOL has been used to verify a simulation model for CMOS cells. Previously, verification of the cell designs involved manual inspection. The application of HOL (in a 10 day effort) uncovered a design specification error which had survived many man-months of non-formal verification. HOL has also been applied to the One Way Regulator (OWR). The OWR is a bridge to link computer systems that operate at different security levels and implements an information flow control policy.

Some of the applied research problems which need to be addressed are how CAFR should be combined with existing CAD methods (loose or tight coupling); the development of a theory and tool infrastructure (standard theories and decision procedures); and the generation of a number of large scale proof experiments.

More basic research problems are (1) What is the right foundation for general purpose CAFR? (set theory, simple type theory, Martin–Löf style type theory, a calculus of constructions, etc.); and (2) Can or should application specific formalisms be mechanized by *definitional extension* of a single formalism?

Some of the technology transfer problems are how large formal proofs should be managed in industry and the absence of a significant community of CAFR practitioners (of which researchers are only a small subset).

The study and use of HOL is encouraged. It is free and easy to get; it has a liberal licensing policy (commercial applications are encouraged); it is intended to be made available on as many platforms as possible (a port to Common LISP has recently been completed); free seed consulting is provided; significant effort is being applied to improve the documentation; and as many of the users of the system as possible have been involved in the development of the system.

Dr. Gordon concluded that CAFR is practical now, using existing tools, but more basic research is needed to develop CAFR. Dr. Gordon observed that HOL is only now becoming widely used even though it is based on research done over 10 years ago at Edinburgh; thus we should be supporting research that will lead to a new generation of CAFR tools in 1999.

Discussion

Dr. Gordon stated that an effort has been initiated to use HOL in the construction of a "stack" similar to the CLI stack (see Section 4.5). The HOL stack will be based on an INMOS device and a simple assembly level language. The focus of this effort will be on dealing with real time properties (i.e., proving that if an input arrives at time t then there is a bound on when an output will occur).

In response to a question about performance or utility of HOL versus Boyer-Moore, Dr. Gordon replied: Although HOL does not have things like an integer box, a number package for doing linear arithmetic (which may mean that, in some cases, it may take several days to do in HOL what may be accomplished in Boyer-Moore in minutes), on large problems, such as VIPER, the difference is not likely to be that great since the majority of the effort is in developing the structure of the proof rather than the proof process itself. Although the Boyer-Moore prover (especially with the Kaufmann interactive front end) is more powerful in performance, it uses a more restrictive logic than HOL. The result is a better performing tool but a more restrictive logical framework. Dr. Gordon noted that if an application could adequately be formulated in Boyer-Moore logic then the Boyer-Moore prover would provide a faster result. He noted that, for many of the applications and styles of specification with which he has been involved, the Higher Order features of HOL are used and he would be unhappy if they were not available. He felt that the increase in performance of the proof support tools would not compensate for the increased time used to formulate a solution.

A library mechanism has been recently incorporated into HOL and a tautology checker developed by ICL has been added. Dr. Gordon felt that this was a useful improvement. If someone were to write a decision procedure for the decidable part of arithmetic, days of work could be avoided. As an example, Dr. Gordon noted that in one area of which he is aware (i.e., protocol correctness) significant effort had been spent reasoning about formulae which probably lie in a decidable subset.[9]

---

[9] *Editor's note:* For more information on HOL, please refer to [Gor 87] and [Gor 89].

4.9   Z

Speaker: J.C.P. Woodcock
Reporter: J.C.P. Woodcock

This talk is divided into two parts: the first describes some of the experiences in using Z; the second describes a technical example.

Experiences in using Z

Managing software developments
Z is a notation which is based on elementary set theory and logic, and is used for producing structured descriptions of software systems. The work on Z at Oxford University has involved the application of mathematics to the development of computer programs, with the intention of reducing overall costs and risks.

Many computer systems are important to society: there may be lives depending on the correct operation of the system, or large amounts of money; it may be so large and complicated that there is little likelihood of its successful completion and subsequent correct operation; or it may be supposed to embody some agreed international standard, and it must conform. Examples of these kinds of systems include the programs that are used to land an aeroplane under computer control, or shut down nuclear reactors during emergencies; patient monitoring systems; banking systems that handle many millions of pounds every hour; airline reservation systems that may coordinate the efforts of several thousand travel agencies; and international standards for the way that automatic telephone exchanges may communicate with each other in order to transmit our telephone calls.

In each of these examples the cost of failure is too high, if it can be contemplated at all. Our mathematical proofs offer an assurance of correctness that cannot be obtained elsewhere. On less important systems, the mathematical approach may be used to simplify the development of a program, and thereby increase its quality and usefulness.

Experience has shown that it is possible to manage such important software developments using mathematics, structure and modularity, and data refinement. Correctness may be ensured through the techniques of proof and derivation; precision through the use of mathematics, in which ambiguous statements simply cannot be uttered; abstraction through data refinement; and re-use through modularity. Of course, many important software systems are too large for this approach to work at present. Either these systems are not critical (in which case it doesn't matter), or they are critical, in which case the cost of failure is too high for them to be developed at all.

Applications of Z
Uses of Z, and the closely related VDM, are not particularly widespread. INMOS have developed the IEEE-Standard Floating-Point Transputer using Z. First they formalized the IEEE Standard itself, then they developed algorithms which were correct with respect to this description, and carried them down to the silicon. Reports from INMOS indicate that this was a very successful application of Z. Not only is the final product satisfactory, but it seems to have saved a good deal of money over a conventional development route.

For some years, a project has been carried out jointly by IBM UK Laboratories at Hursley, and the Programming Research Group at Oxford. The research objectives are to demonstrate the applicability of mathematics to the development of large industrial software products. These objectives are being met, since the last three years have seen the Z notation, which is based firmly on elementary set theory, being used by IBM to develop the latest release of the CICS transaction processing system.

At Tektronix in Oregon, oscilloscopes have been developed using Z; at Manchester University a theorem prover, and in Denmark various compilers, have all been developed using VDM. Many other applications exist, but their successes and failures are less well documented.

The rôle of proof

We can identify two uses of proof in these kinds of developments using notations like VDM and Z. The first concerns *certification*. Many customers, particularly in defence, security, and avionics, require a (usually machine-checked) formal proof of certain properties of their systems; for example, that it implements some security policy. Such proofs are difficult to obtain, and consume vast resources, so vast that significant proofs are carried out only rarely. They form part of the certification process, rather than the development process, and much research, predominantly in the USA, has been carried out into the building of tools to manage them.

The second kind of use is, to quote Lakatos, to *improve* by proving. As part of the process of specification, refinement, and implementation, proofs can be carried out to obtain simpler, more accurate descriptions. The idea is to produce a proof from which the software engineer can learn important insights about the system being developed. In support of this idea tools play a less certain part, the backs of envelopes being preferred instead. The use of formal methods tends to move a developer closer to the essence of the problem, whereas mechanical tools tend to increase the distance from it. This isn't to say that mechanical assistance is wrong, rather that it has to be of the right sort, used in the right way. Of much greater importance is the ability to perform structured proofs using a compositional proof system. In this way, the size of the proof needed at any time may be kept within reasonable limits, following as it may the structure of the specification or data refinement.

An industrial example

As an example of the industrial use of Z, the IBM CICS work is interesting. CICS is a transaction processing system with over 27,000 users throughout the world. It consists of over 800,000 lines of code, a mixture of assembly language and PL/AS. It has enjoyed over 25 years of continuous development, and is expected to continue satisfying customers for many more. It finds its application in banking, airline reservation systems, and stock control, where it may be required to handle large numbers of terminals and massive amounts of data.

Over 200 people at IBM Hursley Park have been trained in the use of Z. Over 20 developers have written Z specifications and designs of new functionality for the most recent release, with perhaps 30 more people having to read and use such documents.

The current release of CICS is the largest ever developed, with over 268,000 lines of code. Of this, 39,000 lines were developed using Z, and 11,000 lines partially using Z. This amounted to 2,000 pages of Z. The release also saw considerable internal restructuring of CICS to allow for future developments.

The development cost benefit was assessed to be a 9% improvement over traditional techniques for the 39,000 lines of code.

Altogether, the experience seems to have been a happy one, with good quality specifications and designs being produced. Notably, there have been no complaints because of lack of tools.

Although there must be a considerable commitment from the managers of an industrial project in order for the use of formal methods to succeed, no formal method can be imposed by the management; programmers must also see the need and want to use it. It is vital for there to be consultants on hand to assist developers; just as vital are real examples that can be used as inspiration. Tools, however, are not vital. When the CICS work started, there weren't really any Z tools available, and even now there are very few. This did not prove to be a hindrance, the work was done anyway. This shouldn't come as much of a surprise, since formal methods are an aid to *thinking*, and we can always do that without the assistance of a computer.

A technical example

As a technical example of the use of Z, consider the specification of the CCITT Signalling System No 7 that Ian Hayes and his colleagues wrote at the University of Queensland, and that we have been verifying. No 7 is a protocol for signalling between trunk telephone exchanges. Let M be the set of messages that the protocol handles. The abstract specification of this protocol is really very small, and we call it the *external view*

$$
\begin{array}{|l}
\hline
\_Ext _____ \\
\quad In, Out : seq[M] \\
\hline
\quad \exists\, s : seq[M] \bullet In = s \frown Out \\
\hline
\end{array}
$$

This states that the protocol promises to deliver messages without loss, corruption or re-ordering; liveness issues are addressed elsewhere. Initially, no messages have been sent

$$
\begin{array}{|l}
\hline
\_InitExt _____ \\
\quad Ext \\
\hline
\quad In = \langle \rangle \\
\hline
\end{array}
$$

A theorem that we must prove is that there is at least one initial state—there would be no point in continuing otherwise

$$\exists\, Ext \bullet InitExt$$

The description of CCITT Signalling System No 7 is a large document; the specification that we have just produced is exceedingly small. We have obtained this economy of expression by using *abstraction*. The specifications of large systems need not themselves be large.

As an aid to understanding the design of this protocol, we introduce a *sectional view*. Let *SPC* be the set of signalling point codes. A sectional view consists of the route that the messages must take through the network, a nonempty sequence of *SPC*s without repetition. Each section in this route may receive and send messages, and those which have been received but not yet sent are in the section; this is depicted in Figure 6.

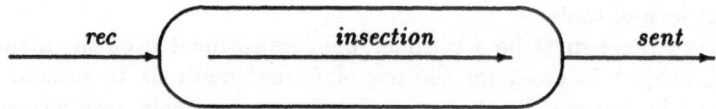

Figure 6: An individual section

The messages sent by a section are those received by the next section on the route; this is depicted in Figure 7.

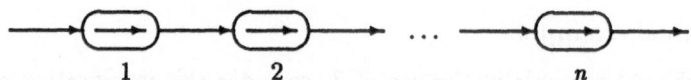

Figure 7: The Sectional View

The description is formalized in the following specification

```
┌─ Section ────────────────────────────────────
│  route : injseq₁[SPC]
│  rec, insection, sent : seq[seq[M]]
├──────────────────────────────────────────────
│  #route = #rec = #insection = #sent
│  rec = insection ⩔ sent
│  front sent = tail rec
└──────────────────────────────────────────────
```

where *insection* ⩔ *sent* is the pair-wise catenation of the two sequences: thus we have that $rec\ i = (insection\ i) \frown (sent\ i)$.

The kind of theorem that we like to prove is that these two views are consistent in some way.

Theorem 1 The sectional view is consistent with the external view.

The external view may be extracted from the sectional view in the following way: the head of *rec* describes *In*, the last of *sent* describes *Out*, and the discrepancy between them is simply those messages in *insection*. To prove this, we must show that

$$Section \vdash head\ rec = (\frown/\ insection) \frown (last\ sent)$$

Proof: by induction on #*route*.

Basis: $\#route = 1.$

$(\frown\!/\ insection) \frown (last\ sent)$

$= [\text{since } \#route = \#insection = \#sent = 1]$

$\quad (\frown\!/\langle insection\ 1\rangle) \frown (last\ \langle sent;\ 1\rangle)$

$= [\text{by definition of distributed catenation}]$

$\quad (insection\ 1) \frown (sent;\ 1)$

$= [\text{from } Section]$

$\quad rec\ 1$

$= [\text{by definition of } head]$

$\quad head\ rec$

Inductive step: $\#route > 1.$ Assume that

$head(front\ rec) = (\frown\!/(front\ insection)) \frown (last(front\ sent))$

$(\frown\!/\ insection) \frown (last\ sent)$

$= [\text{since } \#insection = \#route > 1]$

$\quad (\frown\!/((front\ insection) \frown (last\ insection))) \frown (last\ sent)$

$= [\text{by definition of distributed catenation}]$

$\quad (\frown\!/(front\ insection)) \frown (last\ insection) \frown (last\ sent)$

$= [\text{from } Section]$

$\quad (\frown\!/(front\ insection)) \frown (last\ rec)$

$= [\text{since } \#rec = \#route > 1]$

$\quad (\frown\!/(front\ insection)) \frown (last\ (tail\ rec))$

$= [\text{from } Section]$

$\quad (\frown\!/(front\ insection)) \frown (last\ (front\ sent))$

$= [\text{by the induction hypothesis}]$

$\quad head(front\ rec)$

$= [\text{by a property of } head]$

$\quad head\ rec$

The sectional view is more detailed than the external view, and our theorem demonstrates that it is a genuine *refinement*. The proof is certainly very simple, relying on properties of sequences. The simplicity of the proof gives us confidence in our abstractions.

Discussion

Question: Were any proofs carried out on the CICS project?

Answer: For this release, very few were carried out, although people did reason about things in design reviews. For the next release, I intend that there will be many more proofs, if these add to the value of what has been done.

Question: Is Z frozen now such that you could have a parser for it?

Answer: Z is frozen, or at least pretty cold, but it is of course an extensible notation anyway. There are two books that embody Z as it is: [Spivey88] and [Spivey89].[10] There is a move afoot to produce a British Standard based on these books. Mike Spivey has also produced a parser and type checker based on the notation in his two books. These run on a Sun or IBM PC, seem genuinely usable, and don't cost a great deal of money.

Question: Martyn Thomas said earlier that proof wasn't very important at the top level. You say that, in your view, proof is very helpful in clarifying and structuring descriptions. How are these two views reconciled?

Answer: People get an awful lot out of using a formal method descriptively; as a tool for communication and for sorting out ideas, I don't know of anything better. However, I see no virtue in using a formal method without doing some proof, even on systems where you know that it really doesn't matter terribly much if it fails. To avoid proof would be to get the illusion of formality, with none of its benefits. It is very important to do proofs as part of modelling: it helps you to get a clean, simple model. As a modelling technique, you try to discover consequences, and make sure that desirable properties are preserved in development. You get so much insight as you do this, that it is unwise to turn your back on proof. I don't think that this is the kind of activity that goes on with mechanical theorem provers; too much responsibility for the proof development gets delegated to the machine. This seems inevitable when mechanical provers deal with proofs involving tens of millions of inferences. I wouldn't know what to do with that kind of proof. What I'm most interested in is compositional proof techniques that help me to economize on the amount of proof that I must do. I want to write little pieces of specification and compose them, and do little pieces of proof and compose them in a like manner. Such structured proof techniques are very powerful. What Martyn Thomas referred to was the kinds of proofs that people do with mechanical theorem provers for certification purposes.

Question: In your technical example [a protocol specification], there was an important point: data refinement means that formal specifications of large systems need not themselves be large.

Answer: Used together, data refinement and proof can lead to great simplifications and the discovery of useful levels of abstraction. In the specification that I used in the example, we invented new levels of abstraction simply to explain the system and to simplify our proofs. We learnt a lot.

Question: What is the formal mathematical logic system that Z adheres to?

Answer: The semantics for Z are described in [Spivey88]. The proofs that I carry out use ordinary classical logic and set theory. However, Will Harwood and I are working on a proof system for Z that includes rules for reasoning about the schema notation [the structuring mechanism in Z].

---

[10] *Editor's note:* For more information on Z, please also refer to [Hay 87].

5 Reports From Working Groups

5.1 Working Group 1: What is the applicability of formal methods in systems engineering?

Chair:	John Rushby
Reporter:	J.C.P. Woodcock
Participants:	Graham Birtwistle
	Bernard Carré
	Greg Chisholm
	Steven Hall
	Larry Hatch
	Doug Howe
	Paul Joannou
	Milan Kuchta
	Bill Legato
	Nancy Leveson
	Roger Stokes

Group description

The purpose of this group was to determine the applicability of formal methods technology. How should it be used in the development of trustworthy systems? Should formal methods technology be used in the development of such systems? What aspects of computer-based systems can be successfully described using current, and perceived, formal methods techniques? How does formal methods technology relate to other techniques used in the development of critical systems?

The following report is the consensus of the opinion in the workshop session on the applicability of formal methods.

Issues and problems in systems engineering

The session started by discussing the issues and problems in systems engineering for which formal methods might offer some alleviation.

First, there is the problem of size. Einstein once said that "Systems should be as simple as possible, but no simpler." However, because of the desire to achieve rather complicated ends, there is a certain unavoidable complexity in many modern systems. One of the most important issues is to address the need to manage and control the consequences of this unavoidable complexity.

Second, there is the need to establish what the British call "fitness for purpose" in systems whose failure could have unacceptable consequences.

Third, there is the belief, or the hope, that formal methods may provide the control and assurance that we do not know how to achieve otherwise.

What are formal methods?

Formal methods are, informally, methods that support rational argument, analysis and construction. They provide a basis for decision making, assurance, and design justification. They allow properties of systems to be calculated from those of their components and the inter-connections between them. In principle, there should be some axioms and a set of inference rules to support the method. This is particularly important if you want to mechanize the process.

The rôle of formal methods in systems engineering

The rôle that formal methods might play in systems engineering is in the support of rational design decisions, by enabling one to predict and explore the consequences of design choices. This is made possible by the fact that a formal method permits the calculation of the consequences of these design choices. It is possible to determine whether proposed designs actually implement the required specification, and even whether or not the specification is satisfiable at all. This permits the designer to choose the best design, in some sense, to achieve the specification, and to justify the design both personally and to the reviewers.

For all this to be possible, descriptions of specifications and designs must be amenable to formal deduction, because that is what satisfies these purposes for analysis. It enables the demonstration of consistency between design and specification. Its objectivity is particularly beneficial in an adversarial context, where some independent correctness criterion must be demonstrated.

Formal methods in the system life-cycle

The group agreed on the following generic life-cycle model:

- Requirements
- Specification
- Design
    - Decomposition
    - Evaluation of alternatives
    - Prediction/exploration of properties
    - Selection: rational choice of components and method of composition
    - Internal justification
- Management of development and composition of components
- Integration testing, etc.
- Repeat

The belief of the group is that formal methods can be useful in nearly all stages of the life-cycle.

Perhaps the most interesting point is the rôle that formal methods can play in design. This seems to be the rôle that the practitioners of Z, for example, have been exploring. Z has been used to specify, perform decomposition, evaluate alternatives, predict and explore properties, and then, in particular, select a design in a rational way that allows internal justification. After all this, the work can then go to the reviewers and certifiers for external justification.

Formal methods and assurance

Nobody in the group claimed that formal methods would dispense with the need for testing, or indeed any of the other methods for gaining direct experience of a system. Formal methods must be supported by testing in order to validate the assumptions on which some of the calculations are based. They do not replace, but support many of the established systems engineering forms of analysis, such as failure modes and effects analysis. They should support experimentation in the requirements stage, and testing for quantitative reliability estimation.

It should be noted that formal methods do not provide a number that can be plugged into a reliability analysis of a system. If reliability is a concern, then there should be an analysis of failure modes and effects.

Issues in formal methods

If several formalisms are used in a development, it is not always possible at present to combine their proof systems, so that proofs can be carried all the way from the top to the bottom.

Those formal methods that are effective are at present rather limited in scope, and applicable primarily to sequential systems. If a formalism is applied outside its domain of applicability, then there is a serious danger of failure.

If specialized formal methods are constructed for particular problem domains, then it is important that they have a formal semantics for their foundation in conventional mathematics. For example, it is possible to write the model theory for temporal logic in first order logic, so that there is some common ground for newcomers.

There are certain issues, such as timing, that are still research questions. This limits the applicability of formal methods, and perhaps it also limits the nature of the systems whose development should be attempted by other means as well. The ability to make deductions must take precedence over superficial attractiveness.

Tools

The group felt that it was important to distinguish the different purposes of proof. There is proof as an analytical tool in support of modelling, rational design analysis, and comprehension. There is also proof for certification purposes. These two uses of proof have different goals, and they may need different support.

The first may not need any kind of mechanized support. If it is felt necessary, then it may have more to do with house-keeping: the soundness of the support is less important. The kind of tool that is useful here is a sort of mechanized back of an envelope. The judgment of the value of such a tool may be made on economic grounds: does it help to get the job done better and faster? When dealing with assurance, then perhaps there is a more serious worry about the soundness of the tool.

There is a suspicion that the pain and cost of formal certification may increase exponentially in the extent of the guarantees that are required on the soundness of the entire process.

Obstacles to the adoption and effectiveness of formal methods

The group enquired into the obstacles to the adoption and effectiveness of formal methods. First, of course, must be the lack of experience, demonstrable successes, and confidence in formal methods by the outside world. People worry that these new techniques may be more expensive and may lengthen developments.

External clients may find it, or at least perceive it to be difficult for them to understand, and so to bring to bear their experience on, formal specifications.

The lack of well-documented case studies is being addressed by another group at this workshop (see Section 5.3), but the group discussed the lack of useful libraries of verified components. There is a technical problem to do with the indexing of a library of components: any automatic system would have to be an automatic theorem prover, in order to decide whether the component's specification would satisfy the required specification. However, it was felt that given a limited problem domain, users could index such a library themselves (and presumably prove the theorem themselves).

There is a tension between the desire to build a critical mass of users and tools, and the need to avoid premature industrialization and standardization.

Managing expectations

The group's final discussions concerned the management of expectations. There is a clear need to avoid hyperbole in discussing the merits of formal methods. Overselling has been a problem which has plagued the practice of formal methods since the early days.

There is a need to eliminate the general perception that formal methods are to do with proofs of correctness; there is a larger context in which formalism may be applied and found useful. There should be greater emphasis on calculation and derivation. There is a need for clarifying the benefits of formalism without formal proof.

There is a need for *scrupulous* examples and demonstrations, and for textbooks, education, consultants, etc.

Discussion

Question: Did you try to classify a spectrum of formal methods from very strict to more relaxed?
Answer: No.

Question: What is a "scrupulous example"?
Answer: By "scrupulous" we meant that its assumptions are most carefully stated. That there is a comprehensive and complete documentation of what was achieved and how it was achieved. That you are not left with any uncertainty as to where

the final product came from. I know of no existing developments that would have that character, although the CLI work (see Section 4.5) might qualify.

Question: Did you discuss the means by which you could actually convince systems development groups to accept formal methods?
Answer: We discussed the need for convincing examples. We recognized that you won't convince unless you have a product and demonstrations of efficacy to offer.

Question: Did you discuss technology transfer issues?
Answer: We discussed the need for education, textbooks, and consultancy. We also discussed the need to manage expectations carefully, so that, in our zeal to proselytize, we do not oversell our trade. Otherwise we shall cause eventual embarrassment to ourselves and, perhaps, a loss of faith and interest in what we are proposing. We also covered the issue of technology transfer in what we thought was a list of obstacles to the adoption of formal methods.

Question: Did you get any feeling that the formal methods you talked about could be integrated with the less formal ones?
Answer: I think that the group felt that this might be the case, although they didn't have much evidence to support this. Those who were familiar with informal methods did not see how more rigorous methods could help them.

The British contingent in our group advocated the use of formalism in the design process to help to produce a better product, with less stress on external certification. This approach is easier to integrate with the use of an informal design technique, because it is very flexible.

There seems to be quite a cultural difference between the way that formal methods are perceived in the United States and in Britain. In the States it has tended to be in support of certification. This is probably more to do with accidents of funding and history, than to do with a particular bias on the part of practitioners. But there is quite a difference.

Question: Can you define the notion of "less formal than"?
Answer: We didn't define it; what we were trying to do was to admit the use of useful methods that are not explicit about their mathematical basis. I think that perhaps it isn't the right measure to use. It is the extent to which the formalization is made totally explicit that is important.

It might be worth emphasizing that, although we recognize that the term "formal methods" has a wide range of interpretation and degrees of formality, we achieved a consensus: formal methods allow us to obtain degrees of assurance that we don't know how to achieve otherwise.

Remark: It is important to follow up on the remark on integrating formal methods into the design process: I think that the remark could be interpreted as indicating that that position is not advocated in North America. This is not true. It has been recognized since the early 1970s that the integration of formal methods with design is the only sensible way to proceed with this stuff. I don't think that anyone in the research community has advocated otherwise for the past 15 years. However, some of the *practice* has been in the rôle of certification only, after systems have been built.

5.2 Working Group 2: What are the theoretical and practical limits of formal methods?

Chair: Jeannette Wing
Reporter: K. Speierman
Participants: Mack Alford
Kurt Asmis
Martine Calvé
John Gannon
Will Harwood
Richard Kemmerer
Ian King
David Luckham
Jesse Poore
Mark Saaltink

Group description
The purpose of this working group was to identify the theoretical limits of formal methods and to identify the practical limits of formal methods in the near-, medium- and far-term.

The identification of the theoretical boundaries will define an envelope within which formal methods research and application will expand. The theoretical boundaries will also result in the possibility of identifying risks remaining in the fielding of systems that have been verified formally.

Practical limitations to the technology will be with us for a long time. The working group attempted to identify the limitations of the technology as currently existing, and attempted to map the likely progress over the next few decades. For example, in the realm of computer security, the U.S. Department of Defense has found it convenient to focus on the use of verification systems to prove security properties of specifications; limited verification of higher level code has occurred. Are there similar limitations within the realm of safety critical systems?

Report
Early in the session, we dispensed with what were thought to be the theoretical limitations of formal methods and to divide that into two questions. First, what are the boundaries between the mathematical world and the real world? Our answer is: there are boundaries but they are not unique to formal methods. They are common to all engineering disciplines by virtue of the fact that one has to deal with human beings and the real world. So, there are two boundaries. One is a mapping from the informal to the formal, which is an iterative process not subject to proof: the first codification of the client's requirements. The second is a mapping from the real world to some abstract model or abstract representation of it. This boundary should not be surprising because it is ubiquitous in applied mathematics.

The second question is what, even within our nice mathematical world, do we know that we can never do? There are limitations, but they are not unique to formal methods. They are common to all areas in computer science; in particular, classical undecidability results like the halting problem are obvious limitations. Further theoretical limits may be discovered in the future.

The discussion was structured on the practical limitations by considering the various axes along which we could say "Where are we now? Where do we think we can be? How long will it take to get there?" In other words, try to push this envelope of our boundaries. The working group went so far as to provide estimated numbers. The number "n" means it will be "n" years before we will be applying some formal method somewhere on some significant example. That method may not be widely used. By "significant" we mean that the system or the example to which we are applying this formal method will be used and it will run on some machine. By "applying" we mean using formal methods to specify and refine— in design rather than in code-level verification. Where we make an exception, we will point that out in the tables. Sometimes we mean something like after-the-fact specification where one is handed a huge system and has to figure out how to use it—one way of figuring out how to use it is to specify it formally after the fact. When the number zero appears on the tables that means we can do it now—or, rather, people are doing it now.

The first axis we considered was the hardest and the most interesting; we chose it because we were freshest. This was to consider the problem domains or properties of systems (see Table 8). We started with simple sequential programs, and we agreed that we could specify them. There are various specification languages which we can use today to do so (VDM, Z, Larch, FDM, Gypsy, ANNA, OBJ, etc.). What about something like user interaction? We decided that if we could model the interaction of the user, then we could specify it. What about security? Well, here's somewhat of a qualification. We agreed that there is no agreement on a generic model of security; but given some model of security, we can write a specification, trying to capture that particular security property.

We next considered a property called persistence. This is meant to be a property of the kind of data that a system might manipulate; this was highlighted because there currently seems to be interest in persistent data. Yet, even though there is considerable interest, no one has specified what persistence means. It could be done, but no one has done it; and the same holds for verification. In other words, persistence is another property that is specifiable, much in the sense of security, although we have no general models for persistence.

We turned next to two problem domains that are probably of most interest to the applications people: real time and concurrency.

We decided that we have languages which we can use to specify real time properties (RTL, CSP, LUSTRE, DURRA, VAL, ITL, TL, etc.). They are more adequate for specifying hardware than software. What about verification? We decided that maybe in five years we can verify real time software, but today we can verify synchronous hardware, with very simple real time constraints. Maybe in five years we will be verifying asynchronous hardware. We came up with these numbers in the morning. At the end of the day, we revisited our numbers to see if we believed them, and decided that we needed another column. What is possible versus what is probable. "Probable" means "business as usual" (funding, resources, training and so forth). Thus, if we look at real time again, the numbers increase a bit.

What about concurrency? For a flat specification, where we have all information about all processes available, it should be possible to specify such a system. It should be possible to do proofs given such a specification, that is, to derive other properties

Table 8: Theories/Models

How many years until we have theories/models built for these problem domains?

	POSSIBLE	PROBABLE
1. Simple sequential programs[a]	0	
2. User interaction[a]	0	
3. Security	0	
4. Persistence:		
Specify	3	
Verify	3	
5. Real-time:		
Specify[b]	0	5
Verify:		
Software	5	12
Hardware:		
Synchronous	0	3
Asynchronous	5	8?
6. Concurrency:		
Specification (global)[c]	<5	5
Proofs of properties of specifications	<5	5
Testing with specifications	<5	10
Refinement	>5	12
Composition	>5	12
Metatheory of models[d]	10	10
Verification of implementation		
in program language	>10	>12
Combinations of above	?	?

[a] VDM, Z, LARCH, FDM, GYPSY, ANNA, OBJ, ...
[b] RTL, CSP, LUSTRE, DURRA, VAL, ITL, TL, ...
[c] CSP, UNITY, LOTOS, TSL, CCS, SCCS, COLD, DRAGOON, RAISE, LUCID
[d] Sequences, trees, partial orders, automata, ...

about the system from the specification. And it should be possible to use the specification to do runtime checks on the implementation against the specification. What if you want to specify a large concurrent system? You would want to develop it incrementally, to specify little pieces of it and to put them together. That's what refinement and composition are supposed to indicate, but they are going to take a little longer. There's a lot of theoretical work going on in that area right now. What makes composition hard, for instance, is composing properties specifying race conditions and so forth.

For the theoreticians who like to specify concurrent systems and create various models of concurrency, we believe that many current efforts are attempts to develop a metatheory of models of concurrency. Various people are comparing the notion of equivalence in one model versus the notion of equivalence in another model. That kind of theoretical work will probably go on for the next ten years.

Verification of an implementation of a concurrent system written in a real language will take more than ten years. What is probable is slightly greater than that. We wanted to consider combinations of these, like a real time concurrent system, but did not have time. One formula is to add the numbers and accept that as a possible upper bound. These are just examples using languages which one could use today to specify small, simple concurrent systems using the kinds of models of concurrency that people are now investigating.

Returning to sequential programs, we distinguished between the process of specifying and refining (using specifications for design) and after-the-fact specification. We agreed that we can specify loops and procedures and functions—even procedures and functions which take procedures and functions as arguments—where those procedures may have side effects. And we agreed that, in principle, we could do various parameter passing mechanisms as well. Also, in principle, we could handle pointers; and this gets more interesting.

Table 9: Sequential Programs

	SPECIFY AND REFINE	POST SPECIFICATION/ VERIFY
1. Loops	0	0
2. Procedures/functions	0	0
3. Pointers	0	0
4. Modules (collection of procedures)	0	0
5. Programs (collection of modules)	3	3
6. Systems (collection of programs)	3	3
7. Complexity of specificand pieces of small operating system[a]	0	0

[a] Not UNIX!

We agreed that we could do modules (where a module is a collection of procedures or functions). What about collections of modules, which we call a program?

Given that there is a lot of activity in module-interconnection languages, which are supposed to help hook up these modules, we put the number "3" there.

What about systems which are collections of programs? We, again, said that in three years we should be doing this sort of activity. Then someone asked "What do we mean by a 'system'?" This is where we digressed slightly and talked about the complexity of the specificand.

This is another axis we could have explored in detail. For instance, we all know how to specify a symbol table. We started with a small operating system which we should be able to specify and refine. There is an inconsistency in these numbers because we are talking about an operating system, which is really a collection of programs; and we are saying we can do that, but we can't do programs yet. But we are talking about pieces of the operating system rather than the complete system.

What about more interesting specificands like air-traffic control, command and control, banking and so forth? It's obvious that all of these kinds of specificands have properties like real time and concurrency or distribution, etc; therefore, we should refer to Table 9 for the appropriate numbers.

We also discussed tools and what it is possible to do. We can do syntax checking, type checking, and static semantics checking. We have tools for doing static analysis. Tools for doing static analysis for concurrent and real time systems are coming with the Arcadia project, hopefully. There are tools today for doing runtime analysis, and five years ago we had tools for doing symbolic execution. Of course, we should put a zero there.

We spent a long time discussing proof checkers and what they can do today. We can do user-defined induction rules, user-defined proof tactics, and user-defined logical systems. Some proof checkers are actually integrated with a formal method. There was a difference of opinion as to whether libraries of proofs for reuse are available today or are on the horizon. That is why there is a question mark. What we would like, and what we expect to get in two or three years, are modularizations of proofs and more proof management in our proof checkers.

We did not assign numbers to the wish list of tools (Table 10). We would like to see a combination of provers, tools that generate provers and tools that help us specify and refine using formal methods. In particular, tools for incremental proof and development would be very useful. We kept saying over and over again that we wanted all of these, integrated with the entire software development process.

We made some generic comments as to education; after all, we are supposed to talk about practical limitations. In the research community, we need more dissemination of tools and documentation. In the academic community, below the undergraduate level, at least in the United States, we need to teach more mathematics or the students have to learn more mathematics; at the undergraduate level, there was a proposal is to set up a formal methods lab. At the graduate level, the least we can do is take our own medicine and make our graduate students use formal methods.

What about in industry? There were the usual answers: a little more training, re-education, etc. Some standardization is beneficial, but we don't want to standardize prematurely. We need more people, resources, etc. One proposal was that we need some sort of software engineering certification. Someone even proposed that we need certification in formal methods.

We need more people today who can be trained to the level necessary for using

Table 10: Tools

		POSSIBLE	PROBABLE
1.	Syntax	0	
2.	Type-checkers, static semantics	0	
3.	Static analysis, e.g. ARCADIA (concurrency, timing)	0	5
4.	Routine analysis	0	5
5.	Symbolic execution[a]	-5	
6.	Proof checkers:		
	user-defined induction	0	
	user-defined proof tactics	0	
	user-defined logical systems	0	
	integrated with a formal methods	0	
	libraries of proofs for reuse	?	
	modularization of proofs	2-3	
	proof management	2-3	
7.	Composition of provers	?	?
8.	Prover generators	?	?
9.	Specification and refinement tools	?	?
	incremental proof and develop	?	?
10.	Integration of formal method tools	?	?
	with entire software development process	?	?

[a] Now pushing on more programming language features

formal methods, more documentation and evidence of the commercial benefits of formal methods, and we must make this documentation and evidence widely available. We need more in-depth experiments and collaboration with industry. We need a formal methods environment built using formal methods: this gets back to integrated tools. We need the conviction to carry out a concerted program in formal methods.

Discussion

"In reference to how long it takes before we do these large examples: In doing an example system, such as a banking system, you need to develop a specific theory of the kind of notion of real time or concurrency that is used in that system. You do not have to wait for a global theory of concurrency or real time. And that's very important because it means we can take on certain examples prior to the development of a completely mature theory."

"Did you come across, or discuss, any specific examples of using a specific method on a specific project that failed disastrously?"

"The A7 was a failure because we set out to make a program that would fly in an airplane, and we made a small subset of a program that sort of flew in a simulator. Is that a disaster or not?"

"If the plane crashed, it would have been a disaster, but I don't think your simulator crashed."

"Well, then you have to define 'disastrous'."

"I thought he meant disastrous projects."

"I do actually mean a disaster in terms of the completion of the project, not a disaster in terms of a plane falling out of the sky."

"Another comment like that. It wasn't a disaster but I think quite a few people can point to formal methods exercises where the formal method was being used in an area where it wasn't very appropriate. Thus, the development has finished without the assistance of formal methods."

"It isn't an answer; it's a comment and it relates to the project. I know of projects which actually started using formal methods and were aborted because, by using formal methods, they discovered they really didn't know how to do the project. They didn't understand the problem. Now I count that as a success rather than a disaster."

"I have to make this point. You put it very early in your talk. The thing about undecidability results being limitations—let's forget them, because it comes up every time somebody talks on formal methods to a general audience. Somebody had heard about Gödel's theory somewhere, and they bring it up; they throw it in your face like it's relevant.

And I claim it's absolutely irrelevant. It's irrelevant for mathematics. Aside from the six known hypotheses, like Riemann's conjecture and so on, which are outstanding, the fact of the matter is no conjecture is put forward that is not settled within 10 to 20 years. I mean Gödel's theorem has no relevance to practice."

5.3 Working Group 3: What example applications should we attempt using formal methods?

Chair: Carl Landwehr
Reporter: Tim Gollins
Participants: David Andrews
Robin Bloomfield
Ricky Butler
Brian Graham
Keith Hanna
C. Terrence Ireland
John McHugh
David Musser
Peter G. Neumann

Group description

The purpose of this working group was to identify a set of example applications that exhibit the capabilities of the technology and result in the development of useful applications. The results of these experiments can be used identify future research and development efforts. Possible example applications include an operating system kernel, a database manager, a compiler, an application program, and a microprocessor.

Introduction

A well-chosen example problem, properly solved, can teach a method, test (or stretch) the method's limits, measure its resource demands, or convince a skeptic of its value. Creating example problems that serve these roles for formal methods was the task assigned this group.

While it is too much to expect a single example problem to serve all of these purposes well, it is often possible to find one that can fill two or more of these roles. To work effectively within the single day allotted for discussion, the group first discussed qualities needed in a good example problem, categories of examples and a format for specifying examples. Group members then identified specific examples to be documented in more detail.

Why construct examples?

To be useful, an example must be clearly specified, unambiguous, reasonably easy to understand, and it should have a clear purpose. The group considered four purposes of examples:

1. Worked examples of established methods for others to emulate (i.e., for educational/tutorial purposes). Such examples should convey the essence of the method and be easy to apply to other situations.

2. Examples to test the limits of current methods (exploratory). Such examples should delineate (or push back) the boundary between feasible and infeasible domains of application.

3. Examples that can be used to compare a given formal method with other (formal or informal) methods (benchmarks). Such examples should present realistic resource demands within a specified domain.

4. Examples to demonstrate the practicality of current methods (demonstrations). Similar to tutorial examples, but intended to convince readers of the practicality of a method. Thus "toy" applications may suffice in other categories, but here the applicability of the method to real-world problems is to be shown, so these must be demanding enough and close enough to reality to be convincing.

A single example may, in fact, satisfy several of these purposes, but the group's discussions focused on those in category 4.

Characterizing the space of examples

Before defining particular examples in detail, it is appropriate to survey the space of possible examples. The group developed five roughly orthogonal "coordinates" (in addition to the purposes just defined) to characterize the example-space:

1. Level of application (Hardware/Firmware/Software, with possible sub-areas within software from operating system to application).

2. Degree of rigour to be applied (structured documentation, formal specification, formal specification and proof, formal specification and proof with mechanical checking).

3. Properties of particular interest in the example (security, safety, reliability, fault-tolerance, ...).

4. Scale (small, medium, large).

5. Releasability of results (open, proprietary, classified).

In the course of generating specific examples, the group recognized that whether the example requires the use of several communicating processors or only a single centralized processor is another dimension to consider, but this dimension was not considered during most of the discussions. This is to warn the reader that the above list is not exhaustive.

Examples already available

During the discussion, it became clear that many example applications of formal methods exist already. Although national or commercial distribution limitations apply to many of these, several are freely available. They are listed, with references, in Table 11.

Table 11: Existing examples, with references.

- A7 [BP 81], [PWCB 83], [AFB* 89], [CPPSB 89]
- AMPE [Wal 85]
- CICS [Hay 85], [Wor 87]

- Clock Synchronization Problem   [RH 89]

- Ford Aerospace Trusted Disk System   [WD 89]

- GATE Data Acquisition Problem [McH 74]

- LOCK   [SBL 89]

- Message Flow Modulator   [Lan 83]

- Multi Level Gateway   [BDFKN86], [DFN 88]

- RS232   [Lan 89], [O'Ha 87]

- SEAVIEW   [DLSSH 88], [LSSHW 88], [WL 89]

- VDM   [SJ 89]

- Verification Assessment Study   [Kem 86]

- Z   [Hay 87]

Exploring example space

With such a potentially large space of examples to consider, the group focused on a few interesting regions of the space, listing several possible examples (previously worked, currently under investigation, and recommended for future investigation) in each. A few examples from each region were then chosen to be specified in greater detail by individual members. The regions investigated include:

1. Safety-critical applications
   (*,*,Safety,*,open):
   This region is important because of compelling public interest. Successful examples can increase assurance of the safe operation of widely used systems and can be highly visible. By the same token, failures in this area could have disastrous effects. A difficulty is that failures are much more visible (and often more readily apparent) than successes. Possible examples: transportation-related systems, including railway signalling, aircraft control, air traffic control, and automobile engine control; industrial process control, including nuclear reactor shutdown systems, nuclear process control, and chemical plant process control; and health-care systems, including patient monitoring systems, patient treatment systems, and integrated medical information systems.

2. Hardware-oriented applications of formal methods
   (Hardware, *,*,*,open):
   This region is important for example applications because successes are likely to reduce costs (e.g., through elimination of large-scale product recalls) and thereby promote further use of formal methods, and because the state space of hardware devices is often smaller and more regularly structured than those of software. Possible examples: "smart card" hardware, a simple processor with memory management (specify and verify domain isolation properties), formalization of semantics for VLSI design languages (e.g., VHDL), specification/verification of properties of specific cell libraries, specification/verification of properties of special-purpose hardware, such as a UARTS or graphics accelerator.

3. Medium to large scale software systems, specification only
   (software, spec only, *,medium–large, open):
   There are many systems in this region that could benefit from the application
   of formal methods, though, in discussion, the group was reluctant to exclude
   the use of verification. Examples identified included large libraries of software
   components (though verification could be eventually applied to individual
   components), communication protocols, and programming languages.

4. Software systems to which specification and proof could be applied
   (software,spec and proof, *,*,open):
   This region includes all non-hardware safety-related systems in (1) above, as
   well as a large number of efforts in computer security. Particular new examples listed included a system for monitoring and charging for electric power
   consumption according to time-of-use, smart card software, and software that
   itself is to be used in the production of trustworthy systems.[10]

5. Small software systems
   (software, *, *, small, open):
   Examples in this area should generally require fewer resources, depending
   on complexity and properties to be demonstrated of the system. Examples
   discussed by the group included a simple print spooler and security labeller
   for microcomputers, a separation kernel, and a trusted disk subsystem.

Examples specified
The examples that were specified by the working group are presented in Appendix B.

Conclusions
Many examples of the application of formal methods (broadly construed) exist in
the literature, and many more are not yet circulated for commercial or national
security reasons. Nevertheless, the use of formal methods in software and hardware
development in the United States is very limited in practice. What use there is has
been largely motivated by government-imposed requirements. These statements
also probably apply to Canada and, to a lesser degree, in the United Kingdom.
Additional, openly-documented, realistic examples that expose significant flaws in
critical systems or promise significant gains in software quality or productivity are
justified.

---

[10]This category elicited special attention because the lack of such examples has sometimes been
cited as evidence of a fundamental lack of confidence on the part of the purveyors of mechanized
support systems for the application of formal methods for software development in those very
methods. Further, those purveyors deprive themselves of the direct knowledge they could gain on
the usability of their own products.

5.4 Working Group 4: What should be the R & D strategy and objectives for formal methods?

Chair:	Martyn Thomas
Reporter:	Dan Craigen
Participants:	Susan Gerhart
	Norman Glick
	Joseph Goguen
	Don Good
	Mike Gordon
	Carroll Morgan
	Bob Morris
	David Parnas
	Richard Platek
	Peter Ryan
	Damian Saccocio
	Bill Scherlis
	Chris Sennett
	Vincent Taylor

Group description

This working group had probably the most difficult task. It was to try and identify a research and development program that will ultimately lead to the spread of applications as appropriate within the limits established by the other groups. This is not an issue solely of science; it is also an issue of education, politics and marketing.

Introduction

While this working group did not accomplish its primary task (i.e., the outlining of an R&D strategy for formal methods), a number of interesting observations and opinions surfaced from the spirited discussions. Perhaps the most contentious issue was the timing for transferring formal methods technology to industry. This issue is discussed below in the subsection on technology transfer.

This report is divided by the topics covered during the working group:

- discussion of current systems engineering practices;

- identification of the benefits accruing from the application of formal methods;

- identification of the reasons why formal methods are not being used;

- discussion of debate on technology transfer;

- identification of some recommended R&D efforts; and

- determination of working group recommendations.

Current practice

There was general agreement that the current practice of developing computer-controlled systems is dangerously bad. During the discussion, phrases such as "nothing short of scandalous" and "possibly a crisis on an international scale" were uttered. Specifically, there was general agreement that technology has yet to be developed that would allow for rational decisions concerning the fielding of computer-controlled systems in critical applications. One of the main goals of formal methods research is to enable rational decisions concerning the fielding of critical systems.

There was also concern that the extent of the problem and the risks facing the general public are not understood. The group felt that, while many fielded systems are involved in critical situations, there are no records of the number of such systems extant. In addition, the group was concerned about the high rate of introduction of new critical systems.

From this discussion, three recommendations were forthcoming:

- That a risk assessment on computer technology be performed. This assessment would identify computer-controlled critical systems and identify the consequences of failure of such systems.

- That reporting of failures of critical systems be mandated.

- That computer-controlled critical systems not be developed and fielded if the consequential risks outweigh the benefits.

Having concluded that the current practice of developing computer-controlled systems was bad, the group then focused its attention on why this is the case. Five reasons were identified:

- The systems being developed are exceedingly complex.

- Computer-controlled systems fail in ways that are not intuitive to engineers. In particular, engineers are familiar with systems that are continuous, whereas programs are discrete; small perturbations can lead to massive failure.

- There is no requirement for professional qualifications.

- There is no code of professional practice.

- The rather sorry state of high school mathematics education and of university computing science courses.[11]

What are the benefits of formal methods?

Having agreed that the current practice of developing computer-controlled systems are woefully inadequate, the group proceeded with a discussion identifying the putative benefits of applying formal methods. Perhaps the unifying theme to what follows is that the group believed that formal methods result in a better understanding of the systems we build and, consequently, significantly decrease the risks entailed by fielding critical systems.

The prime *raison d'être* for the application of formal methods is the improvement in our ability to predict the behaviour of computer-controlled systems. In many respects, this view is that of "applied mathematics" and carries the same connotation of developing a theory (to describe some physical system) and using the theory to predict the behaviour of the system. Hence, there is a parallel between formal methods and much of the physical sciences. The group expects that the use of mathematics to describe hardware and software systems will improve our

---

[11]David Parnas has authored a report [Par 89] suggesting one possible computing science curriculum.

forecasting capabilities and, in time, will lead to improved intuition about these systems.

There was agreement that formal methods significantly improve our intellectual control over computer-controlled systems. Particularly, *abstraction*, *induction*, and *precision* were identified as specific techniques leading to such an improvement. Further, by using a mathematical basis, it is feasible to demonstrate (through the means of proof) that systems satisfy certain properties (to within the tolerances of the models used).

Moreover, the application of formal methods potentially reduces the cost of system development and results in better cost control. These claims are based on the observations that formal methods have the potential for greater reuse of system components, of better control (through, for example, the increased levels of precision and rigorous argument) and by improved maintenance.

Finally, formal methods is a means for defining codes of practice and increasing the accountability of those involved in developing critical systems. This is achieved through effective human review and by the articulating of systems development conventions.

Why are formal methods not being used?

Given the aforementioned benefits of formal methods, the group tackled the question "Why are formal methods not being used?" Five reasons were identified:

- The lack of trained personnel. The application of formal methods requires a certain amount of mathematical sophistication that, in general, systems developers have not attained.

- The perception that no real benefits accrue from the application of formal methods techniques. This perception is suggestive of a significant failure in technology transfer.

- The attitude that if one is to adopt formal methods, it must be used throughout the life cycle. This "all or nothing" attitude mitigates against the penetration of formal methods techniques into portions of the life cycle. Consequently, increased experience and examples of the benefits of formal methods are lost.

- The perception that the application of formal methods is not cost effective. This perception remains in place since there have been few controlled experiments that have studied the consequential costs throughout the life cycle.

- Technical limitations that restrict the application of formal methods. However, no specific examples of such limitations were presented.

Debate on Technology Transfer

On most matters of importance, there was considerable agreement amongst the participants of the working group (and, more generally, of the workshop). For example, there was little argument on the general technical directions in need of pursuit and the benefits accruing from the application of formal methods to the development of systems. However, the central controversial issue of the workshop was the timing for transferring formal methods technology to industrial practice. This issue was revisited during the final plenary session.

There were two schools of thought relating to the technology transfer issue. For this report, they will be called the "specification benefit" school and the "specification risk" school.

"Specification benefit" school

Individuals advancing this school of thought took the view that developing systems is an engineering process to be carried out by engineers. Further, the view that it is impossible to do any better than this approach was advanced. Through this engineering process, when a problem that is tractable to some mathematical techniques is identified, an engineer will apply the appropriate mathematics.

The "benefit" school is pursuing a specific technology transfer program. The general idea is to encourage system developers to use mathematically-based specifications without the immediate intent that they should do anything more than that (in a formal methods sense). Over a period of years, encouragement will be given so that the capability and desire to prove particular properties about specifications will grow within the organization. The goal of this technology transfer program is that within a given period there will be a desire and capability to carry out fully formal proofs of correctness throughout the development process.

"Specification risk" school

The individuals advancing this school of thought accepted the general benefits of formal specification but also felt that formal methods are still immature and, therefore, that there are some risks to applying formal specifications in practice prematurely. A formal specification is an accurate description of system behaviour only if it follows from an accurate model of system operation. Accurate operational models of computing systems currently used in practice do not exist. Therefore, investing a large amount of system development resources in formal specifications can result in a large stack of formal specification documents that have little or nothing to do with actual system operation. Those system development resources might well have been better spent elsewhere. If trust is placed in these unfounded documents, overconfidence in system operation can result. It should be noted that the "engineering perspective" for developing systems has also been supported by the supporters of this school of thought.

Unsubstantiated claims

The prime concern motivating the "risk" school perspective is that premature industrialization of formal methods technology will lead to people believing they are achieving levels of assurance from formal methods which, in actuality, they do not. There was concern that if a major catastrophe occurred in a system developed using formal methods (resulting, perhaps, from insecure hardware) then formal methods would be rejected as a way of reducing the risk of these kinds of errors; and, as a consequence, significant harm would result to the further development of the technology. In brief, the "risk" school is arguing for applying formal methods first to develop accurate models of system operation and then to develop formal specifications of various problem domains in which those models will be applied.

As an example of the concern, consider the following: suppose a mathematical model of a spring is developed. If one wants to forecast the physical behaviour of the pendulum, there is an associated risk and danger if the forecast is based on mathematical reasoning and analysis of the spring model. If the model has no relationship to empirical evidence then all predictions on the behaviour of the pendulum are, at best, suspect.

There is some experiential support for the argument. Early work in formal methods, pursued in the United States and supported by the Department of Defense (and as mandated by the Orange Book), focused on formal specifications and the proof of (security) properties about the specifications. (In some respects, this is quite similar to the current British efforts with "Z".) North American experience has shown, however, that the development of a formal specification (and supporting proofs) and the actual development of the system often diverged, were pursued by different (non-communicating) groups and, as a consequence, the formal specification and proof stated absolutely nothing about the fielded system. Obviously, any impression of increased assurance was misplaced.

To the argument that the formal methods field could be harmed by a large-scale disaster of a system where formal methods were used, it was suggested that the concern was misplaced. It should be clear to consumers of formal methods technology that the technology will not prevent disasters from occurring; formal methods does not carry a connotation of perfection.

Unfortunate dichotomy

During the final plenary session, one of the workshop participants suggested that the dichotomy between the "benefit" school and "risk" school was divisive, misleading, unfortunate, and missed the point. Regardless of the formality of an argument, or lack thereof, there must be some coherent and cohesive assessment of the argument, especially for an argument purporting to increase one's assurance of the workings of a critical system.

Risks exist, regardless of timing

Regardless as to what decisions are made with respect to the timing of technology transfer of formal methods, risks exist. If formal methods techniques are not transferred then what other techniques will be used in the meantime? Will those alternative techniques be as beneficial? How safe is safe enough? It is absolutely impossible to guarantee lack of system failure. There was a general feeling that even a limited application of formal methods improves system quality.

There was definite agreement that we must not field systems where we have not developed the technology to reach acceptable levels of assurance. Unfortunately, we are not yet in a position to characterize this situation.

Conclusions about technology transfer

The issue of the technology transfer of formal methods was contentious and is in need of close scrutiny. The few hours that this workshop was able to spend on such a fundamental issue were completely inadequate. The dangers of premature industrialization are significant. For example, a study of the experiences of the Artificial Intelligence field is sobering. For a period, that field suffered from significant overselling. Ultimately, when the field was unable to live up to its "press", there were significant funding reductions which only now are being overcome. The formal methods community must avoid repeating these (unscientific) errors.

Some recommended efforts
Towards developing a research and development strategy for formal methods, a set of recommendations were proposed. These recommendations are divided into four groupings: research and technology development; evaluation; technology transfer; and strategic recommendations.

Research and technology development
While a number of suggestions were forthcoming, the following seemed particularly worthy of note.

It was felt that one of the major benefits of formal methods technology is its application to the formal mathematical descriptions of programming and specification languages. This recommendation is motivated by the observation that one cannot predict the effect of a program if the programming constructs are not comprehended fully. Specifically, it was recommended that these techniques be applied to existing widely used languages. For example, the work by Computational Logic Inc., Odyssey Research Associates and Dansk Datamatik Center, on describing formally portions of Ada have led to a better understanding of the strengths and weaknesses of the language.

A recommendation of particular note to critical systems development was that research be directed at supporting the application of formal methods from the level of system specification down to the level of hardware. In particular, there should be continuity of argument throughout the hierarchy. Work by Computational Logic and proposed work by the European ProCoS project [Pro 89][Pro 90] are early efforts at developing such seamless systems.

While automated deductive systems have advanced significantly over the past two decades, it was felt that significant work remains. Specifically, the group recommended research to improve the inference rules for reasoning systems.

As part of an effort to scale formal methods, so that they can be used in large systems, research into the development of calculi for dealing with large scale modularization was recommended.

In support of the view of formal methods as a form of applied mathematics, it was recommended that researchers develop an applied mathematics for digital systems engineering.

Finally, as with all of science and engineering, basic research must be supported.

Evaluation
Good anecdotal evidence of the benefits of formal methods must be developed. Such anecdotal evidence can be effected by the development of technology demonstrators (i.e., by applying the technology to realistic and experimental applications). For example, the technology can be tested (and problems identified) by applying it to a few straightforward examples. Further, by working on realistic examples with industry, advances will be forthcoming: both from a technology transfer perspective and as a source of new problems.

A number of recommended examples are discussed in Section 5.3 and described in Appendix B.

Technology transfer
The group's principal recommendation with respect to technology transfer is that

mathematics courses, especially at the high school level, be improved. Similarly, at the university level, computing science courses should be upgraded and formal methods should be integrated into the curricula. (This recommendation also has strategic overtones.)

Strategic

From a strategic perspective the group had three specific recommendations:

It was recommended that emphasis be directed towards understanding the roles of formal methods in the systems engineering process. So far, most formal methods research has been performed independently of other research into systems engineering. For both to become more effective, a synergistic union must be developed.

There was a feeling that a certain amount of effort should be directed at applying formal methods techniques to hardware. The particular motivation for this recommendation is the impression that hardware is one of the most promising areas for formal methods to show economic feasibility. Further, by focusing on hardware and the inherent aspects of state space and asynchronous behaviour, research would be directed towards fundamental issues that are manifest throughout the various levels of abstraction for computer-controlled systems.

It was recommended that there be enhanced infrastructure support. By this, it was meant that facilities be developed to enhance the communication between researchers involved in formal methods. Finally, it was recommended that easier access to tools and techniques, being developed on either side of the Atlantic, be supported. Without doubt, the development of the technology has been negatively impacted by export controls.

Recommendations

The working group recommends the following:

Recommendation: Determine the situation for existing and planned critical systems. Perform a survey of such systems and the risks that they entail. Mandate the reporting of the failure of critical systems.

Recommendation: Investigate methods for increasing the competence of those tasked with the development of critical systems. Possible approaches include identifying codes of practice, mandating of certification procedures, and improving education (whether at the university level or through special courses to upgrade the capabilities of those professionals already active).

Recommendation: Develop a project cost model and conduct a survey of system development costs (so as to give a baseline for estimating gains from formal methods).

Recommendation: Undertake the research and development directions described above. There was an opinion that a quarter of the effort be directed towards hardware.

Recommendation: Use shared problems, create shared support facilities and an improved research infrastructure.

6 Concluding Discussions

Speaker: David Parnas
Reporter: Susan L. Gerhart

David Parnas was asked to summarize his reactions to the workshop, both to get the benefit of his experience and to provoke some thinking on the workshop's results.

The notion (in most peoples' minds) of "formal" is far too narrow!
Consider control theory as a formal method that deals with hard-real-time systems. It is not a Hilbert-style system. Indeed, mathematicians didn't do what Hilbert said, so why should we? Each engineering field has developed its own formal systems, such as control theory within electrical engineering and stress analysis within civil engineering. So should we.

It's important to distinguish between notations (which are often mutually translatable) and the information to be represented. For example, whether it's I or J that represents the square root of minus 1 isn't important if there is general agreement on what information ought to be represented.

It was often heard at the workshop that "less formal" methods are needed, thereby suggesting varying degrees of formality. Since we don't know how to measure formality, this suggests that we don't understand the methods yet. The point is that *other* formal methods are needed.

Start with formal methods for documentation.
Better documentation is a prerequisite for everything else—for example, verification and checking—and it has immediate practical benefits. As a research benefit, better documentation provides a source of examples and challenges to be analyzed. Formally expressed documents are needed for communication within the community. This form of documentation may reverse the military view and encourage specifying the mathematical *content* of a document before its *form*. Finally, documentation should be the medium of design, not an after-the-fact write-up.

Readability of documentation is a central issue—readability of formal reference material, where you can look up things. This kind of documentation is not intended for reading "in front of the tube" or by 2-star generals. Note that readability is not inherently dependent on machine support.

Automate conservatively.

We should follow a policy of "conservative automation" based on the two axioms: automation is expensive and automation leads to "rigor mortis". Once something is automated, you are forced to use it even if later experience suggests you should not. To determine what to automate, use it by hand first, demonstrate the usefulness, identify the trivial and tedious, and then begin to automate.

An example is the power of case analysis. For example, the Dutch mathematician de Bruijn has studied the language that mathematicians actually use as contrasted to what Hilbert told them to use. He found considerable use of case analysis to reduce a problem to several smaller problems that can be handled with less memory capability. There is a lesson for formal methods researchers: study the way people get things done rather than how we think they ought to do work.

Tools are important when the proportion of trivia becomes large enough to be recognized as trivia. And that will happen in realistic systems, especially where the problems were not designed for the methods to work smoothly.

Engineering is not a pejorative!

Engineering means being result-oriented. When we make an engineering judgment, we ask ourselves "Does this benefit the quality of the product?" We do not investigate just for the sake of investigating.

Engineering does not mean approximate. It means using precision when it's required. It does not mean using methods that limit application unknowingly and hoping they work. It means knowing the limits. Engineering education often includes exam problems where the formula cannot be applied. That makes engineers go back and look at the hypotheses of the theorem that led to the formula.

Engineering isn't a matter of gluing things together. It's not adding features but rather removing restrictions, so you get a smooth product instead of one that is glued together.

Engineering means systematic procedures, which can only be based on formal methods.

The community of formal methods researchers needs more influence from practicing engineers, from control theorists, even from outside computing.

Problems aren't linked together well.

Black box and white box problems should be separated. Black box problems have hidden state data. This forces you to talk about functions with domains that are time functions or sequences. When you come to white box problems, the domains can contain states. Some methods are being applied to both kinds of problems but there is a fundamental difference.

The pressures are to "publish or perish" in universities, "to succeed or go belly up" in industry. So, we keep looking for areas where we can be successful, often neglecting the harder and more important problems.

This workshop seemed to lack a common framework or classification scheme. For example, one person's slide may say "Z and VDM" in the same breath, while another's may state "Z versus VDM". There should be a way of classifying problems relative to methods.

Models are confused with specifications.
A specification is a predicate whose domain is a set of acceptable behaviours. A model is something that exhibits (part of) the behaviour of the object of interest. An example of the confusion is with concurrency. It's not that one usually wants to specify concurrency but rather to study the properties of a model of concurrency resulting from a specification for a system.

What do you say when someone claims that formal methods take too much time?
The old adage attributed to a pragmatic IBM manager (B.O. Evans?) by F. P. Brooks, Sr.:
"There's never time at the start to do it right, but there's always time at the end to patch it up.".

What should be the direction for R&D strategy?
The issue is not where to put another $5.00 (in U.S. or $5.80 Canadian). It's how to get good research done. The obvious answers are to permit time to work and to provide a supportive environment. It's important to offer more opportunities to interact with others with similar interests, to experiment with our ideas, to work with interested potential users. And there is a need for more open peer review for feedback and discussion. Money might not be the best way to provide this.

For example, the model of real-time system specification presented the first day provides an example of a hypothesis around which to make progress. Whether the model is right or wrong, settling it would be tremendous progress.

Another example is the roles of testing and proving (discussed in the opening session) with random testing to do reliability assessment, but not to substitute for formal methods and not to provide trustworthiness. Agreement on this principle of correctness versus reliability versus trustworthiness, and the roles of testing and formal methods would be progress.

One recommendation for funders is not to fund those people unwilling to demonstrate their methods on problems other people choose. Another is to focus a meeting of this group on a better problem-solution classification scheme. Researchers should be strongly encouraged to use the tools developed by their colleagues.

A final piece of advice to consider is the correct form of statement for selling the results of the field. General claims are statistical. A claim to improve something might or might not do so. Rather, the ideal claim should be of the form "if the following is the situation, with these cost factors, then it will save you money" or "then it will ..."

Parnas recommends "Make no general claims."

7   Conclusions and Recommendations

The emphasis of *FM89* was an assessment of the state of the practice in formal methods and their possible roles in the development of critical systems. The workshop participants were drawn from Canada, the United Kingdom and the United States. Their backgrounds included safety, hardware, software and system engineering, various government agencies, and theoretical and applied computing science.

On completion of the workshop, the organizing committee met for a day of deliberations, to review the workshop and to identify general observations, recommendations and conclusions arising from the workshop.

7.1   Current software development practice is inadequate

There was general agreement that the current practice of software development is unacceptable. Various workshop participants used stronger language: "... nothing short of scandalous" and "... possibly a crisis of international scale" were amongst the comments heard. While no technology is risk free, it was the opinion of the workshop organizing committee that there are unnecessary risks from the fielding of software-controlled critical systems. The risks from the failure of software-controlled critical systems are a consequence of inadequate technology[12] and the generally poor professional backgrounds of those developing such systems.[13]

The inadequacy of existing technology is due, in part, to the following:

- Safety critical systems often must work the first time they are used, unlike many systems which may be phased in.

- The failure modes of software-controlled systems are new to system designers' intuition. Their intuition is often tuned to physical continuity, whereas such continuity is not displayed in the discrete logic of software.

- The benefits gained from increasing the use of software as the controllers of critical systems, namely flexibility and ease of manufacturing, also introduce potential fatal flaws, namely uncontrollable complexity due to excessive functionality and flexibility, and undetectable malicious or haphazard changes.

---

[12]Other factors include whether we have the ability to assess risks in a broad system context and whether we can control environmental factors to control or reduce risks.

[13]This is not meant to be a universal condemnation; there are exceptions such as the workshop participants involved in developing shutdown software for nuclear power plants.

The problem of poor professional backgrounds can be traced to:

- the absence of professional certification criteria or codes of practice for software engineers (which exist in other engineering fields); and

- the lack of agreement on standard engineering techniques for critical systems.

In addition, it was observed that there are no records of the number and types of critical systems that have been fielded. Data is not systematically collected on the causes and effects of failures nor are there requirements or specifications for any form of technical inquest upon failure.

Conclusion:	In general, there are unacceptable risks to the public in the fielding of software-controlled critical systems.
Recommendation:	Systematic records of the number and types of critical systems being fielded, and the causes and effects of failures, should be maintained.

7.2 Formal methods are necessary for the development of trustworthy systems

While the state of the practice of developing critical systems is inadequate, it is recognized that benefits can accrue from the use of software-controlled systems. Hence, it is necessary to develop technologies and supporting infrastructure that will permit the fielding of software-controlled critical systems at a level of risk that is understandable and acceptable to the general public.

It was the view of the workshop that formal methods techniques must be used if we are to field trustworthy critical systems. No alternatives were forthcoming that would permit the same potential increase in confidence in such systems.

This is not to say that formal methods are to be used to the exclusion of other techniques. Formal methods must be incorporated with good software engineering principles and testing techniques. For instance, testing should be used in conjunction with formal methods as an additional validation to formally proved properties, to assess the assumptions upon which formal methods depend and to accumulate data for reliability models. The Cleanroom methodology, one of the formal methods techniques discussed at the workshop, incorporates a statistical testing strategy to derive reliability figures.

The workshop participants felt that formal methods are particularly suited in situations where:

- abstraction is a prerequisite to design;

- extensive review procedures require detailed, well-structured, and precise documentation;

- specialized training and high skill levels substitute for professional certification; or

- the loss of overall intellectual control of a project is sufficient to question the viability of the project.

There are a variety of formal methods that address these situations to varying degrees. Each is characterized by notations for expressing specifications and programs, logical systems that support reasoning about these, and methods that prescribe how to specify, implement, and analyse. Some use notations that are strongly communicative and work best at high levels of abstraction, while others capture the detail of hardware and software implementations with great precision.

Certain methods are geared toward certain kinds of analyses, for example, by supporting division into cases corresponding to modes of a system or·inductive proofs over a data space. The methods are mature to different levels in their theoretical underpinnings, in the instruction materials available to teach them, and in the understanding of their best and worst domains of applicability. Dozens of variations of formal methods have been investigated over the past twenty years and a few are reaching wide industrial acceptance through attractive tool support or intensive technology transfers.

Much can be done today with current methods and tools, as shown in the case studies as documented in the appendices. Much more will be possible as the methods become better understood, as tools improve through better managed investment and through industrial engineering use, and as theory pinpoints the key problems and offers new solutions.

However, difficulties are being encountered in bringing formal methods to bear on the development of critical systems. While there are technological problems, there are also societal problems. Particularly, there is a lack of understanding of the difficulties involved in producing trustworthy systems. This is especially true within the general public, but also with many computing science professionals. Unfortunately, in the area of critical systems, the concept of *caveat emptor* is not sufficiently well developed. This has the further consequence that "business as usual" is deemed sufficient, and so the arguments for applying new or developing techniques, are met with indifference.

Conclusion:	Though still an immature technology, much can be done to increase our confidence in critical systems through the careful application of existing formal methods technology. As the technology matures, application of the technology can expand.
Recommendation:	Motivate the development of improved techniques; increase the general awareness of the risks of critical systems and the inadequacies of current techniques.

7.3 Formal methods viewed as applied mathematics

There was consensus that formal methods should have the same role in software engineering as applied mathematics does to other engineering fields. That is, we expect to design and certify computer systems using the analytic and predictive capabilities that formal methods make available.

As with any form of applied mathematics, one must be aware of the limitations of our models of physical reality. At the extreme, we will be using formal methods to model the physical components of our system. As with any model, we will have to determine what aspects of reality we deem important and will have to ignore others. We must be quite clear, therefore, on the boundaries of our models.

Further, there is a boundary between the informal and the formal. While one can envision a closed connection between the top-most formal specification of a system and the low level physical details, there is a gap between the formal specification and the informal view of what the system is supposed to do. While there are techniques, such as animation and proving properties of specifications, to ameliorate the problem, the gap will always exist.

Further discussion of the boundaries of formal methods is presented in Section 5.2.

Conclusion:	Formal methods are the applied mathematics of software engineering. Their theoretical limitations are the same as those of applied mathematics for other engineering disciplines; the constraints are no greater or less.
Recommendation:	Recast formal methods in predictive and analytic roles.

7.4   What needs to be done

As is usual in workshops of this nature, a comprehensive and cohesive research and development program was not developed. The report from working group 4 (Section 5.4) suggested looking at some particular technical issues in the formal methods area. Here, we present recommendations from a broader perspective.

Improved education in mathematics

There was a consensus that mathematics education is still rather poor (though it was argued that the situation is better in the United Kingdom when contrasted with Canada and the United States). Improvements are required at both the elementary and high-school levels, and there must be efforts to overcome the phobias often associated with mathematics.

With proper background training in mathematics, aspiring systems designers will be in a better position to learn the specific mathematics of formal methods, and will be better placed to reason systematically about their designs. It is not necessary that designers have mathematics training at a graduate level; however, it is likely that several years of experience with critical systems and formal methods will be necessary.

Conclusion:	The teaching of mathematics is in poor shape.
Recommendation:	The teaching of mathematics, both at the elementary and high school levels must be improved.
Recommendation:	Short courses, continuing education, etc. should be developed to train (or retrain) computing scientists and software engineers for the trustworthy critical systems field.
Recommendation:	The appropriate mathematics skills should be identified and integrated in computing science and engineering curricula.

Improved professional status

If critical systems are to be developed then we want the best trained individuals to be involved. Critical systems will require a certain set of skills; it will be necessary to describe what those skills are, to support the education of individuals to obtain the requisite skills, and to certify those approved to work on critical systems. The UK Ministry of Defence Interim Standard 00-55 [MoD 89a] reports upon the skills requirements that the British are intending to mandate.

Conclusion:	The absence of professional certification increases the risks to the public from the fielding of unsoundly developed critical systems.
Recommendation:	Identify the skills required for the designers of critical systems.
Recommendation:	Develop a certification process for the designers of critical systems.

Improved tool support

For system development of any realistic size, formal methods tool support will be necessary. All the existing tools have been developed by researchers and are not capable of meeting the needs of realistic application. Further, all these tools have been developed in isolation and are not necessarily integrated with other tools (e.g., configuration management tools, testing tools) that are necessary through the life cycle.

In addition to the development of tools and methods, there is a requirement to certify both. It is necessary to develop confidence in the tools and methods to be used in critical systems. Arguably, we should have stronger requirements for the tools and methods than for the critical systems being developed, since our confidence in the fielded critical system can only be as good as the confidence we place in our tools and methods.

Recommendation:	Identify candidates for commercialization from existing formal methods tools.
Recommendation:	Develop formal methods workstations and develop tools that are supported commercially.
Recommendation:	Perform a market survey on the number of formal methods workstations required in the 1990s to convince vendors to participate in their development.
Recommendation:	Tools and methods that are to be used in the development of critical systems should be certified.

Realistic examples

While there are exceptions, most applications of formal methods are academic curiosities. One area of enhancing the development of a technology is by attempting to apply the technology to realistic and carefully chosen examples. Such examples help to clarify the strengths and weaknesses of the technology. From identifying the weaknesses, we will be able to determine how to best spend the limited research funds available. Various examples, such as a "time of use electric meter" and a "train signalling protocol" are discussed in the report from working group 3 (Section 5.3).

Recommendation:	Openly documented, realistic examples, performed in conjunction with industry, are necessary for both advancing the technology and for demonstrating the potential benefits of the technology.

Integration of formal methods with software engineering

The existing formal methods tools and formal methods techniques are generally in isolation from current software engineering practices and tools. For the technology of formal methods to be successfully transferred to industry, the technology must be integrated with the development spectrum.

Additionally, the teaching of formal methods should include an engineering flavour in both computing science and computing engineering curricula.

Recommendation:	Enhance the integration of formal methods with software engineering.
Recommendation:	Formal methods-based software engineering curricula should be developed and brought into university or professional degree programs.

Communication between researchers

This workshop was one of those rare times that significant portions of the UK and North American formal methods communities have had a chance to interact at a personal level. As the workshop proceeded, it became apparent that there are some definite distinctions between the two communities.

For instance, most British formal methods apply mathematical specifications early in the software life cycle. The UK research on mathematical specifications is to be supported eventually by tools and to be gradually applied further into the implementation phases of software development. In contrast, most North American research approaches are geared toward formal verification tools to support proofs and they emphasize greater control of implementation details later in the development cycle. North American design methods are expected to build upon the foundations of verifiable languages and verified computing environments. However, this "trans-Atlantic formal methods gap" is viewed as a strength of the field. For example:

- The limits of relying solely on readily-transferred mathematical specifications have been exposed by the ultra-formal security verification community probing into the weaknesses of implementations and model.

- The value of mathematical specifications as arbiters of contracts and as intellectual clarifiers of system purpose and behaviour has been recognized.

Conclusion:	For various reasons, communication between researchers involved in formal methods has been limited (especially internationally). The advances that have been achieved by formal methods researchers have not been sufficiently disseminated.
Recommendation:	Cross-fertilization of ideas and techniques from the UK and North America should be encouraged. Increased cooperation among researchers is necessary.
Recommendation:	The field needs a taxonomy of methods, problems the methods address, modes of use, and results to be expected.

APPENDICES

A Participants

Mack Alford
Ascent Logic Corporation
180 Rose Orchard Way, Suite 200
San Jose, CA 95134, USA
(408) 943-0630

J. Dave Andrews
Andyne Computing Limited
544 Princess Street, Suite 202
Kingston, Ontario K7L 1C7
Canada
(613) 548-4355

Kurt Asmis
Atomic Energy Control Board
270 Albert Street
Ottawa, Ontario K1P 5S9
Canada

Graham Birtwistle
2500 University Drive
Computer Science Department
University of Calgary
Calgary, Alberta T2N 1N4
Canada
(403) 220-6055
graham@cpsc.ucalgary.ca

Robin Bloomfield
Adelard
28 Rhondda Grove
London E35AP, UK
(44) 1 318 7579
reb@lfcs.ed.ac.uk (internet)

Ricky W. Butler
Mail Stop 130
NASA, Langley Research Center
Hampton, VA 23665
USA

Martine Calvé
Communications Security
    Establishment
P.O. Box 9703, Terminal
Ottawa, Ontario K1G 3Z4
Canada

Bernard Carré
(Southampton University)
Program Validation Ltd.
26 Queen's Terrace
Southampton S01 1BQ
UK
011-44 703-330001

Greg Chisholm
Argonne National Laboratory
EBR-II Project
9700 S. Cass Avenue
Argonne, IL 60439, USA
(708) 972-6815
chisholm@antares.mcs.anl.gov

Dan Craigen
Odyssey Research Associates
265 Carling Avenue, Suite 506
Ottawa, Ontario K1S 2E1
Canada
(613) 238-7900
dan@ora.on.ca

John Gannon
National Science Foundation
Room 401
1800 G Street, NW
Washington, DC 20550, USA

Susan Gerhart
MCC, Software Technology Program
3500 West Balcones Center Drive
Austin, TX 78759, USA
gerhart%sw.mcc.com@mcc.com

Norm Glick
National Security Agency
9800 Savage Road
Fort George Meade, MD 20755-6000
USA
(310) 688-8448
norm@cs.umd.edu

Joseph Goguen
Programming Research Group
University of Oxford
8-11 Keble Road
Oxford, OX1 3QD, UK
(865) 54328
goguen@uk.ac.ox.prg (janet)
goguen@prg.ox.ac.uk (internet)

Tim Gollins
CESG, Princess Elizabeth Way
Cheltenham, Gloucestershire GL52 5AJ
UK
(0242) 221491 x4107

Donald Good
Computational Logic, Inc.
1717 W. Sixth Street, Suite 290
Austin, TX 78703, USA
(512) 322-9951
good@cli.com

Mike Gordon
SRI International
Suite 23, Millers Yard
Mill Lane
Cambridge CB2 1RQ, UK
+44 23 324 146
mjcg@cam.sri.com

Brian Graham
2500 University Drive
Computer Science Department
University of Calgary
Calgary, Alberta T2N 1N4
Canada
grahamb@cpsc.ucalgary.ca

Steven Hall
Prior Data Sciences
2000 Barrington Street, Suite 604
Halifax, NS B3J 3K1 Canada

Keith Hanna
University of Kent
Electronic Engineering Department
Canterbury, Kent CT2 7NT, UK
0227-764000
fkh@ukc.ac.uk (internet)

Will Harwood
Imperial Software Technology
3 Glisson Road
Cambridge CB1 2HA, UK
+44-223-462400
will@ist.co.uk (internet)

Larry Hatch
National Security Agency
9800 Savage Road
Fort George Meade, MD 20755-6000
USA
(301) 859-4050

Douglas Howe
Computer Science Dept.
Cornell University
Ithaca, NY 12853, USA
(607) 255-5831

C. Terrence Ireland
NCSC
9800 Savage Road
Fort George Meade, MD 20755-6000
USA
(310) 859-4485
cti@cs.umd.edu

Paul Joannou
Ontario Hydro, Mail Stop H13 F22
700 University Avenue
Toronto, Ontario M5G 1X6
Canada
(416) 592-5910

Richard Kemmerer
University of California
Department of Computer Science
Santa Barbara, CA 93106, USA
(805) 961-4232
kemm@moccasin.ucsb.edu

Ian King
CESG, Princess Elizabeth Way
Cheltenham, Gloucestershire GL52 5AJ
UK

Milan Kuchta
Communications Security
  Establishment
P.O. Box 9703, Terminal
Ottawa, Ontario K1G 3Z4
Canada
(613) 991-7331

Carl Landwehr
Code 5542, Naval Research Laboratory
Washington, DC 20375-5000, USA
(202) 767-3381

Bill Legato
Dept. of Defense
9800 Savage Road
Fort George Meade, MD 20755-6000
USA

Nancy Leveson
ICS Department
University of California at Irvine
Irvine, CA 92717, USA
(714) 856-5517
nancy@ics.uci.edu

David Luckham
Stanford AI Lab.
Computer Systems Laboratory
Dept. of Electrical Engineering
ERL Building, Rm. 456
Stanford, CA 94305-4055, USA
(415) 723-1242
del@sail.stanford.edu

John McHugh
Computational Logic Inc.
3500 Westgate Drive, Suite 204
Durham, NC 27705, USA
(919) 493-4932
McHugh@cli.com

Carroll Morgan
Oxford University
Programming Research Group
8-11 Keble Road
Oxford OX1 3OD, UK
+44 865 272570
carroll@prg.oxford.ac.uk (internet)

Bob Morris
NCSC
9800 Savage Road
Fort George Meade, MD 20755-6000
USA
(301) 859-4373
RMorris@dockmaster.ncsc.mil

Dave Musser
RPI, Computer Science Department
Amos Eaton Hall
Troy, NY 12180, USA
(518) 276-8660

Peter Neumann
SRI International
Computer Science Laboratory
333 Ravenswood Avenue
Menlo Park, CA 94025, USA
(415) 859-2375

Dave Parnas
Department of Computer Science
Goodwin Hall, Queen's University
Kingston, Ontario K7L 3N6
Canada (613)

Richard Platek
Odyssey Research Associates
301A Harris Dates Drive
Ithaca, NY 14850-1313, USA
(607) 277-2020
oravax!richard@cu-arpa.cs.cornell.edu

Jesse Poore
Computer Science Department
University of Tennessee
Knoxville, TN, USA
poore@utkcs2.cs.utk.edu

John Rushby
Computer Science Laboratory
SRI International
333 Ravenswood Avenue
Menlo Park, CA 94025
USA
(415) 859-5456
Rushby@csl.sri.com

Peter Ryan
CESG, Princess Elizabeth Way
Cheltenham, Gloucestershire GL52 5AJ
UK
(0242) 221491 x4295

Mark Saaltink
Odyssey Research Associates
265 Carling Avenue, Suite 506
Ottawa, Ontario K1S 2E1
Canada
(613) 238-7900

Damian M. Saccocio
National Research Council
National Academy of Sciences
2101 Constitution Avenue, NW
Washington, DC 20418, USA
(202) 334-2605

Steve Sadler
Rolls Royce & Assoc.
P.O. Box 31
Derby DE2 8BJ, UK
0332-661461

William Scherlis
DARPA/ISTO
1400 Wilson Blvd.
Arlington, VA 22209-2300
USA
(301) 694-5800
scherlis@vax.darpa.mil

Chris Sennett
RSRE, St Andrews Road
Malvern, Worcs WR14 3DS, UK
+44 614 895184
cts@rsre.mod.uk (internet)

K. Speierman
National Security Agency
9800 Savage Road
Fort George Meade, MD 20755-6000
USA
(301) 688-6434
khs@cs.umd.edu

Roger Stokes
ICL Defence Systems
Eskdale Road, Winnersh
Wokingham, Berkshire RG11 ISL
UK
(44) 734 693131

Vincent Taylor
DND/CRAD DRDCS, 11 CBN
101 Colonel By Drive
Ottawa, Ontario K1A 0K2
Canada
(613) 995-8008
vktaylor@ncs.dnd.ca

Martyn Thomas
Praxis
20 Manvers St
Bath BA1 1PX, UK
+44 225 444700
mct%praxis.uucp@ukc.ac.uk (internet)

Jeannette Wing
Carnegie-Mellon University
School of Computer Science
Pittsburgh, PA 15213, USA
(412) 268-3068
Wing@cs.cmu.edu

Jim Woodcock
Oxford University
Programming Research Group
8-11 Keble Road
Oxford, OX1 3QD, UK
+44 865 272576
Jimw@prg.oxford.ac.uk

B   Potential Applications for Formal Methods

The following potential applications for formal methods were proposed by Working Group 3. Time limitations and a desire not to orient problem statements toward a particular formal method led the group to agree on an informal framework for describing the posed examples. The framework used is as follows:

Title

1. Type of example: (tutorial, exploratory, benchmark, demonstration)

2. Description: (state the problem, including relevant system properties desired in a successful solution)

3. Motivation: (what makes this an example interesting?)

4. Criteria: (what would be a success? a failure?)

5. Lasting value: (for successful completion)

6. Aspects of formal methods stressed by this example:(e.g., ability to handle real-time requirements, ability to handle large systems, ability to verify particular system properties, etc.)

7. Formal techniques/tools that would be interesting to see applied to this problem:

8. Potential impact: (who would be interested in the results?)

9. Estimated resources required:

10. Approach (funding/management/technical)

Nuclear Reactor Protection System
(HW/SW, spec. & mech. proof, safety, med., open)

Type of example: Demonstration (benchmark)

Description:
Specify, develop and prove an example of a nuclear reactor protection system. A redundant voting architecture could be chosen that allows sequential and concurrent aspects of the problem to be separated. The problem could include signal processing, level comparison, and trip logic. The example should not be a *post hoc* application of formal methods to existing software but a full formal development. Full documentation of the example should be in the public domain.

Motivation:
A socially important safety critical example of current public interest and concern. Application of formal methods should lead to increased assurance in the system. The work is feasible with low technical risk and will provide a good example to the nuclear industry to encourage technology transfer. Application of formal methods in this area should reduce the costs of licencing such a system (e.g., gaining approval of regulatory authorities).

Criteria for success:
Complete example system that is acceptable to nuclear regulatory authorities and peer review.

Lasting value:
Technology transfer with an input to safety critical standards.

Aspects of formal methods emphasized:
Application to slow real-time systems with weak concurrency; sequential systems; system synthesis from proven components; and hardware interfaces; use of layered design and specification with an engineering perspective.

Techniques to be used:
Specification and proof at appropriate levels of abstraction.

Potential impact of example:
Mainly technology transfer (see *Motivation*).

Estimate of resources required:
3-6 person years.

Proposed approach:
Multidisciplinary, using existing experiments, e.g., DARTS over the short term.

Transformation Tools (Verified)
(SW, spec. and proof, reliability, small, open)

Type of example: Demonstration

Description:
Hardware designs captured in different forms should be reliably translatable to and from the form used by a verification system. For example, designs in the HOL language should be transformable to and from VHDL, ELLA, the form used by layout design tools (e.g., Electric), or a net list description language. Work is under way at Cambridge to make this transformation possible for HOL to ELLA.

Motivation:
Currently, the parallel or independent definition of designs, or transformation between independent representations, is error prone. The example would seek to demonstrate how this problem could be overcome.

To extend the formal coverage of the range of hardware design representations.

Criteria for success:
The success of the example depends on the size of the transformable subsets of the languages concerned, and the utility of those subsets as perceived by designers and verifiers.

Lasting value:
More reliable production of hardware components.

Aspects of formal methods emphasized:
Usefulness of formalization in a practical field.

Techniques to be used:
Denotational or model theoretic semantic description of the languages concerned.

Potential impact of example:
The production of any verified hardware.

Estimate of resources required:
[None given.]

Proposed approach:
[None given.]

Proof Checker and Interchange Language
(SW, spec. & proof, reliability, small, open)

Type of example: Demonstration.

Description:

Develop a proven, verified proof checker and associated representation language for proof interchange in order to allow comparison between formal reasoning tools and interchange of experience, etc. Should lead to exchange of proofs between different systems.

Motivation:

There is currently a problem with the lack of trusted tools and the lack of credibility of a community not using using its own methods.

Within the formal methods community, there is a need to stimulate cooperation between the various research groups to enable the field as a whole to progress.

Criteria for success:

Delivery of a verified proof checker together with interfaces to key systems (e.g., HOL, Gypsy).

Lasting value:

Will allow the latest tools to be used without the need to wait for large proof libraries to be built; will increase the confidence in machine proof.

Aspects of formal methods emphasized:

The relationship between different formalisms; the generality necessary in a proof representation language; the value of proving the correctness of a "small" proof checking program.

Techniques to be used:

Those applicable to sequential proof, language and logic definitions.

Potential impact of example:

Stimulate research by allowing tool/proof interchange and integration.

Estimate of resources required:

2–4 person years for the basic work, plus effort to alter existing systems to provide required output.

Proposed approach:

Select tools to compare, produce generalized representation and build tool. A single site approach with appropriate liaison should be used.

A Train Signalling System
(Abstract, spec. and hand proof, safety, large, open)

Type of example: Exploratory/demonstration

Description:
  Specify, design and show ability to build an example train signalling system. Axiomatize the rail signalling rule book and show conformity of a real system to rules. Prove the safety of the rules with respect to an abstract definition of safety (possible work needed on the definition of safety).

Motivation:
  This example is publicly accessible and relevant to the general public. The example is potentially "scale-able" and the formal methods approach may have significant commercial advantages. The example has important safety critical aspects that are of both practical and academic interest.

Criteria for success:
  Success of technology transfer to the rail industry; the acceptance of the approach by both public and peers; lack of disaster (e.g., train crash).

Lasting value:
  Theoretical advancement of formal methods in the safety critical field. A focus for research into safety specifications within formal methods. As an input to safety standards. Stimulate the software market into being interested in formal methods, particularly with respect to safety.

Aspects of formal methods emphasized:
  Real world modelling formal methods. Potential for technically interesting logic and representation problems.

Techniques to be used:
  It would be most useful and interesting to apply a good modelling language.

Potential impact of example:
  See motivation.

Estimate of resources required:
  50 person-years or so for full example. Approx. 6 person-months for a pilot study.

Proposed approach:
  Multinational collaborative funding would be necessary, probably in the European context.

Smart Cards

(HW/SW, spec. & mech. proof, integrity security, small, open)

Type of example: Demonstration.

Description:

Verify full functionality of smart card hardware and software to ensure financial integrity and security.

Motivation:

The problem is interesting as it combines VLSI specification, design and construction with firmware and software specification, design and construction. The bounded size of the problem allows reasonable chance of success.

Criteria for success:

Acceptance of both methods and product by banking community. No financial loss by bank or bank customers due to design errors. No recalls of faulty cards.

Lasting value:

Stimulate the market for formal methods within the financial software sector. Increase public trust in smart cards.

Aspects of formal methods emphasized:

Verification of an Integrated VLSI/ firmware/ software system. The structuring of both specification and proofs will be important in order to handle the complexity generated.

Techniques to be used:

Full proof of correctness. This will require a very well-defined spec.

Potential impact of example:

Improved quality of service to both customers and banks.

Estimate of resources required:

20 person years.

Proposed approach:

Funded by banking institutions.

Time of Use Electric Meter (GE product)
(HW/SW, spec. & mech. proof, *, med., open)

Type of example: Demonstration.

Description:

Nature: "Program in product" – software in a high volume (300,000 units) commercial product.

Functionality: Records electricity usage at different rates depending on time of day. Must keep track of time, holidays, standard time/ DST changeovers.

Fault-Tolerance: Continue to keep track of time during power failure (battery backup of clock).

Security: Requires password to access stored data. A high assurance of the integrity of the data needs to be achieved.

Communication/Concurrency: Implemented on more than one microprocessor, protocols between them need to be specified.

Motivation:

Benefits to manufacturer: economic advantage, avoid product recall.

Benefits to customers (utility company): greater confidence in data (accuracy, protection from tampering).

Criteria for success:

Design errors found (possibly) and corrected. No recall of the product necessary. Software engineers are convinced formal methods helped, and continue to use them.

Lasting value:

Demonstration of economic and social benefits of formal methods.

Aspects of formal methods emphasized:

Formal specification and proof, at multiple levels of abstraction. Dealing with concurrency within system. Mapping from high level language to assembly language (via compiler) and hardware. (This high level of assurance in the correctness may not be economically worthwhile.)

Techniques to be used:

Overall organization via formal specification in a mathematical notation plus other informal documentation. Translation into a specification language of one or more mechanical tools such as EHDM, Gypsy, HOL, BM, RRL in order to do proofs.

Potential impact of example:

Convincing demonstration of economic benefit of formal methods in a software engineering project (cost of mass recall = 30M dollars).

Estimate of resources required:

2–4 person years

Proposed approach:

Funding: 50% GE, 50% government.

MACH – Distributed OS
(SW, spec. & mech. proof, *, med./large, open)

Type of example: Tutorial/Demonstration.

Description:
General purpose message-passing OS. Goals include UNIX compatibility and distributed operation.

Motivation:
The need for a distributed OS based on a small OS kernel. The interface to the new OS kernel must be compatible with an existing popular OS to allow easy porting of utilities and applications.

Criteria for success:
Widespread use by vendors. Well-specified operating system with a small kernel.

Lasting value:
Reliable in operational use. Reliable software portability.

Aspects of formal methods emphasized:
Distributed nature of OS (comes from message passing model). Range of specification from abstract levels of interprocess communication down to details of memory management at the hardware level.

Techniques to be used:
Z; Gypsy; Boyer-Moore; CSP.

Potential impact of example:
Significant impact is expected on vendors and research community when advantages (in terms of correctness) of the use of formal methods become apparent when OS is used.

Estimate of resources required:
Unknown.

Proposed approach:
Build on CM/TIS (Carnegie-Mellon/ Trusted Information Systems) work. Include Multi-Level Security.

ASOS

(SW, spec. & mech. proof, security, large, closed)

Type of example: Tutorial/Demonstration.

Description:

A run-time Multi-Level Secure Operating System designed to run only certified software. The OS is not designed for use in software development.

Motivation:

Need for a highly assured (Orange Book A1 level) Ada-based OS.

Criteria for success:

A successful evaluation at A1 level; used operationally.

Lasting value:

Unknown.

Aspects of formal methods emphasized:

Formal security policy; development includes use of Gypsy verified specifications.

Techniques to be used:

Gypsy has been used, but for tutorial/ demonstration purposes Z could be used as the specification language instead.

Potential impact of example:

As a tutorial example; as a useful Multi-Level Secure Operating System; enables trusted distribution.

Estimate of resources required:

Unknown.

Proposed approach:

Contract – NCSC evaluation.

Database
(SW, spec. & mech. proof, security, large, closed (probably))

Type of example: Tutorial/Exploratory/Demonstration.

Description:
Data base management systems with Multi-Level Security.

Motivation:
Support development of Trusted Data base management systems Interpretation (TDI). Work would carry forward research in an important area of Multi-Level Security.

Criteria for success:
Move up through the Orange Book levels; model for vendors.

Lasting value:
Use by vendors as a model for commercial products.

Aspects of formal methods emphasized:
Design specs and design proof at A1 level.

Techniques to be used:
Uncertain.

Potential impact of example:
See lasting value.

Estimate of resources required:
Unknown.

Proposed approach:
Build on current work. Work through Orange Book levels.

Trusted Disk System
(SW, spec. & mech. proof, security, small/med., open)

Type of example: Demonstration.

Description:
Existing prototype provides file and block operations to implement a primitive secure file system. A high level description in terms of Gypsy mappings and a low level implementation in terms of Gypsy arrays exist as does a running version in C (see [Oak 89]).

Motivation:
Demonstrate techniques using Gypsy and hand translation. Provide a component for a trusted, distributed system.

Criteria for success:
Acceptance by research community, successful test operation, use as a building block.

Lasting value:
Minimal.

Aspects of formal methods emphasized:
Gypsy specifications and confidence proofs, proof that application satisfies security model, history based security policy model.

Techniques to be used:
Gypsy.

Potential impact of example:
Research.

Estimate of resources required:
Approximately 3–4 person years.

Proposed approach:
See [Oak 89].

Print Spooler/Labeler

(SW, spec. & mech. proof, security, small, open)

Type of example: Demonstration/Tutorial.

Description:

Filter between computer and printer that ensures each printed page has appropriate labels. Based on model of printer behaviour.

Motivation:

Functional verification of small, stand-alone security-relevant application.

Criteria for success:

Resulting product competitive with commercial, untrusted spoolers within a factor of 2 or 3. Ease of adaptability to a variety of printers.

Lasting value:

Successful use over substantial time period.

Aspects of formal methods emphasized:

Real time (keep up with source/printer) functional correctness, modelling of printer devices, etc.

Techniques to be used:

Could use Gypsy, Z, Cleanroom, or others.

Potential impact of example:

Security utility, potential commercial use.

Estimate of resources required:

Approximately 1–2 person years.

Proposed approach:

Develop printer description paradigm. Develop secure label definition method, i.e., protocol, manual, encryption based. Choose platform, specify, code, verify, test, deliver.

Byzantine Agreement Specialized Hardware
(HW, spec. & mech. proof, safety, small/med., open)

Type of example: Demonstration.

Description:
> Given a system S that has to make a decision based on three independent sensors (or inputs from other systems) X1, X2, X3 which should, in principle, all agree. This hardware is a set of "chips" which guarantees that what appears on "good" X1, X2, X3 are consistent despite the arbitrary failure of S or internal chips, given the number of faults is 1 or less. (This, of course, generalizes to multiple faults.)

Motivation:
> Necessary component of a fault-tolerant system.

Criteria for success:
> Abstract property verified down to gate-level leading to a system that is efficient, i.e., low overhead on CPUs.

Lasting value:
> Yes!

Aspects of formal methods emphasized:
> Asynchronous parts, modelling of asynchrony and fault tolerance.

Techniques to be used:
> Any mechanical theorem provers available, modelling of asynchrony and fault tolerance.

Potential impact of example:
> Could be used as a component in realistic fault-tolerant systems.

Estimate of resources required:
> 1–2 person years.

Proposed approach:
> [None mentioned.]

Seaview, Secure DBMS
(SW, spec. & mech. proof, security, large, open)

Type of example: Demonstration system with commercial potential (prototype exists: SRI/ Gemini). Design, models and prototype completed.

Description:
Seaview enforces a comprehensive security and integrity policy at the granularity of database entities (see [DLSSH 88]). This example extends this work by attempting to produce a verified implementation of a secure DBMS.

Motivation:
Achieves a general-purpose secure DBMS, significantly extending previously available DBMS security. Makes extensive use of existing components (Multi-Level Security Kernel GEMSOS and Commercial DBMS Oracle). Satisfies real needs. A1 candidate.

Criteria for success:
Achieving A1 rating of an application system. Minimum performance degradation when evaluated against comparable DBMSs. Sound proofs of database properties.

Lasting value:
Yes. Real potential impact on commercial marketplace.

Aspects of formal methods emphasized:
Hierarchical specifications and layered mapping of state spaces. Formal modelling of a range of properties other than Multi-Level Security. "Machine" proofs, "balanced assurance" as A1 candidate DBMS based on A1 kernel properties and mapping.

Techniques to be used:
Modelling, formal specs, formal proofs. Design proofs for top-level spec. Hierarchical proof (use of the hierarchical nature of the specification to structure any resultant proofs).

Potential impact of example:
Potential widespread real use.

Estimate of resources required:
A few man-years.

Proposed approach:
RADC is funding the follow-on implementation (SRI/Gemini/Oracle).
See [LSSHW 88].
Separate funding is anticipated for the follow-on specification and proof effort (NCSC). Effort thus far is described in [WL 89].

Software Component Libraries
(SW, spec. only, reliability, medium to large, open)

Type of example: Demonstration, but also tutorial.

Description:
Booch – Slow components in Ada (mostly data structures).

EUB – GRACE (combined product) – may program, not fully specified. Specify (and perhaps prove P7) specification for collection of small components (arrays, linked lists, sort delete, concentrate).

Motivation:
Facilitate re-use of software components.

Criteria for success:
People actually use it (and add to it). Specifying uncovers flaws in existing libraries.

Lasting value:
Re-use of software, elimination of software errors.

Aspects of formal methods emphasized:
Depends on what is in library, e.g., for queue a concurrent procedure may be needed.

Techniques to be used:
Almost any (SDVS/Ada, ORA/Ada, AVA).

Potential impact of example:
DoD software developer can better re-use software with better documentation: greater confidence that use satisfies spec. preconditions.

Estimate of resources required:
Linear in software build, minimum useful 2 person years.

Proposed approach:
Existing generic software libraries for Ada include the Booch Library, described in G. Booch, Software Components in Ada, Benjamin Cummings, Inc., 1987; GRACE, a library of Ada components marketed by EVB, Inc. (Edward V. Brerard); and the Ada Generic Library, described in D.R. Musser and A.A. Stepanov, *The Ada Generic Library: Linear List Processing Packages*, Springer-Verlag, 1989.

C   Respondents' Papers

The following two articles are addenda to the report on the respondents session. John Rushby's contribution was written subsequent to the workshop and further clarifies his views about formal methods and critical systems. Peter Neumann's contribution is the position paper he submitted to the workshop. As a number of his comments referred to the position paper, it is included for completeness.

C.1   Formal Methods and Critical Systems in the Real World

John Rushby
Computer Science Laboratory
SRI International

Programmable computers make it possible to construct systems whose behavior is unimaginably complex. These systems are built because their complexity is believed to confer operational benefits, but this same complexity can harbor unexpected and catastrophic failure modes. The source of these failures can often be traced to software faults—for example, a software bug in the control system of the Therac-25 radiation therapy machine was responsible for the death of three patients and serious injury to several others [Jac 89].

Software doesn't wear out: all software-induced failures are due to design faults, and design faults are largely attributable to the complexity of the designs concerned — complexity that exceeds the intellectual grasp of its own creators. The only way to reduce or eliminate software design faults is to bring the complexity of the software into line with our ability to master that complexity. This might mean choosing not to build certain types of system (such as flight-critical computer control systems for passenger aircraft), and it should mean enhancing the intellectual tools available to software designers.

Engineers in established fields use applied mathematics to predict the behavior and properties of their designs with great accuracy. Software engineers, despite the fact that their creations exhibit far more complexity than physical systems, do not generally do this and the practice of the discipline is still at the pre-scientific or craft stage. Unlike most physical systems, the behavior of software admits discontinuities and so interpolation between known points is unreliable: formal logical analysis is needed to address the discrete, formal, character of software. Thus, the applied mathematics of software is formal logic, and calculating the behavior of software is an exercise in theorem proving. Just as engineers in other disciplines need the speed and accuracy of computers to help them perform their engineering calculations, so software engineers can use the speed and accuracy of computers to help them prove the (large number of relatively simple and not intrinsically interesting) theorems required to predict the behavior of software.

"Formal methods" are nothing but the application of applied mathematics— in this case, formal logic—to the design and analysis of software-intensive systems. Formal methods can be used during the design and documentation of systems, and they can also provide evidence for consideration during the assessment and certification of systems that perform critical functions. The former is surely uncontroversial—one should rather have to defend the absence than the use of formal methods (though see [Nau 82])—and some projects, notably several undertaken in the UK, attest to a practical benefit from using formal methods.

Concern that faults could have very serious consequences has led to the introduction of special standards requiring use of formal methods during the construction and quality assurance of certain classes of computer systems (for example, the US "Orange Book" [DoD 85] for secure systems and the British Defence Standard 00-55 [MoD 89a] for safety critical systems). Such use of formal methods—particularly mechanically checked formal verification—in the certification of critical systems is more controversial.

In established engineering disciplines, the reliability and accuracy of predictions of system behavior are determined by the fidelity of the mathematical models on which they are based, and by the extent to which the necessary calculations are performed without error. For example, the accuracy of the predicted performance of an airfoil depends on how well the chosen aerodynamic model captures the real behavior of air over a wing. It is obvious that similar considerations apply to the reliability and accuracy of predictions concerning the behavior of digital systems made by formal verification. For example, program verification depends on an assumed semantics for the programming language concerned, but these assumed semantics may not coincide with those of its implementation; additionally, the proofs performed during verification may be flawed. The nature and significance of these potential flaws in the efficacy of formal methods are no different from those that attend the use of applied mathematics in other engineering disciplines. Yet—perhaps because the calculations performed in formal verification are proofs, and the inexperienced tend to associate proofs with absolute guarantees—these limitations to formal verification have caused some to excoriate the field [DLP 79, Fet 88] (see [Bar 89] for one of the few well-informed discussions of this controversy). These limitations to verification are not, contrary the assertions of its detractors, denied or minimized by those in the field (see [Coh 89] for example), but the more interesting question—what to do about them—has received scant attention.

Assurance and certification for critical systems

One body of opinion suggests that limitations on the value of the assurance provided by formal verification can be minimized by applying the technique more completely and rigorously. For example, the fear that a verification may be unsound because the assumed and the implemented semantics of the programming language do not agree can be minimized by verifying the language implementation concerned. Of course, this verification will depend on the semantics of the hardware interpreter concerned—and that can be assured by verifying the hardware down to, say, a simple gate model. This approach is valuable and interesting, but it must be careful to address at least two objections.

- The lowest model in a verification hierarchy cannot be verified; evidence for its correctness must be obtained by other means. In addition, purely logical models become increasingly incomplete as increasingly lower levels of implementation are considered. For example, formal gate models do not capture all the relevant properties of hardware implementations: physical properties such as excessive fan-out or power dissipation, violations of topographical design constraints, metastability, or an excessive clock rate, not to mention manufacturing defects, can all undermine formal verification at the hardware level.

- If we build the wrong system, then it avails us little if the semantics of the programming language that supports it are implemented perfectly and run on perfect hardware. In complex systems, the limiting factor may be imperfect understanding of all the properties required for a given component or set of components. System failures can often be traced to the interfaces between components: each component performs as required, but their interaction produces undesired and unexpected behavior [Lev 86]. Again, these issues can be modelled, and perhaps they, rather than the relatively routine aspects of system implementation, should most urgently receive the benefit of formal analysis.

The problem of flawed calculations—i.e., unsound proofs—can be minimized by using mechanical proof checkers built on a very simple and evidently sound foundation. The class of provers derived from LCF are in this category. The disadvantage of this approach is that the provers concerned are orders of magnitude less effective than those built on more powerful—but less assured—foundations.

The root difficulties of the "verify everything" approach and the use of "slow but sure" provers are economic. All engineering is about compromise—wisely chosen and justifiable compromise. In the case of a critical system, we have to consider not only the absolute value of the resources that should be expended on its construction and certification, but also how those resources should best be apportioned. A thousand dollars spent on formal verification will mean a thousand dollars less for testing, or a thousand dollars less for protective redundancy. We have to ask: if some formal verification is good, is more always better?

My own view is that judicious application of formal methods in system design and documentation is essential—indeed, there is no credible alternative. Formal methods used for this purpose do not absolutely require mechanical support; they provide intellectual tools that can be practiced with pencil and paper. The Oxford Z methodology, discussed by several participants in this workshop, has this character.

For assurance and certification, formal methods also have much to offer, but heavy-duty (i.e., mechanically checked) formal verification is just one option among several, to be applied only where it will be the most effective choice. The alternative choices include formally-based methods other than conventional verification (for example, fault-tree analysis, structured walk-throughs, and anomaly detection), empirical testing, and approaches based on error-detection and fault-tolerance. The overall goal should be the construction of Dependable Systems: those in which reliance may *justifiably* be placed on certain aspects of the quality of service delivered [Lap 85].

An important facet of dependability is that it is a systems (i.e., big picture) concept. Perfection in components and subsystems does not necessarily provide a dependable system overall—and may not be the best way to achieve dependability. If dependably safe control cannot be guaranteed of digital avionics (and many believe it cannot), then it may still be possible to build a safe airplane containing digital avionics—provided the digital control system is not a single point of failure. At the least, this requires the airplane to be aerodynamically stable, and that there should be some direct connection between the pilot and the control surfaces.

The concept of dependability also introduces a significant compromise: we do not require that every aspect of system functionality should be provided dependably, only that selected aspects should. Thus, for example, although we would like the digital avionics of passenger aircraft to provide both safe and fuel-efficient control, we might insist that only safety is assured to the highest levels of dependability. In these cases, it is possible to work backwards from hypothesized dependability failures in order to discover whether any errors in design or implementation can allow those failures to occur. This technique of "software fault-tree analysis" [LH 83] can be considered a formal method but, because it reasons backwards from hypothesized failures rather than forward from one supposedly good state to another, it rests on rather different assumptions than other methods and can identify faults that have been overlooked in more conventional analyses.

Direct testing also probes assumptions; it can be used to validate the explicit assumptions of a formal analysis (just as a wind-tunnel may be used to validate the assumptions used in an aerodynamic calculation), and it can expose hidden assumptions and misunderstood or overlooked requirements. Testing is sometimes dismissed by those who espouse the purest of formal methods ("testing reveals the presence of faults, never their absence"), but I can imagine no serious approach to the certification of critical systems that does not require explicit and extensive testing. The interesting challenge is to identify ways in which testing can reinforce and support formally-based analyses.

The same is true of run-time error checking. Even a verified microprocessor is vulnerable to surges on its power line, and to strikes by alpha-particles and bullets. It is only prudent to monitor the progress of a computation in order to ensure that nothing is going drastically awry. By combining run-time checking with formal analysis, it should be possible to make stronger and more reliable statements than is possible with either technique alone [AW 78].

If run-time error checking is performed, it is natural to provide some form of recovery, or fault-tolerance, in response to detected errors. Some degree of fault tolerance is normally considered essential in high-dependability systems. Physical components wear out, and the external environment may introduce unanticipated circumstances. Fault-tolerance requires the monitoring of performance, and the presence of redundancy. Both add complexity, and may thereby reduce, rather than enhance, dependability. The algorithms needed to provide "Byzantine fault-tolerant" synchronization and agreement, for example, are of considerable difficulty, and the software that manages the coordination, voting, error-detection, recovery and reconfiguration in a fault-tolerant system becomes a single point of failure in the overall system. Because of its criticality and difficulty, it is an excellent candidate for heavy-duty formal verification.

From fault-tolerance intended to protect against component malfunction, it is but a small step to contemplate redundancy and fault-tolerance as a safeguard against *design* faults. "Software-fault tolerance" relies on "diversity" (multiple designs and implementations for each program module), run-time checking, and majority voting to safeguard against design faults in critical software [AL 86].

Formal methods and systems engineering

Some researchers in the formal methods community are reluctant to involve themselves with systems that are to be used in the real world. Since the invitation to participate usually comes only from those who are developing systems of unusual criticality (where conventional methods of assurance are known to be inadequate), this reluctance is understandable. Many feel that the complexity of the systems concerned, the constraints that surround them, and the serious consequences that could attend their failure, are such that formal methods can provide only partial assurances that could be misinterpreted.

Others believe that the systems concerned are going to be built anyway, and that it is better to bring some of the benefits of formal methods to bear than none at all; in the absence of participation by the formal methods community, other—perhaps inferior—technologies may become entrenched. It should be noted, for example, that a particular incarnation of software fault tolerance ("N-version programming" [Avi 85]) is the *dominant technology* for dependable systems in aerospace, where the flight control computers for the Boeing 737-300 and for the Airbus A310 and A320 are N-version systems; I am unaware of any deployed flight control system that has been subjected to formal verification.

The presentations that we have heard today all describe serious attempts to apply formal methods to real systems in a limited but responsible manner. In each case, we have seen that it has been important to consider the system context: formal methods should be targeted where they will do the most good. And we have seen that formal methods must be integrated with other approaches to validation and assurance.

I believe that integration of formal methods with other forms of assurance is necessary for truly dependable systems. Calling for verification to simply be used in addition to fault-tree analysis, testing, run-time checking, and fault-tolerance is trite. What we need is not simple redundancy of analysis, but integration: we need to know how to use testing and verification in support of each other, to know how the one can validate the assumptions of the other. And we need to investigate how run-time checking and fault-tolerance can be used to provide principled detection and response to violated assumptions, rather than a gamble on the laws of probability.

In summary, I invite those who are willing to essay the application of formal methods to critical real-world systems to consider the following points:

1. Our techniques are not infallible: any really critical system should be designed so that it can operate safely (though possibly in a degraded mode) without the computer system: even if all the flight control computers fail, it should still be possible to land the plane.

2. Formal methods are not synonymous with mechanically checked formal verification. The "manual" use of formal methods during design, and for documentation, may be of considerable benefit.

3. Formal verification, if it is to be employed at all, cannot be applied everywhere; we need to target its application with great care. Software components that constitute a single point of system failure (such as those that manage the fault-tolerance mechanisms) are natural candidates.

4. We need to develop a foundation for the integration of multiple forms of assurance: formal methods do not stand alone.

The foregoing presentations have shown us some of the opportunities and challenges that await those who are willing to apply formal methods in a systems engineering context. I hope more of us will follow their example.

C.2 Whither Formal Methods?

Peter Neumann
Computer Science Laboratory
SRI International

Summary
By *formal methods*, I mean methods that add mathematical rigour to the development, analysis, and operation of computer systems and to applications based thereupon. I begin with a few background statements, to get the ball rolling.

- The potential of formal methods is enormous, particularly for critical properties of systems with extraordinarily stringent requirements. However, progress has been disappointingly slow to those who unrealistically expected panaceas. (See the proceedings of VERkshops I, II, III for a view of the historical evolution [Ver 80, Ver 81, Ver 85].)

- There is much work still to be done on all fronts—research, tool development, and applications of formal methods to real systems.

- Research in formal methods has progressed somewhat sporadically. There are still unresolved problems relating to the specification, programming, verification, and formally based testing of computer systems and networks. The state of the art is particularly primitive with respect to distributed systems and concurrency. Also, much research is aimed only at localized problems rather than at real systems.

- Overall, formal methods have the reputation of being inherently difficult to apply in practice with real rigour, requiring highly skilled people. Existing tools to support formally based methods are often flaky and difficult to use. Their use may be dangerous if people tend to trust the tools, which after all should be considered as an aid to thinking, not a substitute for it. There is a grave danger of attempting to create methodologies and tools that are resilient to incompetence; even the best approaches can be misused. Nevertheless, greater emphasis could be placed on usability.

- Successes have been small and rather limited in scope. The real problems are big and rather unlimited in scope. Nevertheless, small steps are vital to achieving success in the large. More work is needed on system-level techniques that address the overall system and its desired properties. Hardware specification and verification is also a high-payoff area.

- None of the existing methodologies has yet consistently addressed a meaningfully broad spectrum of requirements across the entire development cycle.

- System designs have not adequately addressed the integration of different real requirements, but this is perhaps a human limitation more than a technological problem. The interactions among different requirements are still not adequately understood—with or without formal methods.

- Some of the formal methods work in the U.S.A. has been too severely constrained by the rather narrow concerns of Bell-and-LaPadula-like models for security and by defense-related applications.

- Some of the formal methods community in the U.S.A. has been seriously hindered by controls on the dissemination of the tools. These controls have impeded widespread use of the tools and the feedback that would result from creative and probing uses as well as from the social process.

This workshop statement pursues the contention that the effective use of formal methods—and probably the long-term survival in terms of R&D funding for formal methods—depends critically on the existence, in the near future, of some carefully documented successes relating to real systems. Some applications that might be suitable vehicles are considered here.

Introduction

Formal methods may be applied throughout the development process, to requirements, design, specification, abstract implementation, concrete implementation, maintenance, evolution, etc. Formal analysis may include reasoning about requirements, design proofs (e.g., that the specifications are consistent with a set of requirements), implementation proofs (e.g., that the code is consistent with its specifications), hardware verification, specification-based testing, etc.

Formal methods are applicable at many layers of abstraction—from hardware to operating system software to application subsystem software to the end-user interfaces. At any particular layer, specific requirements (or properties) may be formalized, relating to (for example) data confidentiality, data integrity, subsystem integrity, reliability, availability, timely responsiveness, and human safety. At the layers forming the human interface, it is also possible to formalize various necessary assumptions on the users that must be satisfied to ensure adequate system behavior. Representation of both the human interface and the assumptions on human behavior is an area of particular R&D importance (cf. the experience with the Aegis shootdown of the Iranian Airbus and the Therac 25, noted below).

Formalism for the sake of formalism is rather sterile. Formalism should have useful manipulative abilities to enhance its existence.

Formal specification and verification have been under attack for many years (e.g., DeMillo, Lipton, and Perlis [DLP 79], and more recently Fetzer [Fet 88])—although many of the would-be attacks are not based on informed technical reasoning. Nevertheless, the formal methods communities have not adequately risen to the challenge (bait?). There have indeed been some limited successes, but they are still all rather narrowly scoped.

Partial successes are generally known to the workshop community, and include—to different degrees of success—Avra Cohn's Viper work, several efforts by Don Good's Computational Logic Inc., the Honeywell SCOMP proofs of security (resulting in an A1 NCSC rating), the Honeywell LOCK effort (LOgical Coprocessor Kernel, in spirit a descendant of SRI's Provably Secure Operating System, PSOS), the SRI-Gemini SeaView secure database management system design (with layered abstraction, modelling of security and integrity, and some formal specification and verification—see Whitehurst and Lunt [WL 89]), SRI's paper design for the Software Implemented Fault Tolerant system (SIFT), the revised and carefully documented proofs of the SIFT n-tolerated Byzantine 3n+1 clock synchronization algorithm (Rushby and von Henke [RH 89]), Blacker, the specification of CICS in Z, uses of VDM, and some of Leveson's modelling and techniques for evaluation of safety properties [Lev 86] [JL 89]) to cite just a few. All of these efforts—and others—deserve more extensive promulgation, carefully qualified and not overstated, to permit a clear understanding of their relative strengths and weaknesses. In addition, the various criteria documents (the NCSC's Orange, Red, and other books; the Department of Trade and Industry (DTI) Commercial Computer Security Centre (CCSC) Green Books, and Communications Electronics Security Group (CESG) confidence levels and the DTI safety standards; and various other national efforts) will hopefully converge compatibly toward common goals.

Formal methods have been most successful in relatively small and well defined contexts such as very critical algorithms, isolation kernels, security kernels, and communication protocols. However, the use of formal methods in the small is deceptively simplistic, and intrinsically lacking in terms of the relations with reality. (Sadly, I am continually astounded to see research providing another allegedly "new" way to specify the stack algorithm—without even being able to accommodate stack overflow.)

Formal methods can also be useful in real systems for describing systems in the large. If system modules and layers of abstraction (e.g., the kernels or the critical algorithms noted above) have been suitably constrained by the design, then formal methods should permit reasoning about the module interconnectivity and constraints enforced on interactions. This should apply both vertically among different layers in an abstraction hierarchy as well as horizontally among different modules at the same layer of abstraction. Reasoning about the interactions among different requirements should also be possible. (Cf. the old HDM concepts and also [Neu 86], which attempts to address different requirements compatibly.)

Unfortunately, much work is directed rather narrowly toward small and well definable problems—in order to achieve some sort of 'success'. However, this can result in systems that in the large do not satisfy their requirements (even though they may satisfy a specific requirement in isolation). This leads to subsystems that might be considered (say) secure, but which when embedded in the larger context are trivially subvertible.

Experience

It is not reassuring to continually find systems that have failed to live up to their expected behavior. (See [Neu 89a] for a lengthy list of disaster cases.) This large body of negative experiences suggests that the human ability to make serious errors or to behave maliciously can undermine even the best of system designs or can lead to horrendous flaws. Conventionally developed systems have resulted in losses of lives, assets, and other valuable resources. Unfortunately, there is little evidence that formally based systems have done much better—although there are great expectations that such systems should be able to do much better. Greater success in the use of formal methods will require further advances in requirement definitions, design, human interfaces, models, specification languages, development and support tools, suitable hardware bases, the use of appropriate programming languages, intelligent people, adequate administrative support, and thorough organizational commitment—among other things. However, each of those factors has often been the source of difficulties that have led to serious consequences. On the other hand, it is dangerous to attempt to assign blame, which in many cases must be distributed. In many cases, several different factors were involved.

Here are a few illustrative cases for which we consider whether formal methods might have played a significant role.

- External security penetrations and internal misuses of authority seem to be increasing. The Internet Worm exploited flaws in the 'debug' option of 'sendmail' and in 'fingerd' (invoking 'gets', which had inadequate bounds checking) in version 4 BSD UNIX network software. The West German Chaos Computer Club attacked NASA systems using flaws in an updated release of a DEC VMS system that had been given a C2 rating. Many other security violations are indicated in the attached list.

- The October 1980 ARPANET collapse resulted from an unforeseen interaction among (1) a natural hardware failure mode (dropped bits), (2) the recreation of check bits from unchecked memory before retransmission, rather than the storage of the checked form, (3) and a garbage collection algorithm that was not resistant to the simultaneous existence of identical messages with different time stamps; this combination had not previously arisen in many years of successful operation. In isolation, the garbage collection algorithm seemed sound—keeping only the most recent of any pair of status messages for a given node, where the definition of recency may be thought of as the larger of two close-together six-bit time stamps, modulo 64. (The bit-dropped versions with time stamps 40 and 8 resulted in the correct version 48 being more recent than 40, which in turn was more recent than 8, which was more recent than 48 end-around.) (See [Ros 81].)

- The Vincennes' shootdown of an Iranian Airbus was blamed on human error, and the computer system was officially vindicated. It is apparently true that the Aegis did represent the Airbus' altitude correctly, from which the operators should have been able to ascertain that the plane was not a military aircraft and that it was not descending. However, the altitude data was not conveniently displayed, and there was no explicit indication over time as to whether the would-be target was ascending, descending, or flying level. There was also confusion between the target whose transponder signal had at some prior time been received (from a plane still on the airport runway) and the plane whose altitude was being tracked, and no indication of how recently that identification had been made. To absolve the system itself of any blame is unrealistic; the human interface is a part of the system.

- The software controlling the Therac 25 therapeutic radiation device was implicated in at least three separate deaths, with other cases of injuries as well. There are two settings for the linear accelerator, a high-intensity X-ray mode and a low-intensity electron-beam mode. The X-ray mode was supposed to be accompanied by the placement of a movable filter (called a 'target') that diffuses the X-rays. The X-ray mode and the presence of the filter should have been linked indivisibly, but were not, resulting in an unsafe state. In general, the lack of atomicity often appears to be an implementation glitch; however, in this case the system and software requirements/specifications were incomplete in that they did not address the safety issues. The Therac 25 design provides another example of an unfortunate user interface, in which safety-critical error messages could be overridden and the complex control commands could be edited without the integrity of any contextual abstraction, thus permitting access to an unsafe state.

The Orange Book criteria for formal models, formal specifications, and formal design proofs (an earlier A2 rating also addressed code proofs) provide some defenses against security vulnerabilities (although there are serious limitations in that approach). These criteria still leave huge gaps in assurance: the models must be sufficiently complete and correct, the design specifications must be consistent with the real models rather than the abstract models, and the code must be consistent with the design specifications. Even if all of those gaps were closed, there would still be many opportunities for system misuse—e.g., improper use and administration such as improper initialization or compromised passwords. (In addition, the Orange Book has also lulled the community into a false sense of security [!] by its being overendowed with sanctity.) Nevertheless, formal methods can contribute significantly to the avoidance of vulnerabilities.

The ARPANET collapse is a fine example of a combination of problems. Formal methods would have been no help whatever unless they represented those combinations. The latent flaw in the garbage collection might have been smoked out by analysis using formal methods—by detecting the possibility of a circular chain of recency and the resulting storage saturation. But the notion of a bit being dropped in the same word in memory on two different occasions surrounding a time-out retry would have had to be covered. This example serves as a challenge to formal methods to realistically represent the interactions among hardware and software and the hidden assumptions that lurk behind all systems.

In the cases of the Aegis and the Therac 25, the 'blame' can be shared among the requirements, the specifications, and the implementation—particularly for the human interface—and also the user/operator. Although research in modelling human users and human interfaces is still fairly primitive, it may have enormous payoff in helping to avoid such tragedies.

Other problems in design and specification are summarized in [Neu 89a, Neu 89b], some of which might also have been avoided by the judicious use of formal methods. It would also be interesting to consider how many of the misuse techniques summarized in [NP 89] could be avoided with formal methods.

Exercises
Success comes most readily on small, well-defined, and somewhat isolatable systems. However, we need both compelling small examples and increasingly realistic large systems—as the technology matures.

Here are a few specific areas in which successful exercises might be expected, in approximate order of increasing difficulty. In each case, formal requirements and specifications are desired, along with clear, well written code, and formal demonstrations that code is consistent with specifications, which are in turn consistent with the stated requirements.

- A simple isolation kernel that satisfies rigorous properties, whose design and implementation are elaborated formally with almost agonizing detail, but with a sense of abstraction so that the individual specifications, implementations, and formal reasoning are crystal clear.

- Clean and elegant examples of trusted computing bases in the Orange Book A1 sense that not merely minimally adhere to the Orange Book but that really transcend the minimal requirements.

- An application in which data integrity properties can be derived explicitly from lower-layer properties (e.g., an underlying multilevel security TCB), as is done in SeaView. The database properties should reflect the explicit layering of specifications.

- A simple distributed system in which all of the assumptions for proper behavior are made explicit, including those regarding secure communications and key management, security mechanisms, reliability (including replicated file servers and data management), etc.

- An application in which safety properties are shown to depend explicitly on lower-layer properties, rather than merely demonstrating that a piece of code satisfies some not-very-abstract properties. For example, explicitly model safety properties and how they depend upon lower-layer properties for security, integrity, and real-time performance.

- A system satisfying requirements encompassing reliability, security, integrity, safety, real-time, and addressing the interactions among them at different hierarchical layers of abstraction—including the hardware. An old argument goes that we cannot even develop models for single simple requirements that can be satisfied by real systems, so how can we address multiple simultaneous requirements? Perhaps the individual component problems have been considered too narrowly. I believe that a suitably general approach should be able to permit the consistent modelling and analysis of the collection of properties.

The proofs of the SIFT [WLG 78, MS 81, RH 89] paper system represent an early attempt to span a significant hierarchical range. Perhaps the VIPER effort will continue in that direction. The last item in this list is in a sense the most demanding—for real systems—in that it attempts to model a range of nontrivial properties and derive the desired user interface properties from the accumulation of all of the underlying layers of abstraction, including the hardware.

It would be appropriate to agree on measures of acceptable progress. The most compelling yardstick would be general acceptance by the technical community that the results are truly significant—the 'social process'. But we need to be much more precise in our expectations of what constitutes 'success'.

Conclusions

I stated above that formal methods are inherently difficult to apply in practice with real rigour, requiring highly skilled people. I do not recommend trying to make formal methods amenable to the uneducated. But I also do not conclude that the use of formal methods is therefore doomed. People are very good at imitating others once they see the way. They tend not to get everything right, because there are various leaps in intuition that cannot be taught. But the importance of having rigorously worked examples cannot be underestimated.

I suggested above that we need some really significant, carefully documented, real-system successes in the near future. Some of the existing efforts could be pursued with great rigour, at least to the point of diminishing returns. Viper and LOCK come to mind as efforts that are well along, and that hold significant promise for rigour.

We need elegant (and therefore small) examples, but we also need to aim toward systems that are larger, or that simultaneously satisfy different requirements. I recommend encouraging joint research efforts that bring together people from different disciplines (e.g., safety, security, integrity, reliability, and system fault tolerance), rather than just encouraging isolated solutions to isolated problems. The unified perspective is likely to simplify each of the previously separate approaches, and recognize the considerable commonality among different requirements.

We have our work cut out for us, but the potential remains enormous. We must establish community goals and go after them together. Germaine Greer speaks of 'horizontal hostility' as the process whereby people who agree almost completely on major issues spend most of their time arguing about their minor differences. There has been far too much of that within the formal methods communities. It is time to pull together. Haranbee.[14]

---

[14]*Editor's Note:* A Swahili word meaning "let us pull together."

D   Illustrative risks to the public in the use of computer systems and related technology

Compiled by Peter G. Neumann
Computer Science Lab, SRI International, Menlo Park CA 94025
Editor, ACM SIGSOFT Software Engineering Notes
Chairman, ACM Committee on Computers and Public Policy

List of RISKS CASES as of 17 May 1990

This list summarizes most of cases that have appeared in the pages of the ACM SIGSOFT quarterly, Software Engineering Notes (SEN), references to which are cited below as (S vol no); one vol per year, vol 15 is 1990. Some incidents are well documented, while others need further study. A few are of questionable authenticity, and are noted as such (e.g., "???") A compendium of these cases is in preparation. Corrections and additions with references please to Peter G. Neumann, SRI International BN168, Menlo Park CA 94025, tel 415-859-2375, Internet Neumann@csl.sri.com.

SEN also considers approaches for developing better computer systems, e.g., safer, more reliable, more secure. There are many approaches, although none is guaranteed. Whereas the emphasis in this list is on problems rather than would-be solutions, the pervasive nature of the problems suggests that techniques for suitably developing and operating systems are frequently ignored. Worse yet, even ideal systems can result in serious risks, through unanticipated technological problems or human misuse.

LEGEND:

!	=	Loss of Life; ∗ = Potentially Life-Critical; $ = Loss of Resources;
S	=	Security/Privacy/Integrity Problem;

Various types of behavior are categorized:

H	=	Intentional misuse (e.g., user/administrator/operator/penetrator)
h	=	Accidental misuse
i	=	Misinterpretation/confusion at a man-system interface
f	=	Flaws in system concept, requirements, design, implementation;
e	=	Improper maintenance/upgrade. (H,h,i,f,e involve human foibles.)
m	=	Hardware malfunction attributable to system deficiencies, electronic or other interference, the physical environment, acts of God, etc.

SPACE:
..... Manned Space Exploration
!!$$fh Shuttle Challenger explosion, 7 killed. (Removed booster sensors might have permitted early computer detection of leak?) (28 Jan 86) (S 11 2) (Probably not? See Paul Ceruzzi, Beyond the Limits – Computers Enter the Space Age, MIT Press, 1989, Appendix.)
$f First Space Shuttle Columbia backup launch-computer synch problem (see Jack Garman, "The bug heard 'round the world", S 6 5, Oct. 1981, pp. 3-10.)
∗f Second Shuttle simulation: bug found in jettisoning an SRB (S 8 3)
∗f Second Space Shuttle operational simulation: tight loop upon cancellation of

an attempted abort; required manual override (S 7 1)

*f Shuttle STS-6 bugs in live Dual Mission software precluded aborts (S 11 1)

*m Columbia STS-9 return delayed by multiple computer malfunctions (S 9 1)

*f Discovery STS-16 landing gear – correlated faults (S 10 3)

*if Discovery STS-18 positioned upside down; mirror to reflect laser beam from
   Mona Kea aimed upward (+10,023 miles), not downward (... feet) (S 10 3)

*$ Two-day delay of Discovery STS-20 launch: backup computer outage
   (NY Times 26 August 1985); Syncom 4 satellite failure as well (S 10 5)

*hife Columbia STS-24 near-disaster, liquid oxygen drained mistakenly
   just before launch, computer output misread (S 11 5)

* Space shuttle computer problems, 1981–1985; 700 computer/avionics anomalies
   logged; landing gear problems in STS-6 and -13; multiple computer crashes in
   STS-9, cutting in backup system would have been fatal; thermocouple failure
   in STS-19 near disaster (S 14 2)

$f Space shuttle launch (25Feb90) delayed; "bad software" in backup tracking
   computer system, but no details yet. (S 15 2)

*f Columbia orbiter suddenly rotates, due to telemetry noise (S 15 4)

* Mercury astronauts forced into manual reentry? (S 8 3)

m Atlantis spacecraft computer problem fixed in space (S 14 5)

$fh $150M Intelsat 6 comm satellite failed; booster wiring error, payload in
   wrong bay; miscommunication between electricians and programmers (S 15 4)

$f Hubble Space Telescope problems, soaring costs, missed deadlines,
   reduced goals, etc. (S 15 2)

..... Others

f Voyager 2 software faults at launch, 20 Aug 1977 (SEN 14 6)

$ Titan 34D, Nike Orion, Delta-178 failures follow Challenger (S 11 3)

* Lightning hits Apollo 12. "Major system upsets, minor damage". See article
   by Uman and Krider, Science 27 Oct 1989, pp. 457-464. (S 15 1)

$m Lightning changed Atlas-Centaur program (51 sec). $160M lost (S 12 3, 15 1)

*$m Lightning hits launch pad, launches 3 missiles at Wallops Island (S 12 3)

*$f Mariner 1: Atlas booster launch failure DO xx I=1.3 (not 1,3) (S 8 5,11 5)
   NO. APOCRYPHAL. Apparently a garbled minus sign (hyphen instead)? (S 13 1)
   NO. HW fault plus programmer missed superscript bar in 'R dot bar sub n'.
   See Paul Ceruzzi, Beyond the Limits – Flight Enters the Computer Age,
   1989, Appendix. (S 14 5) And now we find the comma/period substitution
   problem actually did happen as well–but was detected and fixed. (S 15 1)

*f Gemini V 100mi landing err, prog ignored orbital motion around sun (S 9 1)

$f Atlas-Agena software missing hyphen; $18.5M rocket destroyed (S 10 5)

$f Aries with $1.5M payload lost: wrong resistor in guidance system; (S 11 5)

*f TDRS relay satellite locked on wrong target (S 10 3)

*m Cosmic rays hit TDRS, Challenger comm halved for 14 hours (8 Oct 84)(S 10 1)

$m Sunspot activity: 1979 Skylab satellite dragged out of orbit (S 13 4)

$hfe Soviet Phobos I Mars probe lost: faulty SW update (S 13 4); cost to USSR
   300M rubles (Aviation Week, 13 Feb 89); disorientation broke radio link,
   discharged solar batteries before reacquisition. (Science 16 Sep 88)
   More on Phobos 1 & 2 computer failures (SEN 14 6)

$? Soviets lose contact with Phobos II Mars probe. Automatic reorientation
   of antenna back toward earth failed. (S 14 2)

$f Magellan space software problems: serious design flaw fixed (S 14 5)
$m Magellan spacecraft manual guidance overcomes faulty computer chip (S 15 2)
*h Soyuz Spacecraft reentry failed, based on wrong descent program,
   (orbiting module had been jettisoned, precluding redocking) (S 13 4)
$fe Viking had a misaligned antenna due to a faulty code patch (S 9 5)
*f Ozone hole over South Pole observed, rejected by SW for 8 years (S 11 5)
* Continuing trend toward expert systems in NASA (S 14 2)

DEFENSE
!!$hi Iran Air 655 Airbus shot down by USS Vincennes' missiles (290 dead);
   Human error plus confusing and incomplete Aegis interface (S 13 4);
   Commentary on Tom Wicker article on Vincennes and SDI (S 13 4);
   Aegis user interface changes recommended; altitude, IFF problems (S 14 1);
   Analysis implicates Aegis displays and crew (Aerospace America, Apr 1989);
   Further analysis indicates intrinsic limitations (RISKS-8.74, S 14 5);
   USS Sides Cmdr David Carlson questions attack on Iranian jet (SEN 14 6)
!!$h? Sheffield sunk during Falklands war, 20 killed. Call to London hindered
   antimissile defenses on same frequency. (AP 16 May 86)(S 11 3)
!$ British Falklands helicopter downed by British missile. 4 dead (S 12 1)
!!$f USS Liberty: 3 independent warning messages to withdraw were all lost;
   34 killed, more wounded. Intelligence implications as well. (S 11 5)
!hfi? Stark unpreparedness against Iraqi Exocets blamed on officers, not
   technology, but technology was too dangerous to use automatically (S 12 3);
   Captain blamed deficient radar equipment; official report says
   radar detected missiles, misidentified them. (S 13 1)
*H Fraudulent test SW in Phalanx anti-missile system, Standard missile (S 13 4)
*H West German flies Helsinki-Moscow through Soviet Air Defense (S 12 3)
**f Returning space junk detected as missiles. Daniel Ford, The Button, p.85
** WWMCCS false alarms triggered scrams 3-6 Jun 1980 (S 5 3, Ford pp 78-84)
** DSP East satellite sensors overloaded by Siberian gas-field fire (Ford p 62)
   (Daniel Ford summarized in SEN 10 3)
**f BMEWS at Thule detected rising moon as incoming missiles (5 Oct 1960)
   (S 8 3). See E.C. Berkeley, The Computer Revolution, pp. 175-177, 1962.
** SAC/NORAD: 50 false alerts in 1979 (S 5 3), incl. a simulated attack whose
   outputs accidentally triggered a live scramble (9 Nov 1979) (S 5 3)
*$f Libyan bomb raid accidental damage by "smart bomb" (S 11 3)
* Frigate George Philip fired missile in opposite direction (S 8 5)
*h? Unarmed Soviet missile crashed in Finland. Wrong flight path? (S 10 2)
*f 1st Tomahawk cruise missile failure: program erased (8 Dec 86) (S 11 2)
*m 2nd Tomahawk failure; bit dropped by HW triggered abort (S 11 5, 12 1)
*$f Program, model flaws implicated in Trident 2 failures (SEN 14 6)
*m RF interference caused Black Hawk helicopter hydraulic failure (S 13 1)
*f Sgt York (DIVAD) radar/anti-aircraft gun – software problems (S 11 5)
$f Software flaw in sub-launched ballistic missile system (S 10 5)
$f AEGIS failures on 6 of 17 targets attributed to software (S 11 5)
f WWMCCS computers' comm reboot failed by blocked multiple logins (S 11 5)
$ WWMCCS modernization difficulties (S 15 1)
$f Armored Combat Earthmover 18,000 hr tests missed serious problems (S 11 5)

$fi Stinger missile too heavy to carry, noxious to user (S 11 5)
**$$(Hff?) Strategic Defense Initiative – debate over feasibility (S 10 5)
$ Star Wars satellite 2nd stage photo missed – unremoved lens cap (S 14 2)
$h DoD criticized for software development problems (S 13 1)
$ USAF software contractors score poorly on selections (S 14 1)
$ Systems late, over budget (what's new?); C-17/B-1/STC/NORAD/ASJP (S 15 1)
*h Outdated codes made US missiles useless until annual inspection (S 14 5)
hi? Listing of US Navy safety problems in two-week period (S 15 1)
m Rain shuts down Army computers; lightning effects and prevention (S 15 1)
    DoD Software Master Plan (preliminary draft released 9Feb90. Contact
    George P. Millburn, Deputy Director, DDRE, the Pentagon.) (S 15 2)

MILITARY AVIATION:
!!$f Handley Page Victor tailplane broke, crew lost. 3 independent test methods,
    3 independent flaws, masking flutter problem (S 11 2,p.12;correction 11 3)
!f Harrier ejection-seat parachute system accidentally deployed, blew through
    the canopy, but without ejecting the seat and pilot, who was killed (S 13 3)
*$f Gripen crash caused by flight control software (S 14 2, 14 5)
*$f Software problems in B-1B terrain-following radar, flight-control;
    electronic countermeasures (stealth) jam plane's own signals (S 12 2)
*$h B-1B swept wing punctures gas tank on the ground; blamed on low lubricant;
    problem found in 70 of 80 B-1Bs inspected (S 14 2)! No computer sensors?
$f Stealth development problems, including SW miscalculation in wiring (S 15 1)
$f UHB demonstrator flight aborted by software error at 12,000 feet (S 12 3)
*$f F-18 crash due to missing exception cond. Pilot OK (S 6 2, more SEN 11 2)
*hi F-18 missile thrust while clamped, plane lost 20,000 feet (S 8 5)
*f F-16 simulation: plane flipped over whenever it crossed equator (S 5 2)
*f F-16 simulation: upside-down, deadlock over left vs. right roll (S 9 5)
$hi F-16 landing gear raised while plane on runway; bomb problems (S 11 5)
*fh Unstallable F-16 stalls; novice pilot found unprotected maneuver (S 14 2)
*$f? F-14 off aircraft carrier into North Sea; due to software? (S 8 3)
*$f F-14 lost to uncontrollable spin, traced to tactical software (S 9 5)
* F-111 downed by defense-jamming electromagnetic interference (S 14 2)
* US missile-warning radar endangers explosions of friendly aircraft (S 14 2)
* AF PAVE PAWS radar can trigger ejection seats, fire extinguishers (S 15 1)
!$h 1988 RAF Tornados collided, killing 4; flying on same cassette! (S 15 4)
m Air Force bombs Georgia – stray electromagnetic interference? (S 14 5)

COMMERCIAL AVIATION:
!!$hi Iran Air 655 Airbus shot down by USS Vincennes' missiles (see above).
!!$hi? Korean Airlines 007 shot down killing 269 (1 Sept 1983); autopilot on
    HDG 246 rather than INERTIAL NAV? (NYReview 25 Apr 85; SEN 9 1, 10 3,
    12 1) or espionage mission? (R.W. Johnson, "Shootdown")
!!$h Air New Zealand crashed into Mt Erebus, killing 257 (28 Nov 1979);
    computer course data error detected but pilots not informed (S 6 3 & 6 5)
!!hifm NW 255 computer failed to warn crew of unset flaps; 156 dead (S 12 4);
    Circuit breaker blamed. Simulator, plane behave differently (S 13 1)
    Report blames pilot error, unattributed circuit outage (S 13 3)

Report that the same pilots had intentionally disconnected the alarm on
another MD-80 two days before raises suspicions. (SEN 14 5, RISKS-8.65)
!!mf/h/i? British Midland 737 crash, 47 killed, 74 seriously injured; right
   engine erroneously shut off in response to smoke, vibration (Flight
   International 1 Apr 89); suspected crosswiring detected in many OTHER
   planes (S 14 2); low-probability, high-consequence accidents (S 14 5);
   random memory initialization in flight management computers (S 14 5)
!!h Aeromexico flight to LAX crashes with private plane, 82 killed (S 11 5)
!!h Metroliner&transponderless small plane collide 15 Jan 87. 10 die (S 12 2)
!h Air France Airbus crash blamed on pilot error, safety controls off (S 13 4);
   3 killed. Airbus A320 computer system development criticized (S 13 4);
   Subsequent doubts on computers reported: inaccurate altimeter readings;
   engines unexpectedly throttling up on final approach; sudden power loss
   prior to landing; steering problems while taxiing (S 14 2); reportage by
   Jim Beatson (RISKS-8.49,8.77), barometric pressure backset? (S 14 5)
!? Indian Airlines Airbus A320 crashes 1000 ft short of runway; 97 die (S 15 2)
   More on the A320 crashes and apparent similarities (S 15 4)
!f/h/i? Varig 737 crash (12 dead) flightpath miskeyed? (S 15 1)
! 707 over Elkton MD hit by lightning in 1963, everyone killed (S 15 1)
!!h Two planes collide 19 Jan 87. Altitude data not watched by ATC. (S 12 2)
!!$m DC-10 indicators failed: their power came from missing engine (S 11 5)
! Bird strikes cause crash of Ethiopian Airlines 737, killing 31 (S 14 2)
*f DC-9 chip failure mode detected in simulation (S 13 1)
!!$f Electra failures due to simulation omission (S 11 5)
!$f Computer readout for navigation wrong, pilot killed (S 11 2)
*hi South Pacific Airlines, 200 aboard, 500 mi off course near USSR (6 Oct 1984)
*hi China Air 006 747SP 2/86 pilot vs autopilot at 41,000 ft with failed engine,
   other engines stalled, plane lost 32,000 feet (19 Feb 85) (S 10 2, 12 1)
* Simultaneous 3-engine failure reported by Captain of DC-8/73 (S 14 2)
*f Avionics failed, design used digitized copier-distorted curves (S 10 5)
** 767 (UA 310 to Denver) four minutes without engines (August 1983) (S 8 5)
*f 767 failure LA to NY forced to alternate SF instead of back to LA (S 9 2)
*hi USAir 737-400 crash at NY's LaGuardia blamed on computer interface (S 15 1)
*$f 727 (UA 616) nose-gear indicator false positive forces landing (S 12 1)
*f British Airways 747-400 throttles closed, several times; fixed? (S 15 4)
*$H Masquerading spoof of air-traffic control comm altered courses (S 12 1)
*h Delta plane 60 miles off course, missed Continental by 30 feet (S 12 4)
*f ATC computer system blamed for various near-misses, delays, etc. (S 12 4)
* New San Jose CA ATC system still buggy, plane tags disappear (S 14 2)
*h Open cockpit mike, defective transponder caused 2 near-collisions (S 12 1)
*m Air-traffic control data cable loss caused close calls (S 10 5)
*m Osaka Int'l Airport's radar screens jammed by TV aerial booster (S 12 3)
*m Cellular telephone activates airliner fire alarm (SEN 14 6)
*fi Flawed ATC radars: planes disappear from screens; other problems (S 12 1)
*hi Air-traffic controller errors. O'hare near-miss: wrong plane code (S 12 3)
*m Computer outage in Concorde leads to rocky nonautomatic landing (S 12 4)
*e British ATC 2-hr outage, 6-hr delays: faulty HW/SW upgrade (S 12 1)
*he Southern Cal plane crash due to software change? (S 12 1)

*mf Alaskan barometric pressure downs altimeters; FAA grounds planes (S 14 2)

*fm FAA Air Traffic Control: many computer system outages (e.g., SEN 5 3, 11 5), near-misses not reported (S 10 3)

$m FAA ATC computers in Houston down for 3 hours; long delays (S 12 2)

*$m El Toro ATC computer HW fails 104 times in a day. No backup. (SEN 14 6)

*$m London ATC lost main, standby power, radar; capacitor blamed! (S 12 2)

*f London ATC goof – US ATC program ignores East longitude (S 13 4)

*f Software misdirects air-traffic controller data in Boston (S 13 4)

*h Commercial plane near-collisions up 37.6% in 1986; 49 critical (S 12 2)

*H Radar center controllers (So.Cal) concealed collision course info (S 12 2)

*hi Four 1986 British near misses described – all human errors (S 12 2)

*f/m? Leesburg VA Air Traffic primary, backup systems badly degraded (S 15 1)

*e? DFW ATC 12-hour outage after routine maintenance (S 15 1)

*$ Computer outages force delays in So. Cal, Atlanta (S 12 2)

* Macaque reaches 747 cockpit controls; monkey loose on Cosmos 1887 (S 12 4)

$ Travicom computerized air cargo system withdrawn; 5M pounds lost (S 12 2)

$fe American Airlines' SABRE system down 12 hours; new disk-drive SW launched "core-walker" downing 1080 old disk drives, stripped file names ... (S 14 5)

$H Computer hides discount airline seats from agents; lost sales (S 12 2)

$f Pricing program loses American Airlines $50M in ticket sales (S 13 4)

$m Power outage causes Australian airline reservation system "virus" (S 13 3)

f Delayed DoT airline complaint report blamed on computer (S 12 3)

RAIL, BUS, AND OTHER PUBLIC TRANSIT:

!$m Loose wire caused Britrail Clapham train crash, 35 killed (SEN 14 6)

!!$hi Canadian trains collide despite "safe" computer; 26 killed (S 11 2)

!h Southern Pacific Cajon crash kills 3; tonnage computations wrong (SEN 14 6)

*f London Docklands Light Railway crash; protection system incomplete (S 12 4)

*hf London Underground wrong-way train in rush-hour (S 15 4)

*h London tube train leaves ... without its driver (S 15 4)

*h 1928 British rail interlocking frame problem revisited (S 15 2)

*f SF BART train doors opened between stations during SF-Oakland leg (S 8 5)

f SF BART automatic control disastrous days of computer outages (S 6 1)

*$m BART power mysteriously fails and restores itself 5 hours later (S 12 3) battery charger short + faulty switch subsequently identified (S 12 4)

f SF Muni Metro: Ghost Train recurs, forcing manual operation (S 8 3)

f SF Muni Metro: Ghost Train reappears; BART problems same day (S 12 1)

* Japanese railway communications jammed by video game machines (S 12 3)

* Japanese train doors opened inadvertently several times; EMI? (S 12 3)

h LA Rapid Transit District computer loses bus in repair yard (S 12 2)

$f LA RTD phantom warehouse in database "stores" lost parts (S 12 2)

$*f Puget Sound ferry computer failures – 12 crashes; settlement vs builder $7 million; cost of extra $3 million for manual controls! (S 12 2) Electronic "sail-by-wire" replaced with pneumatic controls (S 14 2,15 2)

*m Water seepage stops Sydney automated monorail computer controls (S 13 4)

h Daylight savings time changeover halts train for an hour (S 15 4)

AUTOMOBILES:

!$f? Mercedes 500SE with graceful-stop no-skid brake computer left 368-foot skid marks; passenger killed (S 10 3)

!$f? Audi 5000 accelerates during shifting. 2 deaths. Microprocessor? (S 12 1)

*$f? Microprocessors in 1.4M Fords, 100K Audis, 350K Nissans, 400K Alliances/ Encores, 140K Cressidas under investigation (S 11 2)

*Sm Sudden auto acceleration due to interference from CB transmitter (S 11 1); *f 1986-87 Volvos recalled for cruise control glitch (S 13 3)

*H Home-reprogrammed engine micro makes 1984 Firebird into race car (S 12 1)

SH Hacking of car engine computers reaches Australia (S 13 4)

*f Anti-skid brakes and computer controlled race cars? (S 12 1)

*f Car with computerized steering loses control when out of gas (S 12 4)

*f Non-fail-safe power-outage modes – car locks (S 13 1)

*m Experimental semi-truck micro died (EMI) when near airport radar (S 12 1)

*$f El Dorado brake computer bug caused recall of that model (1979) (S 4 4)

*$f Ford Mark VII wiring fires: flaw in computerized air suspension (S 10 3)

*f Cadillac recalling 57,000 cars for headlights-out computer problem (S 12 3)

$f Oldsmobile design lost: hard disk wiped, backup tapes blank! (S 12 4)

f GM blames smelly Astros and Safaris on faulty computer fuel mix (S 13 4)

*mh Computer blamed for unbalancing of tires (SEN 14 6)

MOTOR-VEHICLE DATABASE PROBLEMS:

!!h Bus crash kills 21, injures 19; computer database showed driver's license had been revoked, but not checked? Also, unreported citation (S 11 3)

! Murderer got address from Cal DMV DBMS; new regulations on DB access: notify interrogatee, then delay response for two weeks (SEN 14 6)

*SH British auto citations removed from database for illicit fee (S 11 1)

$f California DMV computer bug hid $400 million fees for six months (S 11 2)

$f Toronto motor vehicle computer reported $36 million extra revenue (S 11 3)

f Alaskan DMV program bug jails driver (Computerworld 15 Apr 85) (S 10 3)

f? Parisian computer transforms traffic charges into big crimes (SEN 14 6)

$ Georgia vehicles stopped as stolen; new tags match old ones (S 15 4)

$h 1000 IL residents dunned for bogus parking violations (S 15 4)

*m?e? Mass. Motor Vehicle computer down after maintenance (SEN 14 6)

f NJ DMV computer changes drivers' names to "Watkins Leasing Co." (S 12 3)

*f 100-year-old's age computed as 0, license renewed without test (S 15 2)

$ NSWales computer deregisters ALL police cars; unmarked car scofflaw (S 15 2)

ELECTRICAL POWER (NUCLEAR AND OTHER):

!!$h Chernobyl nuclear plant fire/explosion/radiation (26 April 86) (S 11 3) Misplanned experiment on emergency-shutdown recovery procedures backfired. Fatal (at least 31), serious cases continue to mount. Wide-spread effects. (The town of Chernobyl is now being dismantled.)

*$f 14 failures in Davis-Besse nuclear plant emergency shutdown (S 11 3)

*$hmi Three Mile Island PA, now recognized as very close to meltdown (S 4 2), with 4 equipment failures plus misjudgement. SW flaw noted (S 11 3)

!!,$ Various previous nuclear accidents – American (3 deaths SL-1 Idaho Falls) Soviet (27-30 deaths on Icebreaker Lenin, three other accidents) (S 11 3)

* Subsequent to Chernobyl, US Nuclear Regulatory Commission relaxed fire isolation guidelines, enabling a fire to wipe out two systems (S 11 3)

*$ Crystal River FL reactor (Feb 1980) (Science 207 3/28/80 1445-48, SEN 10 3)
* Nuclear power-plant safety (S 12 4)
*$f? British nuclear reactor software safety disputed (SEN 14 6)
*$f? French nuclear power software safety considered error-prone (S 15 1)
*m Nuclear reactor knocked offline by 2-way radio in control room (S 14 5)
*f Software error at Bruce nuclear station releases radioactive water (S 15 2)
*f Grenoble neutron reactor 10% over limit; equations wrong and instrument
   miscalibrated, ordinary not heavy water assumed in both cases! (S 15 2)
*$f Great Northeast power blackout due to threshold set-too-low being exceeded
*$f Power blackout of 10 Western states, propagated error (2 Oct 1984)(S 9 5)
*f Ottawa power utility loses working three units to faulty monitor (S 11 5)
*$m Squirrel arcs power, downs computers in Providence RI (S 12 1)
$m SRI attacked by kamikaze squirrels who downs uninterruptible power (S 14 5)
m Kamikaze raccoon downs cold fusion experiments (S 14 5)
*m Reactor overheating, low-oil indicator; two-fault coincidence (S 8 5)
*f Bug discovered in Shock II model/program for designing nuclear reactors
   to withstand earthquakes shuts down five nuclear power plants (S 4 2)
hi Trainee raises false alarm on utility emergency printer (S 12 3)

MEDICAL, HEALTH, AND SAFETY RISKS:
!hif Therac 25 therapeutic accelerator programming and operational flaws;
   2 killed, 3 injured (S 11 3, 12 3); (subsequently one more died)
   See also Ivars Peterson, Science News, 12 March 1988,
   Jon Jacky, The Sciences, NY Acad. Sci Sep/Oct 89.
!fh Woman killed daughter, tried to kill son and self; "computer error" blamed
   for false report of their all having an incurable disease (S 10 3)
!hi Girl electrocuted by heart-monitor plugged into electrical outlet (S 12 1)
!f 2 dead, 1 in brain-dead coma from use of bank computer terminal??? (S 12 2)
! Higher miscarriage rate for women in computer-chip manufacturing (S 12 2)
!Sfm Arthritis-therapy microwaves set pacemaker to 214, killed patient (S 5 1)
!Sfm Retail-store anti-theft device reset pacemaker, man died (S 10 2, 11 1)
*if Pacemaker locked up when being adjusted by doctor (S 11 1)
*S Stereo speaker risk to heart device (S 14 5)
*m Failed heart-shocking devices due to faulty battery packs (S 10 3)
*m Medical electronics RF susceptibility: triggers hospital alarms
   respirators failed because of portable radio interference (SEN 14 6)
!Sm Miner killed by radio-frequency interference (S 14 5)
*f Blood test for man born in 1889 "normal" (for 1989 birth!) (S 15 2)
*f 100 US hospital computer systems die; 2**15 days after 1/1/1900 (SEN 14 6)
*f Three medical product recalls due to software errors (S 14 5)
*f Multipatient monitoring system recalled; mixed up patients (S 11 1)
*f Diagnostic lab instrument misprogrammed (S 11 1)
*fi AI medical system in Nevada gave wrong diagnosis, overdose (S 11 2)
*h Nondial emergency phone gives recording to DIAL another number! (S 15 2)
*f/h US occupational hazards much worse than in Europe? (SEN 14 6)
* Video display terminal health safety a continuing concern (S 11 3, 11 5)
   Series of three New Yorker articles by Paul Brodeur, 12-19-26 June 1989
*f Killer terminals –teletypes (old) and Televideo 910s (S 14 1)

* Repetitive strain injury, other risks in video terminal use (S 12 2)
*$ Long Island county legislation on VDT Use (S 13 3)
* VDTs and dermatology: rosacea, acne, seborrheic dermatitis,
  poikiloderma of Civatte. Medical article, useful references. (S 13 4)
* VDTs and deterioration of eye focusing (S 13 4)
* Health hazards attributed to laser printers (S 12 1)
!$ 2 Compaqs (Portable II) exploded after battery circuits rewired (S 12 1)
* Glass cleaner causes static sparks, PC fires (S 13 2)
*f Dangers of computerized robot used in surgery (S 10 5)
,*m? 42 Japanese injured in roller-coaster car crash (EMI?)
* Computer CPU falls on man's foot (S 12 4)
* Computer use and extension phones linked with weight gains (S 15 4)

OTHER ENVIRONMENTAL RISKS:
(!)*$$hif Exxon Valdez oil tanker on autopilot runs aground with captain
  absent; worst oil spill in US history; computer records deleted (S 14 5)
*f/h Computers blamed each time, 3M, 5.4M, 1.5M gallons of raw sewage
  dumped into Willamette River in three separate incidents (S 13 3, 13 4)

ROBOTS AND ARTIFICIAL INTELLIGENCE:
!m Japanese mechanic killed by malfunctioning Kawasaki robot (S 10 1, 10 3)
  (Electronic Engineering Times, 21 December 1981)
!m At least 4 more, possibly 19 more robot-related deaths in Japan (S 11 1)
!m 6 of these deaths due to stray electromagnetic interference? (S 12 3)
!m Michigan man killed by robotic die-casting machinery (S 10 2, 11 1)
! Chinese computer builder electrocuted by his computer (S 10 1) (WWN;AI?)
!f Computer electrocutes chess player who beat it! (from WWN!) (S 14 5)
* Two cases of robot near-disasters narrowly averted by operators (S 11 3)
(!) Budd Company robot commits suicide by dissolving its electronics (S 13 3)
f Servant robot runs amok, winds up in court (S 11 5)
f NBC network-news robot camera runs amok during broadcast (S 13 3)
$S Risks of on-line robotic SW repair: SoftRobots (S 12 4)

OTHER CONTROL-SYSTEM PROBLEMS:
!!$,h? 1983 Colorado River flood, faulty data/model? Too much water held back
  prior to spring thaws; 6 deaths, $ millions damage (NY Times 4 Jul 1983)
!m Computer-controlled computer-room door kills South African woman (S 14 2)
!fe 2 Ottawa elevator deaths; interlock logic bug; flaw unfixed (S 14 5)
*$fm Computer-related British chemical industry accidents: watchdog program
  fails; other SW errors; operator overloads; maintenance error (S 14 2)
*$f Union Carbide leak (135 injuries) exacerbated by program not handling
  aldicarb oxime plus operator error (NY Times 14 and 24 Aug 85) (S 10 5)
*$fe During SW maintenance Alta Norwegian flood gates open in error (S 12 4)
!? Automated toilet seat in Paris killed child? (S 12 2)
$f 3 computer crashes rupture Fresno water mains, 50 plumbing systems (S 14 1)
$f Stanford collider shut down due to innate complexity (S 13 4)
$f "Redundant" air conditioning system with a single thermostat (S 14 2)
$f Computer controls tear movable Olympic Stadium roof in Montreal (S 13 4)

$f Toronto SkyDome movable roof open and shut case: software problems (S 14 5)
*$m 8080 control system dropped bits and boulders from 80 ft conveyor (S 10 2)
*f Automatic doors lock up Amsterdam patrons in new building (S 14 1)
*m Shorts open Seattle drawbridge without warning in rush-hour (S 15 2)
*$f Computer-controlled turntable for huge set ground "Grind" to halt (S 10 2)
*$f Computer stops "Les Miserables" set; 4600 refunds, $60,000 lost (S 12 2)
*$m Secret Service phone interference plunges theater into darkness (S 12 2)
*m Computerized theater winch goes beserk (full-speed-up and crash) (S 12 2)
$f Theatre Royal booking computer downed – no tickets sold for days (S 12 2)
$f Restaurant orders on-line; computer crash overcooks steaks (S 12 2)
h Sydney Restaurant computer data wrong, menu items transformed (S 13 4)
$m CMU library computer power outage – no catalogues (S 12 2)
$fi Ship runs aground; reverse-logic steering problem? (S 15 1)
f Titanic photo expedition control program erratic (S 11 5)

OTHER COMPUTER-AIDED-DESIGN PROBLEMS:
*hf Hartford Civic Center Roof collapse: wrong model (S 11 5, ref. 14 5)
*f Salt Lake City shopping mall roof collapses on first snowfall (S 11 5)
$f America's Cup Stars&Stripes misdesign due to modeling programs (S 12 1)
*f John Hancock Building in Boston – problems in "active control" (S 12 1)

ACCIDENTAL FINANCIAL LOSSES AND ERRORS:
*$h Oct 1987 Dow-Jones index losses amplified by program trading (S 13 1);
    Side-effects of saturated computer facilities; brokerage sued (S 13 1);
    Losses over 100 points truncated to two digits by Signal service (S 13 1);
    Program trading halted by Wall Street firms for own stability (S 13 3)
$f Multiple stock transactions result from blocked confirmation (S 13 1)
$h Mistyped password put two brokers in the same computer files (S 13 1)
$f $32 Billion overdraft at Bank of New York (prog counter overflow) (S 11 1)
$f UK bank SW glitch hands out extra 2B pounds in half hour (S 15 1)
$hi $2 Billion goof due to test tape being rerun live (S 11 2)
$h BofA MasterNet development blows $23M; backup system gone(S 12 4)
    Two BofA executives leave after DP problems costing $25M (S 13 1);
    $60M more spent in botched attempt to fix it (S 13 2)
$f $100M overdraft plus daily interest in Sydney – "computer error" (S 13 1)
$hi .5M transaction became $500M due to "000" convention; $200M lost (S 10 3)
$$ High stakes: Wall St bank wires average over $1.2 trillion/day (S 12 2)
$h Slow responses in Bankwire interface SW resulted in double posting of tens
    of $millions, with interest losses (S 10 5)
$h Computer blunders blamed for $650M student loan losses (S 14 2)
$f California state computer wrote $4M checks accidentally (S 11 5)
$f Canadian Pacific stock price sanity check rejects legitimate data (S 12 4)
$h Australian man can keep $335,000 windfall from computer data error (S 12 4)
$h First Boston loses $10M to $50M on computer securities inventory (S 13 2)
$f New software system blocks commercial loans in California (S 14 5)
$f $2B (3M bank transactions) stalled when computer rejected posting (S 13 2)
$f Australian Comm. Bank doubled all transactions for a day (S 13 2)
$m European ATM repeated debit (S 14 2)

$ Norwegian bank ATM gives 10 times the requested cash; long lines (S 15 4)
$h European bank mounted wrong tape redid monthly transfers (S 14 2)
$he Wells Fargo deposits slip – another software glitch (S 14 5)
$f Wells Fargo 1987 IRS forms stated 100-times-salary for employees (S 15 1)
$f 120,000 long addresses mess up British building society computer (SEN 14 6)
$f Program bug permitted auto-teller overdrafts in Washington State (S 10 3)
$h New Zealand student grants debited instead of credited (S 14 5)
$h Brown University senior's account mistakenly given $25,000 (S 12 2)
$f $80,000 bank computing error reported – by Ann Landers (S 12 4)
$H Chemicals cause checks to disappear, bogus checks clear and vanish (S 13 3)
($) Connecticut lottery computer accidentally gave backdated tickets (S 13 3)
$f+h California Lotto computer crash and its costly effects (S 14 1)
$m Computer problems delay California Lotto payouts (twice) (S 15 4)
$h Programmer unauthorizedly limits sale of certain lottery tickets (S 15 4)
$f $40M Pentagon foreign military sales computer misses $1B (S 13 3)
$fe IRS reprogramming delays; interest paid on over 1,150,000 refunds (S 10 3)
$fe Minnesota PR firm cut over to untested system, bills months behind (S 13 4)
$h San Jose library lost two weeks of records. Books, fines lost. (S 11 3)
$f Racetrack betting seriously impaired by degraded computer system (S 12 2)
$f Saratoga Race Track parimutuel computer down on opening day (SEN 14 6)
$f British Customs computer 'loses' 35.6 million bottles of wine (SEN 14 6)
h Bulk US Mail from CA to Switzerla ND delivered abroad (fraud?) (SEN 14 6)
$h 40,000 copies of book printed from unedited file by mistake (S 15 2)

FINANCIAL FRAUDS AND INTENTIONALLY CAUSED LOSSES:
$SH Volkswagen lost $260M to computer based foreign-exchange fraud (S 12 2)
   5 people (4 insiders, 1 outsider) convicted, maximum sentence 6 years.
($)H Four financial frauds, each foiled (e.g., by luck)
   $70M Chicago First National, $54.1M Union Bank of Switzerland (S 13 3)
   250M kroner Norwegian clearing house Bankenes Betalingsentral BBS (S 13 3)
   $15.2M Pennsylvania lottery scam – post-fabricated ticket (S 13 3)
$SH $15.1M fraud accidentally foiled because of a computer error (S 13 2)
$SH $9.5M computer-based check fraud paid legitimate DCASR invoice (S 13 2)
$SH U.K. computerized bank fraud nets 1M pounds (S 14 2)
$SH Foiled counterfeiting of 7,700 ATM cards using codes in database (S 14 2);
   five admit automated teller scam (Mark Koenig) (S 14 5)
$SH Reservation computer fraud nets 50M AA frequent flier miles (S 14 1)
$SH Frequent flier computer scam nets 1.7 million bonus miles (S 14 2)
$SH $Millions of Bogus airline ticket sold in Phoenix (SEN 14 6)
$fH Reversing air return/depart dates fakes out reservation computers (SEN 14 6)
$SH Bogus computer message nets 44 kilos of gold from Brinks (S 14 2)
$H 'Credit doctors' sell clean credit records to high-risk clients (S 13 4)
SH Wall St audit trail off enables $28.8M computer fraud (S 12 4) (bogus???)
$H Hertz computer system kept two sets of books for accidents (S 13 2)
$SH Dublin tax collectors faked VAT repayments by spoofing computer (S 12 4)
$SH 45 phony computerized IRS filings net $325,000 in refunds (SEN 14 6)
$SH US Coast Guard accessed Customs' computer to transfer $8M (S 12 3)
$SH ATM money dispensers blocked and emptied later by youths (S 11 5)

$SH Barclays Bank hacked for 440,000 pounds? (S 11 5)
$SH ATMs gave $140,000 on VISA card over weekend – software glitch (S 11 2)
$SHf Security Pacific ATM theft bypasses PINs, limits, nets $350,000 (S 14 1)
$SHfe Australian Westpac ATMs big losses (IMS 2.2 installed untested) (S 12 3)
$SH $1800 card maker and spied PIN numbers nets $86K from ATMs (S 12 3)
$SH PC spoofed Italian bancomat ATM, ate cards after capturing PINs (S 14 1)
$SHf ATM accepted lollipop cardboard as $1M (New Zealand) deposit (S 11 5)
$SH ATM scam gets PINs for stolen cards in Boulder (S 13 4)
$SH Harrah's $1.7 Million payoff internal fraud – Trojan horse chip? (S 8 5)
   11 indicted (17 riggings in 3 yrs); 'winner' later found dead (stoolie?)
$SHf Firmware bugs in Dutch gambling machines easy to exploit (S 13 4)
$H Video quiz game scam – teams of "experts" with right answers (S 11 5)
$H West German crackers use knowledge of Poker game machine programs for big
   payoffs. 160,000 machines at risk. (S 12 3)
$H Savings and Loan defaults linked to internal fraud, creative mismangement.
   What could computers have done for S&Ls to prevent fraud/abuse? (S 14 2)
$SH FBI estimates average computer fraud $650K, total $3B-$5B/year (S 12 3)
   and $1.5M average for computer frauds in financial institutions (old data?)
$H Customs Service back-dates computer clock at end of fiscal year (S 14 5)
$H Alleged fraud in computer billing services (S 14 5)
SH Risks in check forgery (S 15 1)

STOCK-MARKET PHENOMENA:
$ Computer-induced big stock-market swings (S 11 2, 11 5)
$f Vancouver Stock Index lost 574 points over 22 months – roundoff (S 9 1)
$f Wild stock trade swing reports suppressed on 13 Oct 89 (S 15 1)
$f Quotron SW problem gives wild swings in Dow Jones Industrial Ave (S 15 1)
$f London Stock Market index quotes down for 2:20 on 23Jan90 (S 15 2)
$m NY Stock Exch. halted for 41 minutes; drum channel errors killed primary
   and backup computer systems (24 Feb 72)
$m London Stock Exchange computer system crashes (23 May 86)
$hfe London Stock Exchange horrors on cutover to new system (S 12 1)
$m Hurricane Gloria in NY closes Midwest Stock Exchange (S 11 1)
$m NASDAQ OTC stock trading halted for 3 hours (S 12 1)
$m Squirrel arcs power, halts NASDAQ computers (S 13 1)
$m Toronto Stock Exchange down 3 hours; multiple disk failures (SEN 14 6)
$m Five NY futures market shut down; uncertainty over cause (S 15 4)
$S GAO finds computer security at stock exchanges vulnerable (S 15 2)

TELEPHONE FRAUDS:
$SH Nevada teens 'blue-box' $650,000 in phone calls (S 13 4)
$SH Zotos switchboard cracked for $75K in calls (S 13 4)
$SH Phone credit-card numbers stolen from computer. $500M total? (S 12 3)
$SH US Sprint, computer penetrations, free calls, arrests (S 12 4)
$SH Crackers attack phone information systems and switches; arrests (S 13 4)
$SH AT&T computers penetrator by Herbert Zinn, Jr. ('Shadow Hawk');
   $1M program previewed (S 12 4); sentenced; more background (S 14 2)
$SH Pac*Bell System computer attacker Kevin Mitnick arrested (S 14 1); further

background (S 14 2); sentenced to year in prison (SEN 14 6)
SH Leonard DiCicco pleaded guilty to aiding Mitnick in DEC SW theft (S 15 1)
$SH Corte Madera CA teenagers arrested for $150,000 in phone calls (S 13 3)
$SH Milwaukee computerized phone phreaking (S 14 2)
SH Telephone answering machines accessible remotely by anyone (S 13 3)
$hH NY Telephone free long-distance calls due to software (S 14 5)

OTHER TELEPHONE PROBLEMS:
!hi Death of 5-year-old boy due to SF 911 computer equipment failure (S 12 2)
    Ultimately blamed on terminal operator failing to press a button.
*$ AT&T congestion (15Jan90); fault-recovery fault propagates (See Telephony,
    22Jan90, p.11.); attributed to "switch"..."if"..."break" (S 15 2)
    Relation of AT&T congestion with SDI testimony of Sol Buchsbaum (S 15 2)
$f/m/h? One customer's telephone problems include nonoriginated two-party
    calls, false billings, incorrect numbers even when correctly dialed,
    multiple phone conversations on the same line, nonoriginated emergency
    calls. This saga prompted discussion of numerous other horror tales, plus
    hacking possibilities. (S 15 4)
$f Pac Bell loses $51 million on lost phone-call charges (S 11 3)
$h AT&T goof disrupts toll-free calls; switchover botched (S 15 2)
$h Bell Canada misbills for 17,000 calls; exchanges exchanged (S 15 2)
$f 400 pay phones in Hackensack lost charges for half of the calls (S 11 3)
$fe GTE Sprint incomplete SW changes lost $10-$20M in Feb-Apr 1986 (S 11 3)
$fe GTE Sprint billing errors from botched daylight savings cutover (S 11 5)
$f 4,800 customers billed in error for telephone calls to Egypt (S 13 2)
$f 2M AT&T customers billed twice (S 13 2)
$f Hangups lost, calls billed at 999 minutes(ave. overcharge C$2,450) (S 13 4)
$m Sharks munch out on fiber-optic phone cables. $250,000/bite (S 12 3)
*f U.Iowa phone system program limitation – ringing forward to busy,
    phones incompatible: explosion or fire if misconnected (S 12 3)
*$fe Michigan Bell ESS office, 2 long outages. SW updates in progress. (S 11 3)
*$ 707 area code (above San Fran.) shut down completely for 5 hours (S 11 5)
$* Atlanta telephone system down for 2 hours (S 11 5)
*$ C&P computer crashes 44,000 DC phones (S 11 1)
*$ Dallas 4-ESS, backup down for most of day, area code 214 isolated (S 12 2)
$f Program glitch disrupts PacBell 619 calls (So.Cal) for most of day (S 12 4)
*f? Computer 'bug' downs 1000s of phones in Vancouver for an hour (S 13 4)
$fe Improper SW upgrade disrupts NY Tel Poughkeepsie-area for 21 hrs (S 12 4)
$fe SW upgrade glitch shuts down phones for 4 hours in Minneapolis (S 12 4)
$f C&P computer "tape flaws" delay 100,000 bills by two months (S 11 5)
$f 1979 AT&T program bug downed phone service to Greece for months (S 10 3)
* World Series ticket orders block phone exchanges, 911 for 3 hrs (S 13 1)
$m Ghost phone calls to 911 from cordless phone interference (S 11 2)
*m Los Angeles computer blamed for 911 system crashes (S 14 2)
*S Telephone sales pitch computer calls emergency broadcast number (S 12 2)
$hi Swedish phone bill of $2600 – program error plus human error (S 11 5)
$ Salem OR library computer racks up $1328 in phone calls (S 12 1)
$i Some risks of reaching someone else's phone number (S 12 4)

fh Computer blamed; Yorkshire cricket fans reach sex hot-line (S 15 1)

ELECTION PROBLEMS:

S(H?) Election frauds, lawsuits (S 11 3, 11 5), mid-stream patches in HW/SW
   (S 10 3, 10 4), David Burnham, NY Times, 7/29, 7/30, 8/4, 8/21, 12/18
   1985. (Most lawsuits later thrown out: not guilty or lack of evidence.)
   See "Accuracy, Integrity, and Security in Computerized Vote-Tallying,
   Roy G. Saltman, NBS special publication, 1988, for a definitive report.
SH Computers in Elections (see Ronnie Dugger, 7 Nov 88 New Yorker, and
   several cited reports); 1988 problems in Florida, Texas, tally error in
   Grand Rapids (S 14 1)
$f Votes lost in Toronto (S 14 1, 14 5); Toronto district finally abandons
   computerized voting; year-old race still unresolved (S 15 2)
S(H?) Alabama, Georgia election irregularities (S 12 1)
Sh Texas beefs up security of computerized voting (S 12 1)
h Clerical error blamed for election computer program mishap (S 11 5)
h Missouri legal decision questions automatic ballot counting (S 13 2)
f Quebec election prediction bug: wrong pick (1981) (S 10 2 pp 25-26, 11 2)
h 6000 moved Australian voters lost from computer election rolls (SEN 14 6)
hi Brazilian computer blocked twins, like-named siblings from voting (S 12 1)
m Computer miscounts SDI vote in Congress (358 ayes + 237 nays ¿ 435) (S 13 3)
*h Computer data-entry error in vote tallying (2828, not 28) (S 13 4)
h Risks of global editing – name change: 'Pollack' -¿ 'Turnoutack' (S 14 5)
f/h? 8 Durham NC precincts had correct totals counted twice (S 15 1)
f/h? VA governor's race also had totals counted twice (S 15 1)
h Date entry error gives wrong winner in Rome Italy city election (S 15 1)
h Leftover test data alters Yonkers NY election results (S 15 1)
f Manual districts required live fudging of Michigan election system (S 15 1)
f Another experience with voting machines in Fairfax County VA (S 15 1)

INSURANCE FRAUDS:

$SH Possible fraud on reinsurance – message time stamp faked??? (S 10 5)
$H N-step reinsurance cycle; software checked for N=1 and 2 only (S 10 5)

OTHER SECURITY/PRIVACY/INTEGRITY violations in computers and
communications: Penetrations, Trojan Horses, Viruses, Time-bombs,
Pranks, Spoofs, Scams, Blackmail, and Other Problems –
..... Security flaws:

*SHf Many known security flaws in computer operating systems and application
   programs. Discovery of new flaws running ahead of their elimination.
   Flaws include problems with passwords, superuser facilities, networking,
   reprogrammable workstations, inadequate or spoofable audit trails, ease
   of perpetrating viruses and Trojan horses, improper handling of line
   breaks, etc. Lots of internal fraud and external penetrations.
Sf Master password generation algorithm uses program bug in LOGIN (S 12 3)
Sf Security Hole in Sun 386i – argument that bypassed authentication (S 14 5)
Sf DEC/Ultrix 3.0 breakins using tftpd, weak passwords, and known flaws (S 15 1)
Sf SunOS 4.0.x rcp problem, exploiting /etc/hosts.equiv , /.rhosts (S 15 1)

Sf Password Snatching? RS-232 data tap advertised for $29.95 (S 12 3)
Sf Trojan horsing electronic countermeasures? Def.Electr. Oct 89 (S 15 1)
  $S GAO finds computer security at stock exchanges vulnerable (S 15 2)
S PRODIGY security and integrity problems discussed (S 15 2)
Sf Old CTSS Password file distributed as message of the day. Editor temp
  name confusion. See Morris and Thompson, CACM 22 11, Nov 1979. (S 15 2)
SH Dictionary-based password cracking (Morris-Thompson) happening (S 15 2)
..... Penetrations by nonauthorized personnel:
SH Australians use dictionary attack on various U.S. computer systems (S 15 2)
SH How to hinder Australian crackers and others (CERT memo) (S 15 4)
SH British Telecom's Prestel Information Service – demonstration for
  a reporter read Prince Philip's demo mailbox and altered a financial market
  database (London Daily Mail 2 Nov 84) (S 10 1)
  Break-in being prosecuted (1st such prosecution in Britain) (S 11 3)
  Conviction reversed by Appeal Court and House of Lords (S 13 3)
SHfe W.German crackers plant Trojan horses, attack NASA systems, exploit flaws
  in new OS release (S 12 4, 13 1); perpetrator arrested in Paris (S 13 2)
$SHf Lawrence Berkeley Lab computer break-ins by Markus Hess; Stoll planted
  phony computer file; file requested (S 13 3, Cliff Stoll, CACM May 1988);
  see Cliff Stoll, 'The Cuckoo's Egg: Tracking a Spy ...', Doubleday 1989.
  Hess and others accused of KGB computer espionage (S 14 2);
  Three of the Wily Hackers indicted on espionage charges (SEN 14 6), 'mild'
  convictions on espionage, not 'hacker' attacks (15Feb90) (S 15 2)
S Report from the Chaos Computer Club Congress '88 (S 14 2)
SHf Hacker enters Lawrence Livermore computers (S 14 1)
SH South German hackers hack TV German Post dial-in poll (SEN 14 6)
fH Fudging a poll on program(med) trading? (S 15 1)
SH USAF satellite positioning system, others cracked by 14-yr-old (SEN 14 6)
SH Belgian Prime Minister's email tapped by penetrator (S 14 1)
SH University of Surrey hacker arrested ... and released;
  Edward Austin Singh penetrated 200 systems (S 14 1)
  $SH AT&T computer break-ins (Herbert Zinn) (S 12 4)
  $SH Pac*Bell System computer attacker Kevin Mitnick arrested (S 14 1)
SH Computer crackers arrested in Pittsburgh, West Coast (S 12 4)
$SH Computer intrusion network in Detroit (Lynn Doucett) (S 14 5)
$SH Fired computer engineer caught downloading proprietary software (S 13 2)
$H Australian hackers face jail or fines (S 13 2)
$SH Australian intruder fined $750 for copying programs (trespass) (S 14 4)
SH TV editor raids rival's computer files (S 14 2)
SH Fox TV computers hacked, access to news stories in progress (S 15 4)
$SH TRW Credit information bureau breakins – one involved gaining information
  on Richard Sandza (Newsweek reporter who wrote "anti-hacker" articles)
  and running up $1100 in charges. (S 10 1)
$SH 14-yr-old cracks TRW Credit, orders $11,000 in merchandise (S 15 1)
$SH FtWorth programmer Donald Gene Burleson plants time-bomb, deletes
  168,000 brokerage records; convicted, fined (S 13 3, 13 4)
SH Milwaukee 414s broke into many computers (some with guessable passwords)
$SH Reps Zschau, McCain computers penetrated, mailings affected (S 11 2)

SH Grade-changing prank at Stanford (around 1960) (S 8 5)

$SH Southwestern Bell computer penetrated: free long-distance calls (S 11 3)

$SH Bloodstock Research thoroughbred horse-genealogy computer system break-in

$SH Computers stolen from SDI Office (S 13 3)

SHf Systematic breakins of Stanford UNIXes via network software (S 11 5)
  Brian Reid, "Lessons from the UNIX Breakins at Stanford", pp 29-35, Oct 1986

$SH Foiled counterfeiting of 7,700 ATM cards using codes in database (S 14 2)

*H Prison escapes via computer manipulation (S 10 1, 12 4)

*$H Masquerading spoof of air-traffic control comm altered courses (S 12 1)

..... Trap-door exploitations, Trojan Horses, logic bombs, worms, viruses

$$SHhf Internet worm attack on BSD-derived Unix systems (editor's discussion
  on software engineering implications (sendmail, finger, .rhosts); references
  to detailed reports by Spafford, Seeley, Eichin/Rochlis) (S 14 1);
  Robert Tappan Morris indicted on felony count (S 14 6)
  Jury declares Morris guilty, Jan 1990; motions, sentencing pending (S 15 2)

SH Unauthorized Internet activity; TELNET Trojan horsed (SEN 14 6)

SH Two Penn State Hackers arrested, service theft, etc. (S 15 2)

SH C compiler Trojan horse for UNIX trapdoor (Ken Thompson, "Reflections on
  Trusting Trust", 1983 Turing Award Lecture, CACM 27 8, August 1984)

$SH PC Graphics program Trojan horse (ArfArf) wiped out users' files (S 10 5)

SH PC-Prankster Trojan horse on PCs (S 12 4)

SH Another Trojan horse trashes DOS – NOTROJ (S 11 5)

SH Trojan turkey program deletes files (S 13 3)

*SH Software time-bomb inserted by unhappy programmer (for extortion?) (10 3)

*SH Los Angeles Water&Power computer system software time-bomb (S 10 3)

SH UK Logic Bomb displays Margaret Thatcher picture when triggered (S 13 3)

SH Trojan horse Christmas-greeting message contains saturating virus (S 13 1)

SH Apple II virus, Amiga virus, a chain letter; Canadian logic bombs; computer
  terrorism; voice mail misuse (S 13 1)

SH Pandair Freight (UK) logic bomb case (S 13 1); backfires (S 13 2)

SH Lehigh time-bomb virus propagates four times, wipes disk (S 13 2)

SH Israeli 13th-of-month PC time-bomb, would delete files 13 May 88 (S 13 2)
  'Jerusalem Virus' Bet declared a draw (S 13 3)
  Time-bomb warning on SunOS for 13 May 1988 (S 13 3)

SH Jerusalum-B virus infects GPO library disk (S 15 2)

SH Jerusalum-B virus infects Chinese computers widely (13Apr90) (S 15 4)

SH Anticipation of time-bomb causes accidental clock bomb (S 13 3)

SH Various Macintosh Viruses/time-bombs – trap handler, INIT32 nVIR –
  Brandow/MacMag 2 March peace message, infected Aldus commercial
  software DREW, FreeHand. (S 13 2)

SH More on viruses dangers of virus construction sets, propriety of assigning
  virus development in courses, plus more on the Atari ST virus, the (c)
  Brain virus and the Providence Journal attack, the Scores virus and the
  "ERIK" and "VULT" attacks, Elk Cloner, Disease DOS, and the growing anti-
  virus business – including contaminated versions of FLUSHOT that
  contained Trojan horses. (S 13 3 refers to on-line RISKS, VIRUS-L.)

SH (c) "Brain" Virus at eastern universities (S 13 2)

SH The Trojan horse named 'AIDS', from 'PC Cyborg Corp' (S 15 1)

SH The "Twelve Tricks" Trojan horse (S 15 2)
SH DECnet 'WANK' Worm on SPAN affected DEC VMS systems (S 15 1)
SH PC pest programs in China and Japan (S 15 1)
S Soviets claim unprecedented computer-virus shield (S 14 1)
SH Self-invoking RUNCOM self-propagates as virus on MIT's CTSS (S 13 3)
$H Use of a virus excuse for nondelivery of software (S 13 2)
$SHf Portable terminals for Hong Kong horse betting spoofable? (S 14 2)
$SH "Big Red" Trojan horse reported (as virus) in Australia (S 12 3). (Bogus.)
   Hackwatch 'expert' Paul Dummet (alias Stuart Gill) claims exposed (S 15 1)
SH Japanese PC-VAN network 'Virus' posts passwords of NEX PC9800s (S 13 4)
SH CerGro voice mail hacked, mailboxes used for illicit purposes (S 13 4)
SH Virus aimed at EDS infects almost 100 NASA computers instead (S 13 4)
S 'Computer Virus Eradication Act of 1988' (S 13 4)
*S Virus hits hospital computers in Michigan, creates bogus patients (S 14 5)
$S "Virus" arrest in New Jersey (Chris Young) (S 14 5)
S Prank 'Virus' Warning Message in government service system (S 14 5)
SH Trojan horses implantable by active electronic jamming? (S 15 1)
..... Spoofs and Scams:
SH April Fool's 1984: Chernenko at MOSKVAX: network mail hoax (S 9 4)
SH April Fool's 1988: self-ref forged April Fool warning message (S 13 2,3)
- - April Fool's 1990: Transmission of IP Datagrams on Avian Carriers (S 15 4)
SH 1984 Rose Bowl hoax, scoreboard takeover ("Cal Tech vs. MIT") (S 9 2)
SH Washington DC street message board displays bogus message (S 15 1)
$SH "Goodbye, folks" software prank costs perpetrator 1000 pounds (S 11 3)
SH Risks of digital video editing – authenticity question (S 14 2)
..... Internal perpetrations:
$SH NY police chief indicted for misuse of confidential database (S 13 4)
SH 3 police officers sentenced for misusing Police Nat'l Computer (S 14 2)
$SH Harrah's $1.7 Million payoff scam – Trojan horse chip? (S 8 5)
$SH Nevada slot-machine ripe for $10 to 15 million phony payoffs? (S 11 2)
$H Amusement game machines have covert gambling mode (S 13 4)
*SH San Fran. Public Defender's database readable by police; as many as 100
   cases could have been compromised (Feb 1985) (S 10 2)
SH Election frauds by vendor or staff charged? ... (see above)
*SH British auto citations removed from database for illicit fee (S 11 1)
..... Other intentional denials of service
*$SH Sabotage causes massive Australian communications blackout (S 13 1)
SH Former estimator destroys billing/accounting data on Xenix (S 15 1)
SH DC analyst in dispute with boss changed password on city computer (S 11 2)
SH Insurance computer taken hostage by financial officer (S 12 3)
$SH Sabotage of Encyclopedia Brittania database (S 11 5)
$SH Prescott Valley AZ computerized financial records wiped out (S 12 2)
..... Incomplete deletions (security residues)
*S White-house backup computer files bypass shredders on Irangate (S 12 2)
*Sh Air Force sells off unerased tapes with sensitive data (S 11 5)
..... Satellite takeovers:
SH "Captain Midnight" preempted Home Box Office program (S 11 3, 11 5)
SH Another satellite TV program interrupted (S 12 1)

$SH Playboy Channel disrupted with bogus program (S 12 4)
SH WGN-TV and WTTW in Chicago overtaken by pirate broadcast (S 13 1)
SH Video pirates disrupt L.A. cable broadcast of 1989 Super Bowl (S 14 2)
..... Privacy violations or questions other than those above
SH Civil liberties issues in National Crime Information Center (S 14 2)
S Calif. to permit prisoner access to confidential drivers' records? (S 14 2)
SH Brian Gumbel's on-line critique stolen, given to Newsday (S 14 2)
SH Are your medical records adequately protected? Probably not. (S 14 2)
Sf Undelivered 'private' E-mail message returned, but NOT to sender (S 14 1)
$ Risks in the British Data Protection Act (S 12 1)
S Concern over privacy of Swedish Databank (S 11 5)
S Discussion on computer privacy and search-and-match in Canada (S 15 1)
S Use of databases for investigative checks on would-be suitors (S 15 1)
$SH Personal attack on USENET raises issues of privacy, ethics (S 12 3)
SH NY Met's parade – brokerage printout substituted for ticker-tape (S 12 1)
S San Diego School payroll printouts sold as Xmas gift-wrap (S 12 2)
S Public pleasure-boat database could help thieves (S 14 5)
S Baby-monitor system bugs house, broadcasts to neighborhood (S 13 1)
  * CA notifies interrogee before responding to data requests (SEN 14 6)
..... Other electronic monitoring
Sf Electronic card designed to spot football hooligans (S 14 5)
..... Other cases
SH British businesses suffer 30 computer disasters/year (S 12 1)
SH UK computer security audit estimates 40M pounds fraud in 1987 (S 12 1)
SH Thief nabs tax preparer's computer, generously returns floppies (S 13 3)
S Accidental breach of Rockwell security bares shuttle software (S 13 3)
$SH Debit card copying easy despite encryption (DC Metro, SF BART, etc.)
$SH ATM cards altered by in-car home computer net $50,000 (S 12 1)
$SH Microwave phone calls interceptable; cordless, cellular phones spoofable
$SH Callback security schemes rather easy to break (S 11 5)
$SH 18 arrested for altering cellular mobile phones for free calls (S 12 2)
SH Risks of lap-top computers being permitted in exams (S 13 3)
$SH Embezzlements, e.g., Muhammed Ali swindle ($23.2 Million), Security Pacific
  ($10.2 Million), City National Beverly Hills CA ($1.1 Million, 23 Mar 1979)
  Marginally computer-related, but suggestive of things to come?
..... Limitations of encryptions
S 100-digit numbers now factorable; crypto implications (S 14 1)

UNINTENTIONAL DENIALS OF SERVICE:
(!)$ Amsterdam air-freight computer crashes, giraffes die (S 12 1)
*f ARPANET ground to a complete halt; accidentally-propagated status-message
  virus (27 Oct 1980) (S 6 1: Reference – Eric Rosen, "Vulnerabilities of
  network control protocols", SEN, January 1981, pp. 6-8)
*f ARPANET loses New England despite 7-trunk "redundancy" (S 12 1)
m Hundreds of duplicate computer-mail copies due to errant gateway (S 12 1)
$f 3 EMAIL problems give extra copies: Internet, UUCP, MCI (SEN 14 6)
f Stanford sendmail buffer overflows saturated systems (S 15 1)
f Posting to vmsnet.announce.newusers unmoderated newsgroup returned half-

hourly nasty messages; 'announce' implies moderation! (S 15 1)
!m Remote clock comm, 22 traffic lights down. 1 killed, 1 injured (S 14 2)
*f Lakewood CO traffic system fails; single disk drive, no redundancy (S 15 2)
*m Austin TX auto traffic-light computer crashes; 2 lights out (S 11 5,12 1)
*ef Another traffic light outage in Austin TX (S 15 4)
$f Overloaded Ontario transit computer delays commuters (S 14 2)
*h Unplugged cable plugs Orlando traffic light computer system (S 14 1)
*$h Hinsdale IL fire seriously affected computers and communications (S 13 3)
$ Rhine flooding disrupts computer networks for two days (S 13 3)
$h Noisy air conditioning shut off by mayor; downs computers (S 13 4)
m Gobblings of legitimate automatic teller cards (S 9 2, 10 2, 10 3, 10 5)
m Mass swallowing of falsely expired ATM cards (S 12 2)
h Australian ATMs snatch 921 cards. "Human error" (S 12 4)
$f+m Bank of America outage shuts down Cal ATMs and nationwide links (S 14 1)
$m Wells Fargo, BofA ATMs out of service (S 14 2)
m Royal Wedding side-effect shuts down computer machine room? (S 11 5)
$m Computer crashes stop gasoline pumps, other businesses (S 11 5)
$ Other problems with fast-food computers as well (S 12 1)
$f UNICEF loses thousands of orders for greeting cards (S 14 1)
* Hospital gets computerized Reagan vote calls, 20/hr for 6 hours (S 12 1)
$ Broker's phone tied up 3 days: errant computerized sales pitch (S 12 1)
f Phone call deluge from program bug in computerized Coke machines (S 10 2)
fh Stray signal loops beeperless remote answering machine (SEN 14 6)
$m Computer network node hit by lightning; down for weeks (S 11 5)
$m Lightning strikes drawbridge controls (twice!!), out for days (S 13 4)
m Basketball scoreboard clock fails as reporters PCs overload power (S 13 3)
$f Australian betting network downed after software inconsistencies (S 13 3)
(h) Fire destroys on-line (sole) copies of secret ice cream flavors (S 13 3)
$h IRS has no contingency plans for computer disasters (GAO report) (S 11 2)
$m NY Public Library loses computerized references; no backup (S 12 4)
$hf Software can burn out PC monochrome monitor (0 horizontal sweep) (S 13 3)
f VMS tape backup SW trashed disk directories dumped in image mode (S 8 5)
f VAX UNIX file system disk purge runs amok at various locations (RISKS-5.4)
$m Electronic flash of BBC documentary crew hangs tape drives (S 12 4)
m EPROMS susceptible to ultraviolet, bright lights (S 14 1)
Sf Spreadsheet program destroys database (S 13 1)
- —¿ Other accidental denials of service/comm interference:
$S Computer interference from McDonalds toasters; paychecks higher (S 15 1)
S Garage door interference again – Mt Diablo and the Navy (S 14 5)
$Sf Sputnik frequencies triggered garage-door openers
$Sf Pres.Reagan's command plane jams 1000s of garage-door openers (S 11 2)
Sf Fort Detrich communications jam garage-door openers? (S 13 1)
$Sm Sunspots disrupt communications, Quebec power station, ... (S 14 5)
Sm Johnny Carson loses his hat to electronic interference (SEN 14 6)
  !! Sheffield (20 deaths), pacemakers (2 deaths),
  *Sfm Air Force bombs Georgia – stray EMI
   *$ Challenger communications, CB auto interference, Ghost phone calls,
   * Fail-unsafe effects of microprocessor controlled autos,

* Nuclear reactor knocked offline by 2-way radio in control room
$ telephone outages, stock exchange outages, Tomahawk 2, Black Hawk
$ "Grind" set ; and other cases noted here ...

OTHER AGGRAVATION to Individuals or to the Populace at Large:
!f Hillsborough soccer computerized turnstiles -¿ space available (S 14 5)
!(H?) 8 deaths, 1 disappearance, 1 injury relating to Marconi systems (S 12 3)
  (now 9) (S 12 4)
!h False computer data shuts off home power; alternative kills girl (S 12 1)
*h Wrong bar codes result in water shut-offs in Utah (SEN 14 6)
$f Software error really messes up 'round the world yacht race (S 14 5)
$h Whistleblowing aerospace SW Quality Assurer fired, life threatened(S 11 3)
*h Weather Service false warnings, disaster reports in live test (S 12 2)
*$h Poor input data blamed for nonprediction of European storm (S 13 1)
*m Carrier control unit blamed for nuclear false alarm (S 11 5)
* Spelling corrector fingers Mafia "enforcer" as "informer" (S 12 4)
SH FAX Attacks – risks of junk mail saturation (S 14 1)
$h Customer declared dead by bank computer; effects propagated (S 11 3)
$h Vancouver woman, dead to revenuer database, can't collect refund (S 13 4)
$f Auto insurance rate triples – man turns 101 (= 1 mod 100) (S 12 1)
$h Auto insurance program misses 18,000 bad-driver surcharges (S 15 1)
$f Comm delays: $1100 debit for aborted withdrawal, side-effects (S 12 1)
$h David Brinkley gets erroneous $2137 penalty from IRS, retaliates (S 12 4)
$h IRS computer issues illegal $47,000 bill (S 13 1)
$h Tampa electric issues bill for $5M instead of $146.76 (S 13 4)
$h Wrap-around problems in meter reading cause erroneous bills (S 13 4)
$f NCStateUniv computer mismatches names, addresses on 6000 bills (S 13 4)
$h/f? British poll tax tales: bill for 4M pounds instead of 70;
  bill delivered to "Occupier" at a bus stop in Kent. (S 15 4)
$SH Blue Cross/Blue Shield victim of computer generated prank letter (S 13 1)
$f Demo NatComm thank-you mailing mistitled supporters (NY Times, 16 Dec 84)
f British NHS computer sent out letters to males with female names (S 12 4)
m Earthquakes: 3 of 5 reported never happened; microwave static (S 11 5)
h Query of vacationing programmer starts beer panic (S 11 5)
$fi Chicago cat owners billed $5 for unlicensed dachshunds. Database match
  on DHC (dachsunds, domestic house cats) with shots but no license (S 12 3)
fh Mass. jury selection computer issues multiple summonses (S 15 2)
$h Computer program misdirects 30,753 Minneapolis school children (S 12 4)
$h 887 Boston school assignments botched; lost tape, no backup (SEN 14 6)
h Indian program to reroute bus lines trounced (S 11 5)
$m Microwave oven erases comic's 3 years of personal computer data (S 12 2)
h Univ. Central Florida did not cut off student registration (S 12 3)
f British school examination program gave erroneous grades (S 11 5)
f Faulty computer program blocks promotion of fifth grader (S 12 2)
h Computer gives law student wrong exam, passes him, after disk fix (S 12 2)
mi "My DOS ate my homework" (Blame it on the computer!) (S 13 3)
h? Saudi Arabian uses computer to organize harem; it runs him ragged (S 13 2)
f Computer error blamed for French diplomatic fiasco (S 13 2)

- - Computer service selects ex-wife as "ideal" mate for divorced man (S 12 1)
$f Virginia State child support payments halted: software problems (S 12 3)
H Stolen disk and digital audio equipment affects Stevie Wonder concert (S 13 4)
H Bogus messages inserted in bank statements, TELEXes, prescriptions (S 13 2)
f Walter Jon Williams' SF novel glitched by letter substitutions (S 15 1)
($)m Effects of single-segment errors in digital displays (S 14 1)
$h Hot-metal print supervisor uses mallet on computerized typesetter (S 15 2)
$h Closed-fist-like pattern observed in damaged keyboard (S 15 2)
- - Sabbath restrictions bypassed by using extensive autotimers (S 15 4)
  - Various cases of gobbled bank cards
  * Various false arrest cases noted below.

LAW ENFORCEMENT AND MISTAKEN IDENTITIES:
$hi Repeatedly detained (S 10 3, S 11 1), Terry Rogan wins rights violation
  case (S 12 4); settles for $55,000 (S 13 2)
$hi Other cases of false arrest due to computer database use: C.R. Griffin
  licence not suspended; Sheila Jackson Stossier mistaken for Shirley
  Jackson; two Shirley Jones, diff birthdays, 6", 70 lbs diff (S 10 3)
hi More computer-inspired false arrests, libel, etc. (S 12 3)
$hi Identical database record names cause nasty tax problem in Canada (S 12 4)
hi Mistaken-identity nightmares: Foster, O'Connor, Taylor, Stapelton (S 13 2)
hi Richard Sklar falsely apprehended three times because of impostor (S 14 2)
$hi Roberto Hernandez falsely jailed twice; won $7000 first time! (SEN 14 5)
$hi Joseph O. Robertson in for 17 months despite contrary evidence (SEN 14 5)
*hi Martin Lee Dement 2 yrs LA County jail; fingerprint sys not used (SEN 14 5)
*SH Santa Clara prison data system (inmate altered release date) (S 10 1)
*SH Drug kingpin escapes LA County prison via bogus release message (S 12 4)
*f Seven Santa Fe inmates escaped; prison control computer blamed (S 12 4)
*hi Oregon prisoner escaped; frequent-false-alarm alarm ignored (S 12 4)
*f New Dutch computer system frees criminals, arrests innocent; old system
  eliminated, and no backup possible! (S 12 4)
f New El Dorado jail cell doors won't lock – computer controlled (S 13 4)
* Undercover police use CHAOSNet BBoards in 'snuff' film bust (SEN 14 6)
f Fault in electronic leg tag indicates false-alarm escape (SEN 14 6)
$ NSWales computer deregisters all police cars; unmarked car scofflaw (S 15 2)

OTHER LEGAL IMPLICATIONS:
!$ Deaths of 3 lobstermen in storm not predicted by National Weather Service –
  3 mos unrepaired weather buoy; $1.25M award (S 10 5) (NY Times 13 Aug 85)
  Overturned by federal appeals court. (AP, 15 May 86) (S 11 3)
$h US court rules computer malpractice in Diversified Graphics case (S 15 1)
$h Lawsuit vs Lotus' Symphony lost (omitted proposal section) (S 11 5, 12 1)
*$ Can a computer system be held liable? (S 15 1)
** Launch on warning legality subject of law suit (S 10 2, 11 5) (suit lost)
H FBI's Cal House sting: ten-fold rise in computer backup deletions (S 13 4)
$ Sex-therapy software risks (S 11 2)
$ Computerized sex ring broken; records seized (S 11 5, SEN 12 1)
S Further risks of computers in prostitution (S 14 1)

$ Heroin smugglers caught; stored computer data used as evidence (S 12 1)
* 7 terrorists arrested via phone numbers in wrist-calculator (S 12 3)
$h Residual evidence still stored in Psion EPROM nabs drug smuggler (S 13 2)
* Detailed telephone bill provides alibi for accused murderer (S 12 1)
$m Israeli supreme court appeal blamed on computer malfunction (S 11 5)
*$ Expert systems for criminal investigations (S 11 5)
$H Blackjack gambler with microprocessor faces trial (S 13 2)
$H Financial-computer penetrator acquitted: "Welcome to the..system" (S 12 1)
$h Man arrested after shooting his computer (S 12 4)
$H America's Cup floppies held to ransom for telemetry data (S 12 1)
$H Computer network used to advertise $250,000 in stolen ICs (S 12 3)
$h Canadian civil servants charged $1,270 for private computer use (S 12 3)
$h NM court's docketing files erased in botched backup; $1300 cost (S 15 4)

MISCELLANEOUS COMPUTER HARDWARE/SOFTWARE PROBLEMS:
$fm Bugs reported in Intel 486 chip and AMD 29000 RISC chip (S 15 1)
f 2-user login max due to HW floating-point flaw used by PW encrypt.(S 15 1)
hi Harmful puns on input: "EDIT" (Everything Deleted Insert T), "⟨cr⟩aboRT"
m Single-bit errors in DQ-11 partition network (S 14 1)
f Clock setting algorithm gets wrong time; other clock problems (S 11 2)
f Hidden horrible bug in Grapevine mail system lurks for 5 years (S 12 1)
f More clock problems – Leap Day, end of century, etc. (S 13 2)
f Every MTS shuts down: 2**15 days from 1 Mar 1900 to 16 Nov 1989 (S 15 1)
 *f 100 hospital computer systems die; 2**15 days after 1 Jan 1900 (S 14 6)
f Windows open and close for runaway mouse in Word 4.0 (S 13 4)
fm Toshiba DOS 3.3 Backup deletes files (S 14 5)
$f Tape unit caught on fire from repeated reading of tape section (S 5 1)
m(i) Stretching cat loads CDROM in Macintosh; interface misleading (S 15 2)
h Incidents on people's willingness to trust computers (S 11 5)
f Program works fine in debug, fails in live execution (S 12 4)
f Harvard Mark I register least-significant digits interchanged on input AND
   output, no effect unless carry propagated; not caught for MANY years.
f Pseudo-randomly generated bridge hands identical except for suits (S 14 1)
f Systran French-English automatic translation oddities (S 15 1)
S/f/m See also anecdotes from ACM Symposium on Operating Systems
   Principles, SOSP 7 (S 5 1) and follow-on (S 7 1).

OTHER COMPUTER SYSTEM DEVELOPMENT FIASCOS:
$ Congress' report Bugs in the System attacks waterfalls, procurement (S 15 1)
$ GAO report on effects of IS technology (S 15 1)
$ Congress repeals catastrophic insurance, SSA gets premiums anyway; too
   difficult to make the software modifications (S 15 1)
$h/f Summary of several 'runaway' computer software projects –
   Allstate, Richmond utilities, Business Men's Assurance, Oklahoma WorkComp,
   Blue Cross/Shield of Wisconsin (S 14 1)
$f Software failures in Britain estimated at $900M per year (S 13 4)
$fh $4.5M Virginia child support system scrapped; bad management (S 14 2)
$fh $5.4M Canadian computerized taxi system won't work (S 14 2)

$fm $800,000 computerized cab service system fouls up (S 15 2)
$fh $15M strip-mining violation computer system deficient (S 14 2)

DEVELOPING BETTER SYSTEMS:
- - Numerous articles on software development, specification, formal
  verification, safety, reliability, security, etc. (S 1 1 to the present)
* More on Proper British Programs – the MoD standard (S 14 1)
- - NewSpeak, a safer programming language (S 13 2)
- - Spark, an attempt at a "safe" Ada subset (S 14 1)
- - Viper and formal methods used in Australian railroad switching (S 14 5)
- - Benefits of computer technology, particularly safety, discussed (SEN 14 6)
- - DoD Software Master Plan (preliminary draft released 9Feb90. Contact
  George P. Millburn, Deputy Director, DDRE, the Pentagon.) (S 15 2)
- - Proposed UK authority for risk management (S 15 4)

E   A Survey of Formal Methods and Techniques

The purpose of this survey was to solicit information on formal methods tools and techniques that have been developed or are under development, and to solicit information on the projects (either research or industrial) towards which the tools and techniques have been applied.

The survey was distributed at *FM89* in Halifax (July 24–27, 1989). Since then, a number of people who did not attend the workshop have responded to the survey.

The results of the survey are presented below, in alphabetical order by project name.

Affirm

Primary participants (project leader, group members):
Dave Musser, Susan Gerhart, Dave Thompson, Rod Erickson, Stanley Lee.

Survey contact:
Susan Gerhart, MCC
Software Technology Program, 3500 West Balcones Center Dr., Austin, TX 78759
email: gerhart@mcc.com

Country (or countries) of origin: USA

Level of effort (person-years, duration):
Approximately, 32 to 35 person-years over 13 years.

Brief description:
Axiomatic data type specifications with rewrite rules, logic, some simplification in its theorem prover. Interactive, natural deduction proof style.

Accomplishments:
Fully usable and well documented including evaluation of experience. Applied to range of problems, e.g., ADTs [Gut 78] and state transition systems.

Representative published articles or reports:
S. L. Gerhart, et al. "An overview of *Affirm*: a specification and verification system." *Proc. IFIP 80*, Australia, October 1980, pp. 343-348.
Recommended as the best introduction to Affirm. Describes the basic system philosophy and architecture and relates early experience.

C. Sunshine, R. W. Erickson, S. Gerhart, D. Schwabe and D. H. Thompson. "Specification and Verification of Communication Protocols in Affirm Using State Transition Models." *IEEE Transactions on Software Engineering* SE-8(5):460-489, September 1982. (Also ISI Technical Report ISI/RR-81-88).
Describes the state transition method as rendered in Affirm. The classical *Alternating Bit Protocol* is specified and verified from the service to the program level.

D. R. Musser. "Abstract data type specification in the Affirm system." *IEEE Transactions on Software Engineering* SE-6(1):24-32, January 1980.
Included in the *Affirm* Collected Papers. Recommended as an introduction to *Affirm*.

Current status of development:
Quiescent

Date of project commencement:
c. 1976

Date of completion (as a research project):
1981 at ISI (further at GE)

Date of completion (as a product or deliverable):
1980

Intended evolution:
Affirm ISI - none
Affirm - 85 -
(ProAffirm components in use for other purposes.)

Particular strengths and weaknesses:
Strengths: Pleasing interface (for its time); exploratory style; documentation of system and method [Tho 81].

Weaknesses: Decision theories weak; portability, performance (InterLisp technology).

Any additional users of technology (outside of development group):
Mitre (toy O.S kernel); Verification Assessment Study [Kem 86]

Additional remarks:
See also [Mil 80, Ger 79].

ANNA

Primary participants (project leader, group members):
David C. Luckham, Sriram Sankar, David S. Rosenblum, Randall Neff, Geoffrey O. Mendal, Walter R. Mann, Neel Madhav, John Kenney.

Survey contact:
David C. Luckham
Computer Systems Lab, Stanford University, Stanford, CA 94305
Tel: (415) 723-1175
Fax: (415) 725-7398
email: dcl@anna.stanford.edu
or
Geoff Mendal
Computer Systems Lab, Stanford University, Stanford, CA 94305
Tel: (415) 723-1414
Fax: (415) 725-7398
email: mendal@sierra.stanford.edu

Country (or countries) of origin: USA

Level of effort (person-years, duration):
3 person-years each year 1983 to 1990

Brief description:
Anna is a language extension of Ada to include facilities for formally specifying the intended behavior of Ada programs. It is designed to meet a perceived need to augment Ada with precise machine-processable annotations so that well established formal methods of specification and documentation can be applied to

Ada programs.

The Anna language includes simple assertions, subtype annotations, subprogram pre- and post-condition annotations, package axioms, generic formal parameter annotations, exception propagation annotations, package state annotations, and virtual code.

Accomplishments:

Anna-I, an experimental toolkit supporting a wide subset of the Anna and Ada languages, has been developed and is being used and evaluated by many research organizations around the world. The toolkit currently contains: Front-End Parser Generator (PGEN), Intermediate Representation (IR) Toolkit (Extended DI-ANA Formal Interface and Implementation packages (AST), Ada/ Anna Parser, Ada/ Anna Pretty Printer, AST Disk ↔ Memory package), Ada/ Anna Static-Semantic Rules Checker, Annotation Transformer, Portable Ada/Anna Testing and Debugging System, Anna Interactive Tutorial System, Ada Logic Reasoning System (formal interface and implementation package), Anna Package Specification Analysis System.

The following highlights some of the collaborative efforts underway with industry:

- Phased technology insertion into Royal Australian Navy's New Construction Submarine Project.

- Exploring Anna run-time assertion checking of the simulated behavior of architectural models.

- Integration into ATF software environment, development of tools that utilize Anna constraint checks to enforce project design guidelines.

- Training engineers in use of formal methods on large software projects, included in hands-on formal methods seminars.

- Integration of Anna into the design review process, formulating a comparative study of the benefits of using formal methods up-front in the design process.

Representative published articles or reports:

Luckham, et al. "ANNA, A Language for Annotating Ada Programs." Lecture Notes in Computer Science, Vol. 260, Springer-Verlag 1987.

Luckham, et al. "Two Dimensional Pinpointing: An Application of Formal Specification to Debugging Packages." CSL-TR-89-379, Stanford University, April 1989.

Luckham, et al. "An Environment for Ada Software Development Based on Formal Specification." CSL-TR-86-305, Stanford University, August 1986.

David Rosenblum. "A Methodology for the Design of Ada Transformation Tools in a DIANA Environment." IEEE Software 2(2):24-33, March 1985.

Sriram Sankar and David Rosenblum. "The Complete Transformation Methodology for Sequential Runtime Checking of an Anna Subset." CSL-86-301, Stanford University, June 1986.

Current status of development:

A stable version of Anna-I is completed. Enhancements of unimplemented language features is continuing.

Date of project commencement:
June 1980

Date of completion (as a research project):
Ongoing.

Date of completion (as a product or deliverable):
Portable Ada/Anna analysis and debugging system, September 1990.

Intended evolution:

- Integration with Task Sequencing Language (TSL) language and toolkit, and technology transfer to Common Prototyping Language (CPL) language and toolkit.
- We are developing formal methods educational materials, focused upon the capabilities of the Anna language and Anna-I toolkit.
- We have been and continue to seek collaborative ventures with industry to insert Anna technology into ongoing Ada projects.
- Longer term, we plan to apply the capabilities of Anna to any implementation language.

Particular strengths and weaknesses:
Strengths: Full Ada typing applies to Anna, simple annotations for debugging such as assertions and input and output annotations for subprograms; advanced annotations for specifying Ada programs: package axioms, subtype annotations, and exception propagation annotations permit development of formal specifications for Ada systems, and analysis prior to implementation. Users can define their own methods of use and applications to program development.

Weaknesses: Anna semantics are limited to the sequential aspects of Ada.

Any additional users of technology (outside of development group):
There is a list of over 30 users.

Additional remarks:
None.

Ariel

Primary participants (project leader, group members):
James Morris, Steve Brackin, Doug Hoover, Mark Howard (Ian Sutherland, formerly project leader)

Survey contact:
James Morris
Odyssey Research Associates, 301A Harris Dates Dr., Ithaca, NY 14850-1313
Tel: (607) 277-2020
Fax: (607) 277-3206
e-mail: oravax!jmorris@cu-arpa.cs.cornell.edu

Country (or countries) of origin: USA

Level of effort (person-years, duration):

4.5 years per year for the last 3 years.

Brief description:

Ariel is a system originally designed for verifying C programs that compute over the reals. Programs are verified by reasoning directly about their semantics which are represented by the execution traces of an ideal C machine. ORA's Clio system is the theorem proving engine used by Ariel. In addition to the usual partial correctness assertions, one can also use Ariel to prove total correctness. Pointers and exception handling are modelled and hence programs that make use of them may be verified.

To model and verify programs that compute with data of type real, Ariel makes a novel use of non-standard analysis. The theory underlying Ariel establishes a notion of asymptotic correctness that is expressed using concepts from non-standard analysis. Asymptotic correctness can be shown to capture what we mean when we say that a program that computes over the reals is logically correct.

Accomplishments:

A prototype system has been constructed. It runs on Sun workstations under Unix, and it accepts programs written in a subset of C.

Representative published articles or reports:

Ian Sutherland. *A Mathematical Theory of Asymptotic Computation.* Technical Report RADC-TR-87-261. Rome Air Development Center, Air Force Systems Command, Griffiss AFB, NY, December 1987.

ORA Staff. *Reals Final Report.* Submitted to Rome Air Development Center, Air Force Systems Command, Griffiss AFB, NY, July 1989.

Current status of development:

Prototype verification system for a subset of C exists.

Date of project commencement:

May 1986.

Date of completion (as a research project):

October 1992

Date of completion (as a product or deliverable):

October 1992

Intended evolution:

The basic approach to semantics and verification developed for C will be applied to Ada. ORA's Penelope system will be adapted as a user interface.

Particular strengths and weaknesses:

Strengths: Total correctness is readily proved. Exceptions can be modelled and reasoned about, as can pointers. The representation of a program's semantics is executable.

Weakness: The (current) lack of an attractive user interface.

Any additional users of technology (outside of development group):

None at present.

Additional remarks:

[None.]

ASLAN

Primary participants (project leader, group members):
Richard Kemmerer, Brent Auernheimer, Dave Stein.

Survey contact:
Richard Kemmerer
Dept. of Computer Science, University of California, Santa Barbara, CA 93106
Tel: (805) 961-4232
email: kemm@moccasin.ucsb.edu

Country (or countries) of origin: USA

Level of effort (person-years, duration):
6 person-years over 4 years.

Brief description:
A specification language and formal verification system for hierarchically speci-fying systems. ASLAN language is an extension of first-order logic with sets and lists as primitive structures, and integer and Boolean as primitive types.

The system deals explicitly with exceptions, and uses a proof methodology, which is an extension of the Alphard methodology for ADT.

Accomplishments:
Two level specification of the secure release terminal.

Representative published articles or reports:
B. Auernheimer and R.A. Kemmerer. "ASLAN User's Manual." TRCS84-10, Dept. of Computer Science, University of California, Santa Barbara, CA, August 1984 (Revised 1985).

B. Auernheimer and R.A. Kemmerer. "RT-ASLAN: A Specification Language for Real-time Systems," *IEEE Transaction on Software Engineering* SE-12(9):879-889, September 1986.

Current status of development:
Maintenance support.

Date of project commencement:
June 1981

Date of completion (as a research project):
1984–1985

Date of completion (as a product or deliverable):
1984–1985

Intended evolution:
Extensions for real-time specification (RT-ASLAN)

Particular strengths and weaknesses:
Deals explicitly with exceptions, exportable to Europe, good teaching tool, well-defined theorem generation.

Any additional users of technology (outside of development group):
Some universities in the US, Germany, Italy and Japan.

Additional remarks:
None.

ASSPEGIQUE, an integrated specification environment

Primary participants (project leader, group members):
Michel Bidoit, Francis Capy, Christine Choppy, Frederic Voisin, Stephane Kaplan, and Francoise Schlienger, with contributions of Clement Roques, Marianne Choquer, Bruno Marre, and Eric Touchard.

Survey contact:
Project designed and realised in Software Engineering group at the Laboratory for Computer Science (Laboratoire de Recherche en Informatique), Université Paris-Sud, Orsay, France.

Christine Choppy
L.R.I., Université Paris-Sud, 91405 ORSAY Cedex, FRANCE
Tel: [33] - 1 - 69 41 66 23 or 69 41 66 29
Fax: [33] - 1 - 64 46 19 92
Telex FACORS 2166F
email: uucp:cc@lri.lri.fr bitnet:cc@frlri61

Country (or countries) of origin: France

Level of effort (person-years, duration):
[Not given.]

Brief description:
Asspegique is an integrated environment for the development of large algebraic specifications and the management of a specification database. The aim of the Asspegique specification environment is to provide the user with a "specification laboratory" where a large range of tools supporting the use of algebraic specifications are closely integrated. The main aspects addressed in the design of Asspegique are the following: dealing with modularity and reusability, providing ease of use, flexibility of the environment and user-friendly interfaces. The Asspegique specification environment supports (a subset of) the specification language Pluss.

The tools available in the Asspegique specification environment include a special purpose syntax directed editor, a compiler (specification modules integration tools), symbolic evaluation tools (including a compiler for conditional term rewriting systems and a "mixed" evaluator where rewriting and code execution are combined), theorem proving tools, an assistant for deriving Ada implementations from specifications and interfaces with the REVE and SLOG systems. All these tools are available to the user through a full-screen, multi-window user interface and access the specification database through the hierarchical management tool. Most of these tools use Cigale, a system for incremental grammar construction and parsing, which has been especially designed to cope with coercion, overloading, and a flexible, user-oriented way of defining operators.

Accomplishments:
[See above.]

Representative published articles or reports:
C. Choppy. *ASSPEGIQUE users's manual.* Rapport L.R.I. no 452, Octobre 1988.

M. Bidoit , C. Choppy, F. Voisin. "The ASSPEGIQUE specification environment, motivations and design." Proc. of the 3rd Workshop on Theory and Applications of Abstract data types (Bremen, Nov 1984), Recent Trends in Data Type Specification (H.-J. Kreowski ed.), *Informatik-Fachberichte* 116, Springer-Verlag, Berlin-Heidelberg, pp. 54-72, 1985.

M. Bidoit, C. Choppy. "ASSPEGIQUE : an integrated environment for algebraic specifications Formal Methods and Software Developments." Proc. International Joint Conference on Theory and Practice of Software Development (TAPSOFT, Berlin, Mars 1985), Colloquium on Software Engineering (CSE), Vol. 2 (H. Ehrig, C. Floyd, M. Nivat, J. Thatcher, eds), *LNCS* 186, Springer-Verlag, pp.246-260.

M. Bidoit, F. Capy, C. Choppy, N. Choquet, et al. "ASSPRO : un environnement de programmation interactif et inte'gre." *Techniques et Sciences Informatiques* 6(1):21-40, Janvier 1987. Also: "ASSPRO: an interactive and integrated programming environment." *Technology and Science of Informatics* 6(4):259-278, 1987.

On the PLUSS language:

M. Bidoit. "Pluss, un langage pour le développement de spécifications algébriques modulaires." Thèse d'Etat, Université Paris-Sud, 1989.

M. Bidoit, M.-C. Gaudel, A. Mauboussin. "How to make algebraic specifications more understandable? An experiment with the PLUSS specification language." *Science of Computer Programming* 12(1), 1989.

Current status of development:
[Not given.]

Date of project commencement:
The project started at the end of 1982

Date of completion (as a research project):
[Not given.]

Date of completion (as a product or deliverable):
ASSPEGIQUE was first demonstrated at the ICSE at Orlando in 1984, and has been distributed since 1985.

Intended evolution:
The project is still under progress. In particular, we are working on a new version that would fully support the PLUSS language.

Particular strengths and weaknesses:
[Not given.]

Any additional users of technology (outside of development group):
ASSPEGIQUE is now distributed in about 16 countries, mainly at research and universities sites (around 30).

Additional remarks:
[None.]

A Verifiable Ada (AVA)

Primary participants (project leader, group members):
Project leader: Michael K. Smith; Group members: Dan Craigen, Mark Saaltink.

Survey contact:
Michael K. Smith
Computational Logic Inc., 1717 W 6th, Suite 290, Austin, TX 78703
Tel: (512) 322-9951
Fax : (512) 322-0656
email: mksmith@cli.com

Country (or countries) of origin: USA

Level of effort (person-years, duration):
5 person-years over 3 years.

Brief description:
Our goal is to develop an effective and sound logical system for reasoning about programs written in a formally defined subset of Ada.

AVA must be sufficiently powerful to support the development of a well defined target application, a several thousand line communications program.

Accomplishments:
We have completely defined a very small subset, called nanoAVA. The definition consists of a subset of the Ada Manual (1815A), a formal mathematical description, and a statement of this mathematical description in Boyer-Moore Logic.

We have completed a draft of the full AVA manual (again, a subset of the Ada Manual), and the formal definition is in progress.

Representative published articles or reports:
Michael K. Smith, Dan Craigen, and Mark Saaltink. "The nanoAVA Definition." Technical Report 21, Computational Logic, Inc., June 1988.

Michael K. Smith. "The AVA Reference Manual." Draft Technical Report, Computational Logic, Inc., January 1989.

Current status of development:
In progress.

Date of project commencement:
May 1987

Date of completion (as a research project):
Ongoing

Date of completion (as a product or deliverable):
Not applicable

Intended evolution:
[None given.]

Particular strengths and weaknesses:
The use of the Boyer-Moore Logic for the formal definition allows us to prove properties of the definition. A powerful mechanical proof checker exists for the logic. It is expected that the existence of this prover will facilitate the develop-

ment of tools based on the formal definition.

Any additional users of technology (outside of development group):
[None given.]

Additional remarks:
[None given.]

BALZAC

Primary participants (project leader, group members):
Paul Taylor (SD, SCICON), Will Harwood (IST), Laurence Jordon, Catriona Fox, Jeremy Bradshaw.

Survey contact:
Peter Ryan (Technical Authority) Rm 10/2W01,
CESG Benhall, Princess Elizabeth Way, Cheltenham, Glos., GL50 5AJ, UK
Tel: (0242) 221491 ext. 4295

Country (or countries) of origin: UK

Level of effort (person-years, duration):
Just over 1 year with approx. 5 people.

Brief description: .
Provides tool support for the writing and editing of "Z" specifications, via either syntax directed editor or parser. Gives syntax checking and type checking. Currently, has crude proof editing capability.

Accomplishments:
[None given.]

Representative published articles or reports:
User guide. Various draft documents. Intend to publish articles shortly describing the kernel language, type system, proof system and semantics. Will present at the Z users meeting in DEC and the VDM and Z conference in Kiel, April 1990.

Current status of development:
Still in R & D.

Date of project commencement:
Approx. June 1988

Date of completion (as a research project):
No fixed completion date at present.

Date of completion (as a product or deliverable):
1st stage delivered July 1989. 2nd stage to be delivered April 1990 (for Beta testing). Potentially, further R&D.

Intended evolution:
Aiming to support a kernel language with extentional capability along with associated semantics and proof system. Will also have a tactical language capability and heuristics. Will also improve interface: make, display of and interaction with proof more "natural."

Particular strengths and weaknesses:
Proof system very elementary at present. Essentially, just a proof editor.

Any additional users of technology (outside of development group):
Beta testing by PRG Oxford, York University, ICL, Logica, Topexpress.

Additional remarks:
At present, quite a good tool for editing Z specs and type checking them. BALZAC '90 should be much better engineered and should provide quite a powerful proof assistant.

The Boyer-Moore Theorem Prover (NQTHM)

Primary participants (project leader, group members):
Robert S. Boyer and J Strother Moore

Survey contact:
J Strother Moore
Computational Logic Inc., 1717 W. 6th St., Suite 290, Austin, TX 78703
Tel: (512) 322-9951
email: moore@cli.com

Country (or countries) of origin: Edinburgh, Scotland (3 years); USA (17 years)

Level of effort (person-years, duration):
18 years X 2 persons

Brief description:
Automatic/interactive theorem prover for a first-order logic resembling Pure Lisp. The logic is based on recursive function definition and inductively defined data types. The theorem prover consists of about 1 megabyte of Common Lisp and contains many heuristics for controlling rule-based rewriting and induction.

Accomplishments:
Proofs of Gödel's Incompleteness theorem, Wilson's Theorem, Gauss' law of quadratic reciprocity, unsolvability of the halting problem, correctness of the Boyer-Moore fast string searching algorithm, invertibility of the RSA encryption algorithm, Piton assembler, Micro-Gypsy compiler, FM8502 microprocessor, KIT operating system, Bitonic sort, several programs in Unity.

Representative published articles or reports:
Boyer and Moore. *A Computational Logic.* Academic Press, 1979.

Boyer and Moore. *A Computational Logic Handbook.* Academic Press, 1988.

Current status of development:
Ongoing

Date of project commencement:
1971

Date of completion (as a research project):
Never

Date of completion (as a product or deliverable):
[Not given.]

Intended evolution:

Toward support of a practical applicative programming language, practical von Neumann verification system, and open architecture theorem prover.

Particular strengths and weaknesses:
Sound, extensible, interactive via incorporation of user-suggested but mechanically proved rules. Complicated; requires experience.

Any additional users of technology (outside of development group):
Over 300 copies have been distributed over the net in the last year. Mainly university research groups. Some industry interest. Much government interest.

Additional remarks:
[None.]

CASE

Primary participants (project leader, group members):
Praxis, ICL, UK Treasury (CCTA)

Survey contact:
Anthony Hall
Praxis, 20 Manvers Street, Bath BA1 1PX, UK
Tel: +44 225 444700
Fax: +44 225 465205
email: uunet!mcvax!ukc!praxis!jah

Country (or countries) of origin: UK

Level of effort (person-years, duration):
Approximately, 10 person-years over 2 years.

Brief description:
CASE is the infrastructure for a toolset to support SSADM on a SUN-3. It was specified in Z and implemented in objective-C.

Accomplishments:
Delivered and accepted by the client.

Representative published articles or reports:
None at present.

Current status of development:
Finished.

Date of project commencement:
1987

Date of completion (as a research project):
[Not applicable.]

Date of completion (as a product or deliverable):
1989

Intended evolution:
The CASE system will be populated with tools to support SSADM document production, and sold by ICL.

Particular strengths and weaknesses:
[None given.]

Any additional users of technology (outside of development group):
[None given.]

Additional remarks:
An interesting project combining Z specification and object-oriented implementation.

CLI Verified Stack

Primary participants (project leader, group members):
J Strother Moore, Bill Bevier, Warren Hunt, Bill Young.

Survey contact:
Dr. Bill Young
Computational Logic, Inc., 1717 W. 6th St., Suite 290, Austin, TX 78703
Tel: (512) 322-9951
email: young@CLI.COM

Country (or countries) of origin: USA

Level of effort (person-years, duration):
4 people, over approximately 2 years

Brief description:
The CLI "verified stack" is a collection of system components, each built upon the previous one, each subsequently providing more abstraction, and each being formally specified and mechanically verified. The system we have constructed contains a microprocessor with machine code, an assembly language, and a simple high-level programming language, together with the compiler, assembler and linker necessary to connect them. The stack properly consists of four abstract machines:

1. Gates–a register-transfer model of a microcoded machine.

2. FM8502–a machine code interpreter comparable to a PDP-11 in the complexity of the ALU and instruction set.

3. Piton–a high-level assembly language.

4. Micro-Gypsy–a simple high-level language which is a subset of the Gypsy 2.05 programming and specification language.

Relating each pair of adjacent machines is an implementation, represented as a function in the Boyer-Moore logic, which maps a higher-level state into a lower-level state. The implementation function is known as a "compiler" for the step from Micro-Gypsy to Piton, but as a "link-assembler" for the step from Piton to FM8502.

In addition, we have specified and proved correct the implementation of a small operating system kernel (KIT) written for a uniprocessor von Neumann machine. KIT is proved to implement a fixed number of conceptually distributed communicating processes on this shared computer. In addition to implementing processes, Kit provides the following verified services: process scheduling, error handling, message passing, and an interface to asynchronous devices. KIT is not currently integrated into our stack.

Accomplishments:
  We believe that this is the first hierarchically verified system of such complexity.
  It is possible using these components to compose and verify a high level program,
  and generate a core image for a microprocessor which provably preserves the
  semantics. We believe that future progress in this direction will lead to a higher
  degree of reliability than any existing approach.

Representative published articles or reports:
  Journal of Automated Reasoning 5(4), November 1989, contains five papers describing the stack and the individual components.

Current status of development:
  The various components are being extended and improved.

Date of project commencement:
  Earliest work began (on FM8502) in 1984. Most of the other work was in 1986
  and after.

Date of completion (as a research project):
  The last major piece (the Micro-Gypsy compiler) was finished in September,
  1988. The extensions, etc. are continuing.

Date of completion (as a product or deliverable):
  Uncertain.

Intended evolution:
  The CLI short stack can be represented as the following collection of components:

  Stack-0: Gates → FM8502 → Piton → Micro-Gypsy → Applications

  Our long-range goals include a verified stack similar to:

  Stack-n: Gates → RISC → MACH → Piton' → RCL → Boyer-Moore prover

  The position of the FM8502 processor is filled by some more standard RISC
  architecture supporting a verified version of the MACH operating systems. The
  Piton assembly language is enhanced to utilize operating system capabilities such
  as interrupts and I/O. The high level language supported is RCL, a subset of
  Common Lisp adequate for coding key portions of the Boyer-Moore theorem
  prover. Investigation of each of these components is currently ongoing at CLI.

Particular strengths and weaknesses:
  Strength: ability to preserve the semantics of verified high-level language programs through the various translation steps.

  Weakness: the various components of our current stack are rather specialized
  and provide limited services.

Any additional users of technology (outside of development group):
  None.

Additional remarks:
  [None given.]

Daffodil

Primary participants (project leader, group members):
Praxis, STC

Survey contact:
Martyn Ould
Praxis, 20 Manvers Street, Bath BA1 1PX, UK
Tel: +44 (225) 444700
Fax: +44 (225) 465205
email: ...uunet!mcvax!ukc!praxis!mao

Country (or countries) of origin: UK

Level of effort (person-years, duration):
Approximately, 6 person-years over 2 years.

Brief description:
Daffodil is a VDM specification for a configuration management tool.

Accomplishments:
Possibly the only formal model of configuration management.

Representative published articles or reports:
None.

Current status of development:
Complete.

Date of project commencement:
c. 1985

Date of completion (as a research project):
c. 1987

Date of completion (as a product or deliverable):
c. 1987

Intended evolution:
None. The work will possibly lead to a verified CM tool at some time (e.g., if a customer can be found to pay for the development).

Particular strengths and weaknesses:
[None listed.]

Any additional users of technology (outside of development group):
Daffodil has been used as the starting point for a further Praxis project by other staff.

Additional remarks:
[None.]

DAIDA (ESPRIT 892)

Primary participants (project leader, group members):
Matthias Jarke (University of Passau), technical manager
Universities: Frankfurt (Germany), Passau (Germany)
Research institutes: FORTH-CRC, Iraklion (Greece)
Software houses: BIM (Belgium), GFI (France), SCS (Germany)

Survey contact:
Matthias Jarke
University of Passau, P.O. Box 2540, D-8390 Passau, W. Germany
Tel: (49) (851) 509 322
Fax : (49) (851) 509 171
email: unipas!jarke@uunet.uu.net

Country (or countries) of origin: Germany, Greece, Belgium and France

Level of effort (person-years, duration):
ESPRIT project 892 (1986-1990), 46 person-years funded.

Brief description:
The DAIDA project investigates computerized Development Assistance for (a) providing validation and verification tools for requirements analysis and system specification, (b) supporting the formal refinement of quality-assured database software from object-oriented conceptual designs, and (c) maintaining knowledge about tool-assisted design decisions in a software process information system.

Important formal tools used and extended in the project include: the extensible knowledge representation language Telos which integrates predicative assertions and an interval-based time calculus with a structurally object-oriented kernel; the transaction-oriented database programming language DBPL which integrates an extended relational model of data with the system programming language Modula-2; and Abrial's theorem proving assistant B which aids in the consistency checking and formally verified refinement of modular designs expressed in an Abstract Machine/ Generalized Substitution Calculus formalism.

Accomplishments:
The project has developed a decision-object-tool (DOT) model in which large-scale software processes using heterogeneous methods and tools can be formally controlled and represented. Within this framework, a rule-based assistant supports consistent choices of how to embed a system specification in a formal model of requirements which may include aspects of the system environment. A set of theories and proof tactics dedicated to the needs of data intensive information systems (object identification in sets, data structure selection for large sets, static typing support) helps transform these specifications into efficient and correct database programs. The software information system based on the DOT model, ConceptBase, assists the developer in making, evaluating, and propagating incremental changes needed for maintenance. The DAIDA environment is completed by graphic-supported formal tools for requirements modelling, Prolog-based prototyping, version and configuration management, and programming-in-the-many support. An integrated prototype has been completed in fall, 1989, and is currently tested with application examples from the industry partners. Some DAIDA results are directly commercialized, others used in large-scale industrial projects

in the ESPRIT II program; a close collaboration exists with the REMAP project at New York University, and with the University of Toronto.

Representative published articles or reports:

Borgida, A., Mylopoulos, J., Schmidt, J.W., Wetzel, I. "Support for data-intensive applications: conceptual design and software development." *Proc. 2nd Intl. Workshop Database Programming Languages,* Portland, OR, 1989 (to be published by Springer-Verlag).

Dhar, V., Jarke, M. "Dependency-directed reasoning and learning in system maintenance support." *IEEE Trans. Software Eng.* 13(2):211-227, 1988.

Jarke, M., DAIDA Team. "The DAIDA demonstrator: development assistance for interactive database applications." *Proc. ESPRIT Conf. '89,* Brussels, Belgium, 1989.

Jarke, M., Jeusfeld, M., Rose, T. A software process data model for knowledge engineering in information systems. 1989.

Rose, T., Jarke, M. "A decision-based configuration process model." *Proc. 12th Intl. Conf. Software Engineering,* Nice, France, 1990.

[Remainder of survey not submitted for DAIDA.]

Distributed System Design Method

Primary participants (project leader, group members):
J. David Andrews, M. Higginson.

Survey contact:
J. Dave Andrews
Andyne Computing Limited, 544 Princess Street, Suite 202, Kingston, Ontario K7L 1C7
Tel: (613) 548-4355
email: andyne\!andrews@qucis.queensu.ca

Country (or countries) of origin: Canada

Level of effort (person-years, duration):
2 person-years over 1 year.

Brief description:
Component-wise specification technique, based on graphical, hierarchical model (Mascot) with component description in m-Verdi.

Accomplishments:
[None listed.]

Representative published articles or reports:
[None listed.]

Current status of development:
Emerging, research method; support tools planned.

Date of project commencement:
c. 1986

Date of completion (as a research project):
c. 1987 (experimental phase)

Date of completion (as a product or deliverable):
[Not available.]

Intended evolution:
Support tool on Sun workstation.

Particular strengths and weaknesses:
Strengths: Modularity, precise specification of low-level components, and interfaces.

Weaknesses: Relationships between components (especially involving concurrency) as yet poorly described. Development to implementation not yet explored.

Any additional users of technology (outside of development group):
None as yet.

Additional remarks:
[None.]

EHDM

Primary participants (project leader, group members):
Friedrich von Henke, John Rushby, Natarajan Shankar, Judy Crow (plus many others in the past, notably Melliar-Smith, Schwartz, Chastak).

Survey contact:
Friedrich von Henke, Computer Science Laboratory,
SRI International, 333 Ravenswood Ave., Menlo Park, CA 94025
Tel: (415) 859-2560
email: vonHenke@csl.sri.com
or
John Rushby
SRI International (same address as above)
Tel: (415) 859-5456
email: Rushby@csl.sri.com

Country (or countries) of origin: USA

Level of effort (person-years, duration):
Approximately 12 person-years (since 1983)

Brief description:
Self-contained specification and verification environment; specification language based on many-sorted higher order logic with parameterized modules. Hoare logic is also directly supported, as are implementation mappings based on theory interpretations. Three theorem proving components (ground prover, instantiator, Hoare-sentence prover) provide mechanized deduction. Several additional tools and services are provided (including Ada translator). Full documentation and a complete formal semantics and soundness theorems are available.

Accomplishments:
Re-verification of certain properties of SIFT (using early version of EHDM). Verification of a clock synchronization algorithm: formal specification and analysis of part of SeaView database design.

Representative published articles or reports:

John Rushby and Friedrich von Henke. "Formal verification of the interactive convergence clock synchronization algorithm using EHDM." SRI-CSL-89-3, SRI International, February 1989.

"The EHDM Verification Environment: An Overview." In *Proc. 11th NBS/ NCSC Computer Security Conference,* October 1988, p. 147-155.

Current status of development:
In Beta test at a number of sites. Public release expected late 1989

Date of project commencement:
c. July 1983

Date of completion (as a research project):
c. 1991

Date of completion (as a product or deliverable):
Late 1989

Intended evolution:
Internal reorganization for increased performance and interaction. Much improved theorem proving capability. Extension to distributed systems and concurrency.

Particular strengths and weaknesses:
Strengths: Very sophisticated specification languages and environment. Supports wide variety of specification styles. Supports hierarchical development and verification. Theorem prover provides powerful decision procedures for arithmetic.

Weaknesses: Proof construction (i.e., proof paradigm) is hard (for novices) and inefficient.

Any additional users of technology (outside of development group):
NASA Langley (serious use); NCSC; NRL and MITRE (minor experimentation only)

Additional remarks:
Currently subject to restriction of distribution.

ERGO

Primary participants (project leader, group members):
Dana Scott, Peter Lee, John Reynolds, William Scherlis (on leave at DARPA since 1986)

Survey contact:
Peter Lee
Computer Science, Carnegie-Mellon University, Pittsburgh, PA 15213
Tel: (412) 268-5025
email: peter.lee@cs.cmu.edu

Country (or countries) of origin: USA

Level of effort (person-years, duration):
10 people (approximately) including students.

Brief description:
ERGO is an aggregation of experimental and theoretical activity focused on

the application of formal techniques to software development and maintenance. There are several focal points of activity, including (1) development of an open-architecture implemented system (called ESS) to enable experimentation with a variety of formal methods approaches using a common set of tools and interfaces; (2) exploration of issues related to the formal manipulation of specifications and programs, including data structure refinement and other techniques; (3) exploration of the connections between proof manipulation and program manipulation; (4) development of data structures and tool support for formal documentation of specifications, structural designs, design commitment records, and informal documentation; (5) foundational work, particularly related to concurrency and types; (6) environment metalanguage design.

Accomplishments:
ESS prototype soon to be released. Higher-order abstract syntax and other internal interfaces defined. Program transformations (for abstract type representations and signatures, and for destructive data operations). Many foundational results.

Representative published articles or reports:
C. Elliott and F. Pfenning. "Higher-Order Abstract Syntax."

P. Lee, F. Pfenning, E. Rollins and W. Scherlis. "The ERGO Support System." SDE3, November 1988.

D. Scott, et al. "ERGO in 1988." Carnegie-Mellon University, Tech.Report, 1988.

Current status of development:
ESS prototype exists; will soon be available for preliminary, controlled use.

Date of project commencement:
1983

Date of completion (as a research project):
Ongoing

Date of completion (as a product or deliverable):
Ongoing

Intended evolution:
Experiments based in ESS are being done in the following areas:

- Program manipulation (ADT transformation, destructive operations).
- Proof manipulation, including program generation from proofs.
- Derivation/proof metalanguage support (e.g., Lambdaprolog, ELP, LEAP).
- Experimental prototyping of new programming language designs.

Particular strengths and weaknesses:
Strengths: Careful attention to ESS architecture and interface designs yields flexibility. Internal representations (higher-order abstract syntax) well suited to program manipulation.

Weaknesses: ESS is just emerging, so there is insufficient experience, particularly in program manipulation

Any additional users of technology (outside of development group):
Several groups will receive the technology in the next few months.

Additional remarks:
[None.]

EVES

Primary participants (project leader, group members):
Dan Craigen, Sentot Kromodimoeljo, Bill Pase, Irwin Meisels, Mark Saaltink

Survey contact:
Dan Craigen, Odyssey Research Associates,
265 Carling Ave., Suite 506, Ottawa, Ontario K1S 2E1, Canada
Tel: (613) 238-7900
email: dan@ora.on.ca

Country (or countries) of origin: Canada

Level of effort (person-years, duration):
Approximately 10 person years over 2.5 years

Brief description:
EVES is a verification system based on first-order, untyped set theory (with the Axiom of Choice). Programs are specified, implemented and proven using the language Verdi. A denotational description of the linguistic components for specifying and implementing programs has been developed. A formal characterization of the proof obligations resulting from each declaration, so as to maintain a semantic conservative extension property, has also been developed. (This includes a mathematical justification of the analysis performed by the Verdi verification condition generator.) Amongst other constructs, Verdi supports a library facility, mutual recursion, a form of strong typing for executable constructs and various constructs to support the expression of general mathematical concepts.

The theorem prover NEVER, while strongly influenced by its predecessor m-NEVER, has been modified to mirror the change in logical framework from m-EVES to EVES. EVES is implemented in Common Lisp and has been successfully run on Symbolics and Suns.

Accomplishments:
As with m-EVES, EVES is based on a solid mathematical foundation and has a powerful theorem proving tool. Though just completed, EVES has been used to specify and implement significant portions of an interpreter for PICO (as described in FR-90-5444-02 below). The resulting specification, implementation, and system commands consists of over 10,000 lines.

Representative published articles or reports:
Dan Craigen. *The Verdi Reference Manual.* TR-90-5429-09, Odyssey Research Associates, February 1990.

Mark Saaltink. *The Mathematics of Verdi.* TR-89-5429-10, Odyssey Research Associates, October 1989.

Sentot Kromodimoeljo, Bill Pase. *Using the EVES Library Facility: A PICO Interpreter.* FR-90-5444-02, Odyssey Research Associates, February 1990.

Current status of development:
Completed March 1990. Ongoing research, development and application.

Date of project commencement:
November 1987

Date of completion (as a research project):
Ongoing.

Date of completion (as a product or deliverable):
March 1990

Intended evolution:
Continued evolution of the system's capabilities and investigation of its inclusion into the broader system's engineering perspective. Expected to be released as a commercial product.

Particular strengths and weaknesses:
Strengths: Sound mathematical basis, expressive language, and a powerful theorem prover.

Weaknesses: EVES is an isolated tool and Verdi is not a mainstream development language.

Any additional users of technology (outside of development group):
[None given.]

Additional remarks:
Sponsored by the Canadian Department of National Defence and the Communications Security Establishment.

Formalisation of a Transaction Processing System

Primary participants (project leader, group members):
IBM UK Laboratories, Hursley Park; Oxford University Computing Laboratory Programming Research Group.

Survey contact:
J.C.P. Woodcock, Oxford University Computing Laboratory,
Programming Research Group, 8–11 Keble Road, Oxford OX1 3QD
Tel: +44 865 272576
e-mail: Jim.Woodcock@prg.ox.ac.uk

Country (or countries) of origin: UK

Level of effort (person-years, duration):
[Not stated]

Brief description:
This co-operative research project with IBM was launched in 1982 to test the application of formal methods to the development and development of software on an industrial scale.

IBM is engaged in the design, implementation, delivery and maintenance of a large transaction processing system known as the Customer Information Control System (CICS). To increase the range of services offered by CICS, and to adapt it to new hardware products, the programs in the CICS system are subject to constant modification. For this reason, CICS was particularly suitable for testing the mathematical methods proposed by the PRG. Today, parts of the IBM CICS development team use the mathematical notation known as Z, and part of the work now is in assisting the IBM programmers with the theoretical and notational problems encountered in the development of new system modules.

The research objectives are to demonstrate the applicability of mathematical methods to large industrial products. This includes developing formal specifications of CICS modules and the systematic refinement of specifications into code.

The research is conducted jointly by project programmers at IBM and researchers at the PRG. Professor C.B. Jones (of Manchester University), and Professor C.A.R. Hoare and Dr. J.C.P. Woodcock (both of Oxford University) are engaged as consultants to the project.

Accomplishments:
  Largest CICS release ever developed: 268,000 lines of new and modified code; 39,000 lines specified in the Z notation; 11,000 lines partially specified in Z.

Representative published articles or reports:
  M. Phillips. "CICS/ESA 3.1 Experience." *Procs 4th Annual Z Users' Meeting*, 14 December 1989, Rewley House, Oxford.

  J.C.P. Woodcock. "Calculating Properties of Z Specifications." *ACM Software Engineering Notes* 14(5):43–54, 1989.

Current status of development:
  Currently in Early Support Program.

Date of project commencement:
  1982

Date of completion (as a research project):
  [Not applicable.]

Date of completion (as a product or deliverable):
  1991

Intended evolution:
  [Not stated.]

Particular strengths and weaknesses:
  [Not stated.]

Any additional users of technology (outside of development group):
  Over 40 industrial companies use Z. Oxford University has taught the Z notation to approximately 1,000 industrial students; alternative courses are taught by at least three software companies.

Additional remarks:
  [None given.]

Formaliser

Primary participants (project leader, group members):
David Brazier, Mike Flynn, Tim Hoverd, Roy MacLean.

Survey contact:
Roy MacLean
Logica Cambridge Ltd., Betjeman House, 104 Hills Road, Cambridge CB2 1LQ
Tel: 0223 66343
Fax: 0223 322315
Email: roy@logcam.co.uk

Country (or countries) of origin: UK

Level of effort (person-years, duration):
2.5 person-years over last 2 years

Brief description:
Formaliser supports the interactive construction and editing of Z specification
documents that interleave formal text and free text paragraphs. The tool operates in a "WYSIWYG" point-and-click style. Mathematical symbols and constructs are displayed as they would appear on a printed page. Syntactic correctness is ensured by structure editing and parsing of typed input. Compliance
with the type and scope rules of Z can be checked interactively, and type/scope
information can be queried.

Specification documents are held within libraries and can be linked together via
inclusion relationships. The "Mathematical Toolkit" is itself a set of specification
documents to be included in other documents. Documents are automatically
loaded and unloaded from disk. The core of the tool is generic, and can be
configured for formal languages other than Z. A particular instantiation of the
tool is driven from a compiled attribute grammar for the language.

Accomplishments:
Formaliser has demonstrated: the feasibility of providing tool support for formal
methods on desk-top machines; the effectiveness of generic facilities working from
attribute grammars; the advantages of an object-oriented approach to design.

Representative published articles or reports:
Mike Flynn. "Formaliser - An Interactive Support Tool for Z." Proceedings of
the Z Users Group meeting, PRG, Oxford, December 1989.

Current status of development:
A beta-test version has been produced. It is implemented in Smalltalk/V, and
runs on a Compaq 386 (or equivalent PC clone).

Date of project commencement:
Mid-1988

Date of completion (as a research project):
Ongoing

Date of completion (as a product or deliverable):
[Not given.]

Intended evolution:
The presentation and management of large Z specifications will be investigated;

an instantiation of the tool for CSP will be considered; porting to Macintosh will be considered.

Particular strengths and weaknesses:
  Strengths: Good user interface; highly interactive style.

  Weaknesses: Type/scope error reporting is unsophisticated; configuration control of documents and library management not yet addressed.

Any additional users of technology (outside of development group):
  None at present.

Additional remarks:
  None.

Full Authority, Fault-Tolerant Reactor Control System (FAFTRCS)

Primary participants (project leader, group members):
  G.H. Chisholm, B.T. Smith, A.S. Wofcik, F. Klfaich.

Survey contact:
  Greg H. Chisholm
  Argonne National Laboratory, 9700 S. Cass Ave., Argonne, IL 60439
  Tel: (708) 972-6815
  email: Chisholm@mcs.anl.gov

Country (or countries) of origin: USA

Level of effort (person-years, duration):
  10–15 person-years over 3 years.

Brief description:
  Formal analysis of a computer-based (fault-tolerant) reactor control system. Real-time ultra-reliable, safety critical system. Utilizes a method to analyze the totality of the system. Specific attention to interfacing hardware, software proofs. Based upon automated theorem prover ITP.

Accomplishments:
  Generation of proofs of fault-tolerance for hardware/software, their interaction based upon independent behaviour; development of dependency lists. Note: Functionality not proven.

Representative published articles or reports:
  [None available.]

Current status of development:
  Clock synchrony proof and detailed proofs remain.

Date of project commencement:
  June 1986

Date of completion (as a research project):
  October 1989

Date of completion (as a product or deliverable):
  May 1990

Intended evolution:
  Complete detailed software proof.

Develop temporal logic and apply to synchrony.
Present to review group for preliminary response.
Incorporate comments.
Final proof/safety case presentation.

Particular strengths and weaknesses:
Strengths: Applies to total system; general, extensible.

Weaknesses: Utilizes clausal form and research-oriented theorem prover.

Any additional users of technology (outside of development group):
No.

Additional remarks:
[None.]

GATE Data Acquisition System

Primary participants (project leader, group members):
John McHugh

Survey contact:
John McHugh
Computational Logic Inc., 3500 Westgate Dr., Suite 204, Durham, NC 27705
Tel: (919) 493-4932
email: McHugh@cli.com

Country (or countries) of origin: USA

Level of effort (person-years, duration):
3–4 person-months over 4 months.

Brief description:
Program acquired data from up to seven asynchronous sources and a time source, and output it to nine track tape. A constructive, top down proof (early H. Mills style) of the program showed that data was correctly transferred from inputs to output and properly formatted. A separate proof, based on path analysis, instruction timing, and worst case data rates shows that no data will be lost up to a total aggregate data rate.

Accomplishments:
Program ran for in excess of six months total machine time (until all experiment data was processed). No run time failures were observed, either in operation or in subsequent data analysis.

Representative published articles or reports:
John McHugh. "Design and Construction Proof of a Real-time Program." Master's paper, Computer Science Dept., University of Maryland, 1974.

Current status of development:
Program/Hardware retired

Date of project commencement:
April 1972

Date of completion (as a research project):
July 1972

Date of completion (as a product or deliverable):
July 1972

Intended evolution:
None. System was constructed as a backup to a contractor developed program. It was placed in service when the primary program failed acceptance tests. It was designed as part of a custom suite of instrumentation for a large scale (multi-ship, 3 month) meteorological experiment. A single modification, to accommodate a higher precision time code, was made after deployment.

Particular strengths and weaknesses:
Demonstrated the utility of hand proofs, including real time properties of a substantial (approximately 3K lines) assembly language program. The program may or may not have been "correct." The proofs were undoubtedly flawed. The program accomplished its mission.

The technique did not address tensions between performance and correctness until fairly late. This resulted in substantial reproof when code and data structures were modified to gain performance.

Any additional users of technology (outside of development group):
The program was operationally used by Center for Experiment Design of NOAA for the Global Atmospheric Research Project's Atlantic Tropical Experiment. I left prior to the field phase to return to graduate school. As far as I know, no similar systems have been constructed.

Additional remarks:
I am embarrassed by my failure to publish this work. At the time it was done, I assumed that everyone would work this way in the near future. In recent years, the work has been rejected as "stale" by several conferences in the real time area.

Genesis

Primary participants (project leader, group members):
Imperial Software Technology, Philips, Imperial College

Survey contact:
Will Harwood
Imperial Software Technology, 3 Glisson Road, Cambridge CB1 2HA, UK
Tel: +44 223 462400
Fax: +44 223 462500
email: will@ist.co.uk

Country (or countries) of origin: UK and Holland

Level of effort (person-years, duration):
30 person-years over 3 years.

Brief description:
Genesis is an ESPRIT funded research project to create a meta-tool for creating tools to support formal methods. The meta-tools allow the creation of syntax directed editors, parsers, pretty printers and proof editors for formal notation.

Accomplishments:
The languages VDM, Z and COLD-K have been supported using the Genesis meta-tool. The VDM tool includes an LVF proof system, the Z system provides

syntactic support for Z with the proof system under development. COLD-K has syntactic support.

Representative published articles or reports:
[None listed.]

Current status of development:
Prototype product (dependent on language)

Date of project commencement:
January 1986

Date of completion (as a research project):
July 1989

Date of completion (as a product or deliverable):
Z and VDM tools are available as products.

Intended evolution:
Generally, the look-and-feel of Genesis developed tools is good but interface performance is too low. This is undergoing performance improvement.

The major evolution will be driven by using Genesis to construct support tools for further formal methods, e.g., Lotos (however, this will require finding further funding).

Particular strengths and weaknesses:
The Genesis system allows the support of formal notations and proof systems in a style that is close to the textbook presentation of the notation or proof system.

Its major weakness is that it requires a Lucid Common Lisp (Sun Common Lisp) development environment to run.

Any additional users of technology (outside of development group):
Approximately 6 other sites (outside of IST/Philips) have access to Genesis generated tools.

Additional remarks:
[None.]

Gypsy Information Flow Tool (GIFT)

Primary participants (project leader, group members):
John McHugh, Robert L. Akers, Bret Hartman, Tad Taylor, Art Flatau, Craig Singer.

Survey contact:
Robert L. Akers
Computational Logic Inc., 1717 W. Sixth St., Suite 290, Austin, TX 78703
Tel: (512) 322-9951
email: akers@cli.com
Fax: (512) 322-0656

Country (or countries) of origin: USA

Level of effort (person-years, duration):
Roughly two person-years over roughly two years

Brief description:

Covert channels are mechanisms that allow users of a supposedly secure computer system to communicate with each other in violation of the system's security policy. The Gypsy Information Flow Tool (GIFT) embodies one method for identifying and evaluating such channels. GIFT is based on an analysis of the specification of the trusted computing base (TCB) of a secure system. The tool also provides the analyst with a detailed description of the information dependencies that are present within the TCB and the circumstances under which the potential channels identified by the GIFT can be exercised. The GIFT is designed to analyze TCB specifications written in the Gypsy language and is a fully integrated component of the Gypsy Verification Environment.

The Gypsy Information Flow Tool is based on a combination of a dependency analyzer and a security formula generator. Informally, we define dependency analysis to be the process of tracing the flow of information into, through, and out of a system based upon a formal specification for that system. In the context of the GIFT, we provide a more formal definition of dependency analysis that relies upon Gypsy language semantics and Gypsy specification conventions designed to model state machines and security policies. The information provided by dependency analysis is combined with user supplied information about the security levels of system entities to generate formulas which, if proven to be true, ensure that the information flows identified during the dependency analysis conform to the system's security policy.

Accomplishments:

The tool has been used to perform flow analysis tasks on the ASOS and LOCK software systems.

The Honeywell LOCK project is using non-interference proofs to help establish the security of their system. As with any non-interference proof, it is important that the concept of what is "visible" to a user be captured correctly, since proofs are performed with respect to that definition. The dependency analysis capabilities of the GIFT were used to help validate the completeness of the visibility definition.

Representative published articles or reports:

McHugh, Akers, "A Formal Justification for the Gypsy Information Flow Tool", Computational Logic, Inc. Report No. 13a.

McHugh, Akers, Taylor, "GVE User's Manual: The Gypsy Information Flow Tool, a Covert Channel Analysis Tool", Computational Logic, Inc. Report No. 12c.

Hartman, "Non-Interference and Information Flow Analysis: A Hybrid Approach", In *Proceedings of the Computer Security Foundations Workshop*, Franconia, NH, June 1989.

Current status of development:

The GIFT is a stable component of the Gypsy Verification Environment. No further development is planned.

Date of project commencement:

January 1987.

Date of completion (as a research project):
September 1988.

Date of completion (as a product or deliverable):
July 1989.

Intended evolution:
Although the basis exists for extending its capability into the area of tranquillity analysis, there are no plans for this extension.

The GIFT has its own methods for tracking the effects of the incremental development of the TCB specifications. Since the completion of the GIFT, a new incremental development tool has been installed in the GVE which could supplant the GIFT methods, however the new incremental development tool was not integrated into the GIFT. This could easily be done, but is not on the current task schedule.

Particular strengths and weaknesses:
The GIFT represents several advances in the state of the art and practice of flow analysis:

The GIFT theory provided a more satisfactory approach to information flow into structured objects than had been previously utilized. It also extended the conventional theory into the area of dynamic data objects by treating Gypsy sequences, sets, and mappings.

The pragmatic issues of "labelling" objects with their security levels were addressed in a manner much more conducive to formal and automatic analysis than in any previous tool or theory.

The expressive power of the Gypsy language provided a basis for explicit dependency analysis of some cases which were outside the limits of previous tools.

The GIFT was fully integrated into a popular verification system, the GVE. The theory embodied in the GIFT was totally consistent with the theory and semantics of verification in Gypsy, and the software tools were smoothly integrated with the existing system, thus eliminating on both fronts a cognitive dissonance which had plagued other flow analysis tools.

As previously mentioned, the tool does not yet address tranquillity analysis.

Any additional users of technology (outside of development group):
TRW (ASOS), Honeywell (LOCK)

Additional remarks:
The GIFT was supported by the TRW Defense Systems Group in conjunction with work on the Army Secure Operating System (ASOS), Contract No. DAAB07-86-CA032, US Army Communications-Electronics Command.

Gypsy Verification Environment

Primary participants (project leader, group members):
Don Good and his associates at The Institute for Computing Science, The University of Texas at Austin, and at Computational Logic, Inc.

Survey contact:
Bill Young
Computational Logic, Inc., 1717 W. Sixth Street, Suite 290, Austin, TX 78703
Tel: (512) 322-9951
email: young@cli.com

Country (or countries) of origin: USA

Level of effort (person-years, duration):
Started in 1974. 50–100 person-years of effort have gone into the GVE implementation.

Brief description:
The Gypsy Verification Environment is a large computer program that supports the development of software systems and formal, mathematical proofs about their behaviour. The environment provides conventional development tools, such as a parser for the Gypsy language, an editor and a compiler. These are used to evolve a library of components that define both the software and precise specifications about its desired behaviour. The environment also has a verification condition generator that automatically transforms a software component and its specification into logical formulas which are sufficient to prove that the component always runs according to specification. Facilities for constructing formal, mechanical proofs of these formulas also are provided. Many of these proofs are completed automatically without human intervention. The GVE also contains a Feirtag-style Information Flow Tool.

The Gypsy language is a combined specification and programming language descended from Pascal. It supports a large variety of data types, data abstraction, exception handling, and concurrency. All parts of the language have associated proof rules.

Accomplishments:
Encrypted packet interface for ARPANET hosts (see report below).

Message flow modulator (see report below).

Scomp Trusted Processes: Formal Specifications for Secure Communications Processor Trusted Software Release 2.2, Honeywell Information Systems, Inc., March 1985.

Used heavily in the specifications on Honeywell LOCK and ACCAT Guard.

One of two tools endorsed by the National Computer Security Center for use in achieving A-1 certification under the DoD Trusted Computer System Evaluation Criteria.

Representative published articles or reports:
"The Proof of a Distributed System in Gypsy." Technical Report CMP-30, Institute for Computing Science, UT-Austin

"Message Flow Modulator." Technical Report CMP-34, Institute for Computing

Science, UT-Austin.

"Report on Gypsy 2.05." CLI technical report 1, January 1989.

"Using the Gypsy Methodology." CLI technical report 2, January 1988.

Current status of development:
Under maintenance.

Date of project commencement:
1974

Date of completion (as a research project):
Transition from research to production use, approx. 1985-89.

Date of completion (as a product or deliverable):
? mid-1990s

Intended evolution:
Starting in 1989, the GVE is moving from an enhancement phase to a maintenance phase. A new generation of tools to replace it will be developed in the 1990's.

Particular strengths and weaknesses:
Strengths: Demonstrated effectiveness on sizable projects. Applicable to a wide range of problems, including design and code level proofs. Supports data abstraction, concurrency, and condition handling.

Weaknesses: Because of its research roots, the GVE was never designed to handle the large applications to which it is now being applied. Its implementation shows the signs of many graduate-student programmers over the years.

Any additional users of technology (outside of development group):
One of two tools endorsed by the National Computer Security Center for use in achieving A-1 certification under the DoD Trusted Computer System Evaluation Criteria. Used by Government contractors on security-related projects.

Additional remarks:
[None.]

Hardware verification

Primary participants (project leader, group members):
Graham Birtwistle, Brian Graham, Todd Simpson, Konrad Slind.

Survey contact:
Graham Birtwistle, Dept. of Computer Science
University of Calgary, 2500 University Dr., Calgary, Alberta T2N 1N4, Canada
Tel: (403) 220 6055   Fax: (403) 284 4707
email: graham@cpsc.ucalgary.ca

Country (or countries) of origin: Canada, NSERC funding

Level of effort (person-years, duration):
3 years

Brief description:
Re-implement HOL in SML (we will complete a "throw-away" first-order system

first, before attempting HOL). We will then put effort into putting some automation into HOL, some of it tailored to hardware (automatic verification of ALU's, etc.) and complete a library of theorems and tactics for self-timed circuits.

Accomplishments:
Project just underway (5 months). We have a FOL prototype running. This will be reviewed (early 1990). The new HOL system will be written and documented in early 1990.

Representative published articles or reports:
[None given.]

Current status of development:
Just started.

Date of project commencement:
May 1, 1989

Date of completion (as a research project):
April 30, 1992

Date of completion (as a product or deliverable):
April 30, 1991

Intended evolution:
FOL system: December 1989
HOL system: B version - April 1990
HOL system: released - April 1991

Particular strengths and weaknesses:
Our first effort at a theorem prover, although we are quite experienced with compilers. We can, however, make much use of the existing HOL system, much of which is written in old ML and can easily be mapped into SML.

Any additional users of technology (outside of development group):
The system will be given to Cambridge, UK (Mike Gordon). If he is satisfied, it will become the HOL standard. If not, it won't.

Additional remarks:
This effort is heavily based upon the current version of HOL, made available to us by Mike Gordon of Cambridge. It would not be possible without his generosity.

HOL verification of ELLA designs

Primary participants (project leader, group members):
Praxis, British Aerospace, Cambridge University.

Survey contact:
John Richards
Praxis plc, Bath, UK
or
Mike Gordon
SRI International, Suite 23, Millers Yard, Mill Lane, Cambridge CB2 1RQ, UK
Tel: +44 23 324 146
Fax: +44 223 460 402
email: mjcg@cam.sri.com

Country (or countries) of origin: UK

Level of effort (person-years, duration):
2–3 persons for 3 years

Brief description:
To interface HOL to ELLA and to perform design and verification case studies with the resulting tool.

Accomplishments:
Not available.

Representative published articles or reports:
Not available.

Current status of development:
Project started August 1, 1989

Date of project commencement:
August 1, 1989

Date of completion (as a research project):
July 31, 1992

Date of completion (as a product or deliverable):
Not available.

Intended evolution:
It is hoped to develop a hardware verification methodology that combines both traditional (e.g., simulations) and formal methods.

Particular strengths and weaknesses:
To be discovered.

Any additional users of technology (outside of development group):
[Not available.]

Additional remarks:
[None.]

IPSE 2.5

Primary participants (project leader, group members):
Praxis, ICL, Manchester University, STC

Survey contact:
Clive Roberts
Praxis, 20 Manvers Street, Bath BA1 1PX, UK
Tel: +44 225 444700
Fax: +44 225 465205
email: mct%praxis@uunet.uu.net

Country (or countries) of origin: UK

Level of effort (person-years, duration):
For this task, 10 person-years over 4 years.

Brief description:
IPSE 2.5 is an advanced IPSE, which can be tailored to a desired development

model (or life cycle) by writing some process model description in Role Modelling Language. RML is a formal language for describing activities and interactions, based on RADS (Role-Activity Diagrams).

Accomplishments:
The language exists, an interpreter exists.

Representative published articles or reports:
Ould and Roberts, Defining Formal Models of the Software Development Process, pp 13 - 26 in Software Engineering Environments, Ellis Horwood, 1988

Current status of development:
Continuing

Date of project commencement:
c. 1985

Date of completion (as a research project):
Possibly late 1989

Date of completion (as a product or deliverable):
1990

Intended evolution:
This work is the central part of the IPSE deliverable.

Particular strengths and weaknesses:
This is an unusual application domain for formal methods. RML allows organizations to be modelled and the models to be animated.

Any additional users of technology (outside of development group):
The IPSE 2.5 project.

Additional remarks:
This work is partially funded by the UK Alvey program. Another task is addressing theorem proving (MURAL). The MURAL work can be discussed by contacting Cliff Jones at Manchester University.

IV & V on space station software

Primary participants (project leader, group members):
Prime contractor: SPAR Aerospace; Sub-contractor: Prior Data Sciences

Survey contact:
Steven Hall, Prior Data Sciences,
2000 Barrington St., Suite 604, Halifax, N.S. B3J 3K1, Canada
Tel: (902) 423-1331
Fax: (902) 425-3664

Country (or countries) of origin: Canada

Level of effort (person-years, duration):
Still being defined. Current estimate is 20+ person-years.

Brief description:
Project is just starting.

Accomplishments:
IV & V plan.

Representative published articles or reports:
None yet.

Current status of development:
Requirements phase.

Date of project commencement:
1989

Date of completion (as a research project):
[Not available.]

Date of completion (as a product or deliverable):
Current phase: March 31, 1990

Intended evolution:
IV & V will be applied to all phases of the software life cycle. We hope to influence the addition of formal methods to the development.

Particular strengths and weaknesses:
Not available yet.

Any additional users of technology (outside of development group):
None yet.

Additional remarks:
Prior is in the process of planning a Software Engineering Centre for the Halifax area. This centre will include and emphasize IV & V and Formal Methods.

Larch

Primary participants (project leader, group members):
John Guttag, MIT; Jim Horning, DEC/SRC;
Jeannette Wing, Carnegie-Mellon University; Steve Garland, MIT.

Survey contact:
Jeannette Wing, School of Computer Science,
Carnegie-Mellon University, Pittsburgh, PA 15213-3890
Tel: (412) 268-3068
email: Wing@cs.cmu.edu

Country (or countries) of origin: USA

Level of effort (person-years, duration):
3–4 principals in language design since 1980
2–3 serious users since 1985
1–2 serious tool developers since 1985

Brief description:
Language design supports "two-tiered" approach for specifying program modules, e.g., procedures, functions, ADTs. One tier is algebraic and is program language semantics independent. One tier is predicative (pre/post) and is program language semantics dependent. Tool support is an important focus of the project.

Accomplishments:
Formal semantics for algebraic tier and formal semantics for one predicative tier: done. Others in progress.

Tools: Larch prover (semantic checking support for algebraic tier): Version 1 done.

Larch checker (syntax checker for algebraic tier): two prototypes done.

Generic Interface Language Checker (syntax checking for predicative tier): one prototype done.

Representative published articles or reports:
Guttag, Horning, and Wing. "Five easy pieces." DEC/SRC TR-5, July 1985.

Guttag, Horning, and Wing. *IEEE Software*, September 1985.

Current status of development:
Language design has gone through a revision since 1985 report. Tools are in prototype stage.

Date of project commencement:
c. 1980

Date of completion (as a research project):
Ongoing

Date of completion (as a product or deliverable):
Larch prover is the tool that has progressed the furthest. Version 1 is due late 1989.

Intended evolution:
Language design: focus on adding concurrency.

Tools: integrate existing tools (or better versions of them).

More users outside of Larch community, e.g., through SEI or CMU's MSE program.

Particular strengths and weaknesses:
Strengths: Larch prover – state of the art in proof checker techniques for rewrite-rule theory (beyond Affirm and Reve); two-tiered approach is a big success.

Weaknesses: Can specify only program modules, not collections of programs; cannot deal with concurrency.

Any additional users of technology (outside of development group):
Unknown how extensive. The project group has a list of examples specified in Larch. Other groups that have done examples in Larch include ORA (Larch/Ada work), a group in London, a group in Mexico, and 1 or 2 groups in SEI or one of their affiliates.

Additional remarks:
[None.]

Low-level Verification (Clio)

Primary participants (project leader, group members):
Edward A. Schneider, Mark Bickford, Charles Mills, M. Srivas, Tanja de Groot.

Survey contact:
Edward A. Schneider, Odyssey Research Associates,
301A Harris B. Dates Dr., Ithaca, NY 14850-1313, USA
Tel: (607) 277-2020
e-mail: oravax!ed@cu-arpa.cs.cornell.edu

Country (or countries) of origin: USA

Level of effort (person-years, duration):
10 person-years, 3 year duration.

Brief description:
Design and build a rewrite-rule verification system based on a lazy functional programming language and then apply it to hardware and compiler verification. The compiler was for a typical imperative language and a typical assembly language. The hardware is a pipelined RISC chip being developed at Cornell University.

Accomplishments:
The Clio verification system has been built. A major portion of the Cayuga RISC chip, including interrupts, has been verified to the register transfer level. A simple compiler has been specified and the correctness conditions formulated.

Representative published articles or reports:
Mark Bickford and Charlie Mills and Edward A. Schneider, *Clio: An Applicative Language-Based Verification System,* Odyssey Research Associates TR 15-7, June 1989.

M. K. Srivas and Mark Bickford, "Formal Verification of Microprocessors," *Proc. Fourth Annual COMPASS Conf.,* Gaithersburg, MD, June 1989.

Mark Bickford and M. K. Srivas, "Microprocessor Verification Using Clio," *Proc. Workshop on Hardware Specification, Verification, and Synthesis,* Ithaca, NY, July 1989.

Current status of development:
The Clio verifier is in use. Hardware verification is continuing.

Date of project commencement:
June 1986.

Date of completion (as a research project):
Ongoing.

Date of completion (as a product or deliverable):
Clio to be delivered September 1989.

Intended evolution:
The full Cayuga chip will be verified. A tool for graphical input of hardware specifications will be added. Improvements to the prover, such as tactics and special purpose decision procedures, will be made. Clio will continue to be used in a variety of projects and will improve in response to the user's needs.

Particular strengths and weaknesses:

Strengths: Executable specifications. Specifying and reasoning about a wide range of data types, including infinite lists, free algebras, and function types, is simple and natural. Structural induction and fixed-point induction are handled well. Arbitrary partial recursive functions are allowed.

Weaknesses: Special decision procedures, e.g. integer arithmetic, linear order, should be incorporated. Checkable proofs are not created or saved (although replayable proof scripts are created). The fully automatic mode is not powerful as there is no tactic facility.

Any additional users of technology (outside of development group):
Members of the US Air Force at Syracuse University.

Additional remarks:
[None.]

Mathematically Proven Safety Software (MPSS)

Primary participants (project leader, group members):
Laboratory Foundations Computer Science (LFCS), Edinburgh; Adelard, London, UK

Survey contact:
Robin Bloomfield
Adelard, 28 Rhondda Grove, London, E3 5AP, UK
Tel: (44) 1-318-7579
Fax: (44) 1-852-4738
e-mail: reb@ed.lfcs.ac.uk

Country (or countries) of origin: UK

Level of effort (person-years, duration):
10 person-years but building on a much larger research effort.

Brief description:
To develop and apply the Concurrency Workbench to safety-critical systems, building up the relevant theories. To build on the Logical Framework project and apply to safety-critical problems, in particular to consider reuse of proof.

Accomplishments:
None yet.

Representative published articles or reports:
None yet.

Current status of development:
About to start in earnest

Date of project commencement:
September 1989

Date of completion (as a research project):
September 1992

Date of completion (as a product or deliverable):
September 1992

Intended evolution:
[To be determined.]

Particular strengths and weaknesses:
Based on Milner's CCS and addressing concurrent aspects of systems.

Any additional users of technology (outside of development group):
The Concurrency Workbench is a joint venture between LFCS and other groups in the UK, the USA and Sweden. This project will develop and apply the workbench to the safety-critical field. It is intended to build upon the large investment made to date in the study of concurrency and the development of the workbench.

Additional remarks:
The project is looking for realistic case studies.

The Mechanical Verification of Concurrent Programs

Primary participants (project leader, group members):
Jimi Crawford, David Goldschlag.

Survey contact:
David Goldschlag, Computational Logic, Inc.,
1717 West Sixth Street, Suite 290, Austin, Texas 78703-4776
Tel: (512) 322-9951
Fax: (512) 322-0656
email: dmg@cli.com

Country (or countries) of origin: USA

Level of effort (person-years, duration):
Four person-years over three years.

Brief description:
This project formalizes, on an automated theorem prover, a proof system for concurrent programs. This proof system allows one to specify concurrent programs and their correctness properties and then prove (and mechanically verify) that the programs satisfy their correctness properties.

The proof system formalized is based on Unity (*Parallel Program Design: A Foundation*, Chandy and Misra, Addison-Wesley, 1988), which emphasizes non-operational correctness arguments. This project includes demonstrating this proof system by mechanically verifying several concurrent programs, including a solution to the n-processor mutual exclusion problem, a spanning tree algorithm, and a real-time program.

Accomplishments:
To the best of our knowledge, this project provides the first mechanically verified solution to the n-processor mutual exclusion problem with non-deterministic processors. This solution was proved to satisfy both mutual exclusion and absence of starvation. Though the correctness of the algorithm was not in doubt, the mechanically verified proof of correctness demonstrates the generality of this proof system and suggests that this proof system is not limited to the proof of a limited class of concurrent programs.

The formalization of the Unity proof system within the Boyer-Moore logic and the validation of this formalization on the Boyer-Moore prover proves the soundness of Unity.

Representative published articles or reports:

David M. Goldschlag. "A Mechanically Verified Proof System for Concurrent Programs." Technical Report No. 32, Computational Logic, Inc., Austin, Texas, January 1989.

J. M. Crawford and D. M. Goldschlag. "The Underlying Semantics of Transition Systems." Technical Report No. 17, Computational Logic, Inc., Austin, Texas, December 1987.

J. M. Crawford and D. M. Goldschlag. "The Mechanical Verification of Distributed Systems." Technical Report No. 7. Computational Logic, Inc., Austin, Texas, July 1987.

Current status of development:

The Unity proof system has been formalized on the Boyer-Moore prover. This formalization is currently being used to verify a concurrent spanning tree algorithm and a real time program.

Date of project commencement:

October 1986

Date of completion (as a research project):

December 1989

Date of completion (as a product or deliverable):

[Not given.]

Intended evolution:

This project will become one level of a stack of machines which defines a computer system at different levels of abstraction. This level will let one specify concurrent programs and prove their correctness properties; lower levels will specify correct implementations of these programs, while higher levels will specify more global system properties.

Particular strengths and weaknesses:

This proof system inherits from Unity a clean and simple view of a concurrent program, whose execution is defined to be the repeated execution of a set of statements where each statement is scheduled in an arbitrary but fair manner (no statement is ignored forever). This view, together with various proof rules, provides a coherent structure within which one argues correctness properties.

Because of the arbitrariness of statement selection in an execution it is difficult to specify real-time properties. A solution may be to constrain the selection mechanism to satisfy those real-time properties.

The mechanically verified proofs are long and contain much detail that would usually be skipped in a hand proof. However, a mechanically verified proof closely resembles the structure of a corresponding hand proof; the detail is necessary as part of a more rigorous proof.

Any additional users of technology (outside of development group):

None currently.

Additional remarks:

[None.]

m-EVES

Primary participants (project leader, group members):
Dan Craigen, Sentot Kromodimoeljo, Bill Pase, Irwin Meisels, Mark Saaltink

Survey contact:
Dan Craigen, Odyssey Research Associates,
265 Carling Ave., Suite 506, Ottawa, Ontario K1S 2E1, Canada
Tel: (613) 238-7900
email: dan@ora.on.ca

Country (or countries) of origin: Canada

Level of effort (person-years, duration):
Approximately, 15 person-years over 4 years.

Brief description:
m-EVES is a prototype verification system, based on a first-order, many-sorted, predicate calculus extended to include a definitional principle. Programs are specified and implemented in the language m-Verdi. The language has a denotational semantics description and the m-EVES logic has been proven sound. A library mechanism has been included.

The theorem prover, m-NEVER, integrates concepts drawn from the Boyer-Moore prover, Nelson-Oppen decision procedures, Affirm and work by Bledsoe. m-NEVER incorporates significant automated support but also supports user interaction. m-EVES is implemented in Common Lisp and has been successfully run on Symbolics, Suns and Vaxes. A compiler for m-Verdi runs on Vaxes (under VMS and UNIX).

Accomplishments:
m-EVES is based on a solid mathematical foundation and has a powerful theorem proving tool. m-EVES has been used to prove, amongst other efforts, results from set theory (e.g., Schroeder-Bernstein, Cantor), UNIX programs (WC, TR), hardware examples (e.g., an n-bit adder), security properties (e.g., non-interference). m-EVES is being used externally to specify a lambda calculus based chip and is to be used on a security example and to prove properties relating to real time constraints.

Representative published articles or reports:
Dan Craigen, et al. "m-EVES: A Tool for Verifying Software." In *Proc. of the 10th International Conference on Software Engineering,* Singapore, May 1988.

Dan Craigen. "An Application of the m-EVES Verification System." In *Proceedings of the 2nd Testing, Verification and Analysis Workshop,* Banff, Alberta, July 1988.

Bill Pase and Mark Saaltink. "Formal Verification in m-EVES." In *Current Trends in Hardware Verification and Automated Deduction.* G. Birtwistle and P.A. Subrahmanyam (Eds), Springer-Verlag, 1989.

Current status of development:
Completed November 1987 and ported to the Sun in 1989.

Date of project commencement:
1983/4

Date of completion (as a research project):
November 1987

Date of completion (as a product or deliverable):
November 1987

Intended evolution:
m-EVES is a proof of concept system. It formed a basis for work leading to the development of EVES. (EVES is described separately.) An m-Verdi compiler that generates code for the 68020 will be written in 1990. There will not be any further evolution of m-EVES.

Particular strengths and weaknesses:
Strengths are sound mathematical basis, powerful theorem prover, and compiler support. Weaknesses are that m-EVES is an isolated tool and m-Verdi is not a mainstream development language.

Any additional users of technology (outside of development group):
Andyne Computing Limited, Kingston, Ontario
Communications Security Establishment, Ottawa, Ontario
MCC, Austin, Texas
The Mitre Corporation, Bedford, MA
Naval Research Laboratory, Washington, DC
Royal Signals and Radar Establishment, Malvern, England

Additional remarks:
Sponsored by the Canadian Department of National Defence and the Communications Security Establishment.

μral (Mural)

Primary participants (project leader, group members):
Cliff Jones, Juan Bicarregui, Neil Dyer, Bob Fields, Jane Gray, Kevin Jones, Ralf Kneuper, Peter Lindsay, Richard Moore, Brian Ritchie, Alan Wills

Survey contact:
Prof. Cliff Jones
Dept. of Computer Science, The University, Manchester M13 9PL, England
Tel: ++44-61-275-6128
email: JANET - cliff@uk.ac.man.cs   ARPA - cliff%cs.man.ac.uk
fax: ++44-61-275-6280

Country (or countries) of origin: England

Level of effort (person-years, duration):
c. 30 person-years; 4 years duration

Brief description:
Support for formal software development, comprising:

- Specification support tool support for the construction of formal specifications in (a subset of) BSI standard VDM and generation of proof obligations for these specifications. This latter takes the form of a "theory of the specification" in μral 's proof assistant.

– Interactive proof assistant support for the construction of proofs, both fully formal and rigorous.

Some research work has also been done on animation of specifications via symbolic execution.

Accomplishments:
Proof assistant generic over a wide range of logics. Provides a hierarchical store of inference rules to which the user can add, and prove, new rules. Emphasis on user interface and user interaction. Automatic generation of theories and inference rules from a VDM specification.

Representative published articles or reports:
J.C. Bicarregui and B. Ritchie. "Providing support for the formal development of software." In: *Proc. the 1st International Conference on System Development Environments and Factories*, 1989.

P.A. Lindsay. "Formal Reasoning in an IPSE." In: *Software Engineering Environments: Research and Practice.* Ed. K.H. Bennet, Ellis Horwood Ltd, 1989, pp. 235–253.

Current status of development:
Proof assistant and specification support tool largely complete, but still some tidying up needed. A prototype symbolic execution tool has been built, but this is not integrated with the system at present.

Date of project commencement:
September 1985

Date of completion (as a research project):
March 1990

Date of completion (as a product or deliverable):
March 1990 as end of project deliverable. Hopefully sometime later in 1990 as a product.

Intended evolution:
Extension of specification support tool to full BSI standard VDM syntax, possibly also to support other formal specification languages, e.g., Z. Possible further development of the symbolic execution tool. Development as a product, and as a vehicle for formal methods teaching.

Particular strengths and weaknesses:
Strengths: Genericity supports proofs in a wide range of logical systems. "Natural" language proofs appear in mathematical notation, as in maths textbooks. Openness: much of the functionality of the system (e.g., pattern matching) available to user on request. Natural user interface system functions as an electronic "sketch pad", allowing freedom for the user to explore various alternatives and facilitating the discovery of proofs. Controllability: user steers system at all times by selecting an action from a list of (system generated) possible actions. Tactic language: user can write tactics to deal with a lot of the tedious aspects of proof construction. Interface to LaTeX paper copies of proofs/theories/inference rules, etc., can easily be generated for inclusion in LaTeX documents.

Weaknesses: Only supports a subset of the full BSI standard VDM. Single user.

Any additional users of technology (outside of development group):
Interest within the research community in using μral in future research projects. Intended to be used in the teaching of formal methods as from early 1990. A number of software companies and commercial research laboratories have expressed an interest in the system, both for learning about formal methods and for application of formal methods to their work.

Additional remarks:
[None given.]

Murphy

Primary participants (project leader, group members):
Nancy Leveson

Survey contact:
Nancy Leveson
ICS Department, University of California at Irvine, Irvine, CA 92717
Tel: (714) 856-5517
email: leveson@ics.uci.edu

Country (or countries) of origin: USA

Level of effort (person-years, duration):
[Not given.]

Brief description:
A methodology and set of integrated tools for building safety-critical, real-time systems. It spans the entire software life cycle, providing both synthesis and analysis techniques. Murphy includes software hazard analysis, analysis of software requirements specifications, design techniques for safety-critical software, and verification and validation of safety. It spans the life cycle, and information from analysis at one stage is used to guide the rest of the development.

Accomplishments:
– Software hazard analysis; Formal modelling and analysis techniques
– Software Fault Tree Analysis
– Methodology for building safety-critical software
– Analysis of Software requirement specification

Representative published articles or reports:
N. G. Leveson. "Software Safety: Why, What, and How." *ACM Computing Surveys*, June 1986.

N. G. Leveson and J. Stolzy. "Safety Analysis using Petri-Nets," *IEEE TSE*, March 1987.

N. G. Leveson and P. R. Harvey. "Analysing Software Safety." *IEEE TSE*, September 1983.

N. G. Leveson. "Engineering Software for Safety." In *Aerospace Software Engineering*, ed. C. Anderson, AIAA, 1990.

Current status of development:
In progress

Date of project commencement:
 1981

Date of completion (as a research project):
 To be determined

Date of completion (as a product or deliverable):
 To be determined

Intended evolution:
 More requirements analysis including an interface model. Design analysis and verification for safety. Constraint-driven analysis and verification throughout development. Layers of protection.

Particular strengths and weaknesses:
 Emphasizes hazards and safety. Integrates with system safety engineering analyses and risk assessments.

Any additional users of technology (outside of development group):
 Software fault tree analysis: defence projects (e.g., F-16, F-15E, weapons systems), medical systems (e.g., patient monitoring, radiation therapy), nuclear power plants, and so forth. PN analysis: China Lake Naval Weapons Center and Naval post-graduate school. Software hazard analysis, design techniques, etc.: applied to various real-world projects.

Additional remarks:
 [None.]

NRL Hardware Verification

Primary participants (project leader, group members):
 Andrew Moore

Survey contact:
 Andrew Moore
 Code 5542, Naval Research Lab., Washington, DC 20375-5000
 Tel: (202) 767-6698
 email: moore@itd.nrl.navy.mil

Country (or countries) of origin: USA

Level of effort (person-years, duration):
 Approximately 1 person-year

Brief description:
 Project is just getting underway; plans are to attempt verification of security-related properties of specific custom hardware. Specific tool has not yet been chosen.

Accomplishments:
 [To be determined.]

Representative published articles or reports:
 [None yet.]

Current status of development:
 Ongoing, just started.

Date of project commencement:
Fall 1987

Date of completion (as a research project):
To be determined.

Date of completion (as a product or deliverable):
To be determined.

Intended evolution:
[To be determined.]

Particular strengths and weaknesses:
[To be determined.]

Any additional users of technology (outside of development group):
[To be determined.]

Additional remarks:
[None.]

NRL COMSEC SW Verification (ASVT)

Primary participants (project leader, group members):
Andrew Moore

Survey contact:
Andrew Moore
Code 5542, Navel Research Lab., Washington, DC 20375-5000
Tel: (202) 767-6698
email: moore@itd.nrl.navy.mil

Country (or countries) of origin: USA

Level of effort (person-years, duration):
Approximately 1 person-year

Brief description:
Simple voice processing system (abstracted from real system) specified. Split system into red and black parts and proved unencrypted information never entered into black partition when terminal's mode selection dial was set in the cyphertext position.

Accomplishments:
Specified problem in CSP, spec and verified in Gypsy, InaJo/FDM. Developed framework procedure for comparing verification systems in this context.

Representative published articles or reports:
A. P. Moore. "Specification of an example of COMSEC Software Security." NRL Memo Report 6516, July 1989.

A. P. Moore. "Investigating Formal Specification and Verification Techniques for COMSEC Software Security: The ASVT." In *Proc. of 1988 National Computer Security Conference,* Baltimore, MD, 1988.

Current status of development:
Ongoing

Date of project commencement:
Fall 1988

Date of completion (as a research project):
[To be determined.]

Date of completion (as a product or deliverable):
[To be determined.]

Intended evolution:
[To be determined.]

Particular strengths and weaknesses:
[To be determined.]

Any additional users of technology (outside of development group):
[To be determined.]

Additional remarks:
[None.]

OBJ

Primary participants (project leader, group members):
Joseph Goguen, Oxford; J. Meseguer, SRI; T. Winkler, Oxford;
J. Jouannaud, Orsay; K. Futatsugi, ETL Tsukuba.

Survey contact:
Joseph Goguen
PRG, 8-11 Keble Road, Oxford University, Oxford OX1 3QD, UK
Tel: (0865) 54328
email: goguen@prg.ox.ac.uk

Country (or countries) of origin: US, UK, France, Japan.

Level of effort (person-years, duration):
18 years over 10 years.

Brief description:
Specification language with executable and non-executable parts, based on order-sorted equational logic, with generic (parameterized) modules, mix-fix syntax, overloading, views. Executable part based on initial algebra semantics, non-executable part on theories. Implementation based on order-sorted term rewriting. Has pattern matching modules, associative and/or commutative axioms. Fast interpreter (about 400 rewrites per second on Sun 3/60).

Accomplishments:
Used for rapid prototyping, design, specification (e.g., of OBJ and many other systems); used for theorem proving, including VLSI (e.g., CMOS serial adder).

Representative published articles or reports:
J. Goguen and T. Winkler. "Introducing OBJ3." SRI Tech. Report.

"OBJ as a Theorem Prover." In *Current Trends in Hardware Verification and Automated Deduction*, ed. G. Birtwistle and P. A. Subrahmanyam, Springer-Verlag, 1989.

Futatsugi, Goguen, Jouannaud, and Meseguer. "Principles of OBJ2." *POPL,*

1985.

Current status of development:
Mature and stable release of OBJ3

Date of project commencement:
1974

Date of completion (as a research project):
Ongoing

Date of completion (as a product or deliverable):
OBJ3 released early 1989

Intended evolution:
More features will be added to support theorem proving, and the system will extended to the object-oriented paradigm. Meanwhile, there will be further releases with bug fixes, implementation improvements (faster code), and new features; the documentation will be revised accordingly.

Particular strengths and weaknesses:
Strengths: Absolutely rigorous semantics; well-tested, robust implementation; much experience in use; very powerful type system (generics); many small to medium examples are well-documented; industrial experience.

Weaknesses: No existential quantifiers (yet); no states (yet), i.e., purely functional; no well-documented large examples; no compiler.

Any additional users of technology (outside of development group):
OBJ3 released to over 75 sites; major Alvey project on application of OBJ1 produced several industrial studies (to appear in book); at least five other implementations of OBJ, including one that is commercially supported.

Additional remarks:
This system is very unusual in that it integrates specification, design, prototyping, verification (and maybe programming—if we had a compiler for a sublanguage) in a *single* system having a *single* rigorous underlying logic, namely (first-order) order-sorted equational logic.

We may soon organize a user's meeting and/or a user's newsletter.

OSU-CIS Reusable Software Research Group

Primary participants (project leader, group members):
Faculty: William F. Ogden, Bruce W. Weide, Stuart H. Zweben
Graduate Students: About 10 Ph.D. students in Computer and Information Science

Survey contact:
Bruce W. Weide, Dept. of Computer and Information Science,
The Ohio State University, 2036 Neil Ave. Mall, Columbus, OH 43210-1277
Tel: 614-292-1517
fax: 614-292-9021
e-mail: weide@cis.ohio-state.edu

Country (or countries) of origin: USA

Level of effort (person-years, duration):
Funding from the National Science Foundation and the Applied - August 1990. We expect the work to continue for the foreseeable future.

Brief description:
The Group's mission is to address various technical problems impeding progress toward software reuse. The overall objective is to demonstrate the practicality of formally specified, verified, and efficient reusable software components.

Our work is based on a comprehensive approach to reusability. We have defined a programming language, RESOLVE, that permits us to write formal specifications of reusable components, to verify them, and to build efficient implementations for them. We are currently implementing a first version of RESOLVE and exploring a variety of issues in the process: guidelines for designing reusable components, influences of reuse on programming language design and implementation (and vice versa), architectural considerations for the run-time environment of programs built from reusable components, component quality assessment, mechanical modular verification, formalization of testing issues for reusable components, and many related topics.

Accomplishments:
We have written formal specifications for a few dozen reusable components (based largely on the functionality of basic data structures and algorithms). These designs have been influenced by a set of general design guidelines for reusable components that were discovered in the process, and that are direct products of the use of formalism and abstraction in specifications. We have also developed and used proof rules for our language to verify (manually) the correctness of component implementations involving non-trivial data structures and algorithms. Finally, we have demonstrated and solved several problems related to testing of reusable components and have shown some interesting connections between verification and testing in the reusable component framework.

Representative published articles or reports:
Muralidharan, S., and Weide, B.W., "On Distributing Programs Built from Reusable Software Components." Dept. of Comp. and Inf. Sci., Ohio State Univ., OSU-CISRC-11/88-TR36, Nov. 1988, 32 pp., submitted for publication.

Harms, D.E., and Weide, B.W., "Types, Copying, and Swapping: Their ... " Dept. of Comp. and Inf. Sci., Ohio State Univ., OSU-CISRC-3/89-TR13, Mar. 1989, 22 pp., submitted for publication.

Zweben, S.H., et al., "Exploratory Studies of the Software Testing Methods Used by Novice Programmers." in *Software Engineering Education*, N.E. Gibbs, ed., Springer-Verlag, July 1989, pp. 169-188.

[Remainder of survey not submitted for OSU-CIS Reusable Software Research Group.]

pc-nqthm

Primary participants (project leader, group members):
Matt Kaufmann

Survey contact:
Dr. Matt Kaufmann
Computational Logic Inc., 1717 W. Sixth St., Suite 290, Austin, TX 78703
Tel: (512) 322-9951
Fax: (512) 322-0656
email: kaufmann@cli.com

Country (or countries) of origin: USA

Level of effort (person-years, duration):
Rough estimate 1.5 person-years over 2 3/4 years.

Brief description:
This "proof-checker" is loaded on top of the Boyer-Moore Theorem Prover, which is a prover for a logic that resembles pure Lisp. The user can give commands at a low level (such as deleting a hypothesis, diving to a subterm of the current term, expanding a function call, or applying a rewrite rule) or at a high level (such as invoking the Boyer-Moore Theorem Prover). Commands also exist for display-ing useful information (such as printing the current hypotheses and conclusion, displaying the currently applicable rewrite rules, or showing the current abbrevi-ations) and for controlling the progress of the proof (such as undoing a specified number of commands, changing goals, or disabling certain rewrite rules). A no-tion of "macro commands" lets the user create compound commands, roughly in the spirit of the tactics and tacticals of LCF and its descendants. An on-line help facility is provided, and a user's manual exists.

As with a variety of proof-checking systems, this system is goal-directed: a proof is completed when the main goal and all subgoals have been proved. Upon completion of an interactive proof, the lemma with its proof may be stored as a Boyer-Moore "event" that can be added to the user's current library of definitions and lemmas. This event can later be replayed in "batch mode." Partial proofs can also be stored.

Accomplishments:
This system has been used to check theorems stating the correctness of a transi-tive closure program, a Towers of Hanoi program, a ground resolution prover, a compiler, irrationality of the square root of 2, an algorithm of Gries for finding the largest "true square" submatrix of a boolean matrix, the exponent two version of Ramsey's Theorem, the Shroeder-Bernstein theorem, Koenig's tree lemma, and others.

The name "nqthm" is sometimes given to the Boyer-Moore Theorem Prover, while "pc" stands for "proof-checker". The name "pc-nqthm" thus stands for "an interactive enhancement to the Boyer-Moore Theorem Prover."

Representative published articles or reports:
The first report below is a detailed user's manual, including soundness arguments. The second extends this by describing an extension of the system which admits free variables, an important addition for doing full first-order reasoning. The

third describes a major proof effort carried out using the system.

Matt Kaufmann. *A User's Manual for an Interactive Enhancement to the Boyer-Moore Theorem Prover.* Technical Report 19, Computational Logic, Inc., May, 1988.

Matt Kaufmann. *Addition of Free Variables to an Interactive Enhancement of the Boyer-Moore Theorem Prover.* Technical Report 42, Computational Logic, Inc., May, 1989.

William D. Young. "A Verified Code Generator." Ph.D. Thesis, University of Texas at Austin, 1988.

Current status of development:
A publicly available, completed version has been available via ftp from rascal.ics.utexas.edu since May 1988, and is described in Technical Report 19 (Computational Logic, Inc.). A more recent (and quite stable) version is currently in use at Computational Logic.

Date of project commencement:
c. November 1986

Date of completion (as a research project):
May 1988, for the first (and publicly available) version. The version currently in use at Computational Logic was completed in July 1989.

Date of completion (as a product or deliverable):
Same as above.

Intended evolution:
Boyer and Moore will probably release a new version of their theorem prover this fall (1989). Within two months of that time, I expect to release a new version of pc-nqthm which corresponds closely to what is currently in use at Computational Logic, Inc. Additional extensions may be developed and made publicly available from time to time. In particular, we are currently investigating the addition of full first-order quantification and set theory to the Boyer-Moore logic and prover, and have begun to develop some preliminary capabilities in pc-nqthm in these directions.

Particular strengths and weaknesses:
I believe that this system is unsurpassed in its ease of use by people who are not researchers in automated reasoning. Several factors contribute to this opinion:

- A detailed user's manual, carefully layered so that the first 11 pages (which include an example) suffice to get someone started.
- The Boyer-Moore prover available for a primitive "prove" command.
- An on-line help facility constructed in two layers, so that the user can either get basic command descriptions with examples or else rather complete specifications of commands.
- Primitive commands which provide much freedom in moving around in the proof.
- A capability to extend the system by "macro commands" (patterned after LCF's "tactics" and "tacticals"), which range from simple combinations of primitive commands to those which have complex heuristics.

- Robustness (e.g., in handling bad input by the user).
- Full integration into the Boyer-Moore system. Thus completed interactive proofs become completed Boyer-Moore "events" that can be replayed. Also, Boyer-Moore libraries of theorems may therefore be used in pc-nqthm.

A second major strength of the system relates to soundness. The logic is exactly the Boyer-Moore computational logic, carefully described in their book *A Computational Logic Handbook*. The design of the system implies that terms certified as theorems by the system are indeed theorems in this logic. The implementation of the system has been done with great care to try to ensure that it implements this design. And although the system is extensible by macro commands, these commands expand into primitive commands which must ultimately be accepted by the system. Hence, it is not possible for someone using the system to make it unsound.

A weakness of the system is the same as the weakness of nearly all existing verification or theorem proving systems: more user interaction is required than might be desired. One might try to argue that this system allows a rather painless kind of interaction, both because of the clean design and inclusion of appropriate commands and because the Boyer-Moore prover is available to take care of some of the details. However, this ease of use may encourage the user to put insufficient effort into structuring his proofs effectively. More precisely, the Boyer-Moore prover shines in those settings where the user has proved appropriate rewrite rules to help automate the process. The pc-nqthm enhancement of the Boyer-Moore prover allows the user to avoid thinking too hard about proving such rules, at least at first, since he can do manual proofs that do not require such rewrite rules. But good rewrite rules become very important in large proof developments, so such a user may lose in the long run.

Another weakness of the system is that the Boyer-Moore logic does not have first-order quantification (which can be very desirable for certain specifications). A recent enhancement allows the user to define notions that involve first-order quantifiers, but still one cannot reason about the quantifiers in as direct a way as one might like. Just how inconvenient that restriction is remains to be seen.

Any additional users of technology (outside of development group):
Although there have been requests for information on this system and how to obtain it, all the major proof efforts which use pc-nqthm at this time seem to be happening at Computational Logic, Inc. Current uses of this system include formalization of floating point arithmetic as well as program verification and verification of hardware, compilers, and distributed systems.

Additional remarks:
Even though I have some pride in this system, I believe that the difficulty in proving theorems using this or any other existing system is often underestimated. I would encourage those who are interested in applying this technology to Formal Methods work to try some examples. Those who are interested in trying pc-nqthm are welcome to write to me (Matt Kaufmann) for information.

Penelope (Ada Verification)

Primary participants (project leader, group members):
Wolfgang Polak, David Guaspari, Carla Marceau, Norman Ramsey, C. Douglas
Harper, Doug Weber, Pietro Cenciarelli and Maureen Stillman (project manager)

Survey contact:
Maureen Stillman, Odyssey Research Associates,
301A Harris Dates Dr., Ithaca, NY 14850-1313
Tel: (607) 277-2020
email: oravax!maureen@cu-arpa.cs.cornell.edu

Country (or countries) of origin: USA

Level of effort (person-years, duration):
18 person-years over 3 calendar years

Brief description:
The goal of the project was to develop a sound mathematical basis for verifying
sequential Ada programs and to implement it in an editor. The user of the editor
is able to develop the specification, code and proof of correctness concurrently.
We have adopted the Larch two-tiered approach to specification. The approach
we have taken to verification is to develop predicate transformers based on a
denotational semantics for Ada. A verification condition is generated from the
specification and the program text. A proof editor and extensive simplification
capabilities are available to aid the user in program development and proof.

Accomplishments:

We have developed the specification language based on Larch called Larch/Ada
and an extensible technique for defining its semantics. Predicate transformers
have been defined for our subset of (sequential) Ada. To demonstrate the validity of our techniques we have proved the soundness of these transformers for
a small, but difficult subset. We have defined what it means for a program to
satisfy its specification when a two-tiered approach to specification is used. The
Penelope editor implements the basic control constructs (if statement, loops,
exit statement), arrays and records, packages, global variables, user-defined exceptions, built-in arithmetic functions, and user-defined subprograms (including
recursive programs). Some constructs supported by the theory (e.g., go to and
case statements, constraint checking) have not been implemented.

We have used the Penelope system to formally specify and verify Bell-LaPadula
security invariants for a small set of kernel subprograms from the interprocess
communication code of the Army Secure Operating System (ASOS).

Representative published articles or reports:
Norman Ramsey. "Developing Formally Verified Ada Programs." In *Proceed-
ings of the Fifth International Conference on Software Specification and Design*,
Pittsburgh, May 1989.

Carla Marceau and C. Douglas Harper. "An Interactive Approach to Ada Verification." *NCSC Proceedings*, October 1989.

Wolfgang Polak. "A Technique for Defining Predicate Transformers." Submitted
to *TOPLAS*, available as Odyssey Research Associates TR 17-4, 1989.

Current status of development:

Reports on the formal basis of the system and the Penelope Verification System software were delivered to the project sponsor, Rome Air Force Development Center (RADC), in August 1989.

Date of project commencement:
August 19, 1986

Date of completion (as a research project):
September 19, 1989

Date of completion (as a product or deliverable):
The final deliverables were delivered on September 19, 1989.

Intended evolution:
Future R&D work will include the theory and implementation of private types, a library facility, generics and tasking. The theory for constraint checking has been completed, and we will work on the implementation. Penelope also needs static semantic checking of the Larch/Ada specification language and further work on simplification of verification conditions.

Particular strengths and weaknesses:
Strengths: Penelope allows the user to develop programs and proofs concurrently and to reuse proof steps as the program changes. For example, it is often trivial to reprove a program if an input condition is replaced by the raising of an exception.

Weaknesses: Penelope is a research prototype, not a production quality system. Penelope does not support verification of full Ada; for example, generics and tasking are not supported.

Any additional users of technology (outside of development group):
No.

Additional remarks:
For further information or to be included on the mailing list, please contact Maureen Stillman at above address.

RAISE

Primary participants (project leader, group members):
CRI, Denmark; STL, England.

Survey contact:
Howard Gill
STL address: London Rd, Harlow, Essex CM17 9NA, England.
Tel: +44-279-29531-XT3344
email: mhg@stl.stc.co.uk
or
Henrik Maegaard
CRI Address: Bregneroscwj 144, DK - 3460 Birkeroed, Denmark.
Tel: +45-45-822100
email: Henrik Maegaard@cpe.csd.cri.dk

Country (or countries) of origin: England and Denmark

Level of effort (person-years, duration):
20 people 5 years

Brief description:

RAISE is a formal specification language, RSL, an associated method, a tool set and a formally defined implementation relation. RSL has a formally defined semantics which unifies applicative, concurrent and sequential styles of specification. It has a defined set of proof rules which cover the full language. It is a wide spectrum language which encompasses axiomatic specification and implementation level descriptions. The axiomatic techniques encourage an object-oriented style of specification.

The tool set consists of a number of editors based on the CSG (Cornell Synthesizer Generator) tool, mainly, the Structure editor, Development editor, Justification editor. Several proof tools are based on Prolog, mainly, the implementation condition generator, the simplifier, the animator and the proof transformer. The tools access a versioned data base, currently Oracle.

The method is a rigorous one which uses the implementaion condition generator to generate proof obligations from the implementation relation assertion. These are discharged by the justification editor using the simplifier and the proof transformer.

Accomplishments:

A prototype system is operating on Sun workstations. A description of a mainframe system architecture has been completed with three levels of abstractions and partial proof of correctness.

Training and technology transfer materials have been created.

The semantics and proof rules have been fully documented.

Representative published articles or reports:

C.W. George and R.E. Milne. "Specifying and Refining Concurrent Systems – An Example From the RAISE Project." *Proceedings of the Third RRG/BCS-FACS Refinement Workshop*, January 1990 to appear.

Current status of development:

A toolset mounted on an Oracle database is available. A book on the language and method is being prepared.

Date of project commencement:

April 1985.

Date of completion (as a research project):

March 1990.

Date of completion (as a product or deliverable):

Intended evolution:

To use RAISE on large scale user trials over the next two years and then prepare draft ISO standards proposals.

Particular strengths and weaknesses:

Strengths: Usable formulation of concurrency. Documented semantics. Documented Proof Rules. Method Document.

Weaknesses: Editors based on CSG. Large number of proof rules.

Any additional users of technology (outside of development group):

ICL

Additional remarks:
None.

Romulus

Primary participants (project leader, group members):
Tanya Korelsky, Carl Eichenlaub, Bruce Esrig, Carl Klapper, Marcos Lam, Daryl McCullough, Garrel Pottinger, Owen Rambow, and David Rosenthal

Survey contact:
Tanya Korelsky, Odyssey Research Associates,
301A Harris Dates Dr., Ithaca, NY 14850-1313
Tel: (607) 277-2020
oravax!tanya@cu-arpa.cs.cornell.edu

Country (or countries) of origin: USA

Level of effort (person-years, duration):
333 staff months (for base contract and extension)

Brief description:
Romulus is a computer security modelling environment developed at Odyssey Research for RADC. As part of the Romulus effort, we have developed a theory of security called *hook-up security*, as well as a methodology and tools enabling a user to create system models, specify their functionality, perform security analyses on the models, and prove security properties about them. Hook-up security is an information flow theory which is used to determine whether high level information can leak to low level users. It is *composible* in that the security of a complex, multi-component model can be established by proving the security of each component.

The Romulus system consists of:

- a *Security Modelling Assistant* which permits the construction and analysis of a system using a structured data-flow description. Methods are provided to establish the security of a system, by instantiating components which have been proved secure, by establishing the security of manifestly secure components, and by using the hook-up theorem. A natural language text generator is used to summarize the models and for data-flow analysis.
- a *Specification Language Interface* for constructing specifications, proving theorems, and generating sufficient properties that a specification could satisfy to be secure.
- an *Extensible Theorem Prover Environment* for developing new inference rules, managing theories, and constructing the proofs.

Accomplishments:
- the development of a new theory of computer security
- the implementation of an expressive specification language
- the implementation of an extensible, higher-order constructive logic theorem prover
- a graphical system modelling environment which is linked with a formal semantics

Representative published articles or reports:

Daryl McCullough. "Specifications for Multi-Level Security and a Hook-Up Property." In *Proceedings of the IEEE Symposium on Security and Privacy,* p. 161-166, 1987.

Ulysses Staff. "Ulysses: A Computer-Security Modelling Environment." In *Proceedings of the 11th National Computer Security Conference,* September, 1988.

James Hook and Garrel Pottinger. *Ulysses Theories: The Modular Implementation of Mathematics.* Odyssey Tech Report TR 11-14, February, 1989.

Current status of development:
[Not given.]

Date of project commencement:
It is being ported from the Symbolics to the Sun.

Date of completion (as a research project):
April 24, 1985

Date of completion (as a product or deliverable):
Base Contract: July 31, 1989. Extension: April 24, 1990

Intended evolution:
We would like to adapt it to handle other areas of security.

Particular strengths and weaknesses:
The strengths of our approach include the expressiveness and flexibility of our specification language and theorem prover, and the combination of rigour and heuristics in our security methodology. The major weakness is the slowness of theorem proving and the overhead involved in maintaining rigour while improving the functionality.

Any additional users of technology (outside of development group):
It has not yet been released.

Additional remarks:
[None.]

Rose Common Lisp, RCL.

Primary participants (project leader, group members):
Matt Kaufmann, Robert L. Akers, Larry Smith.

Survey contact:
Dr. Matt Kaufmann
Computational Logic Inc., 1717 W. Sixth St., Suite 290, Austin, TX 78703
Tel: (512) 322-9951
Fax: (512) 322-0656
email: kaufmann@cli.com

Country (or countries) of origin: USA

Level of effort (person-years, duration):
Approximately, 0.8 person-years over 11 months.

Brief description:
This is a system for reasoning about programs written in a language which we

intend to meet the definition requirements for a subset of Common Lisp. The existing prototype system is actually a translator from definitions in this language to definitions in the Boyer-Moore logic. The basic idea is to translate Common Lisp definitions into definitions in the Boyer-Moore logic, with a minimum of change. That is, we wish the translated definition to be structurally similar to the original definition, in order to make reasoning about the programs as simple as possible.

The current prototype supports a number of primitive Lisp functions such as arithmetic and list processing functions. It also includes a number of programming constructs, some outside the realm of Pure Lisp: special variables, non-local return constructs CATCH and THROW (and BLOCK and RETURN-FROM), LET (local binding), SETQ (assignment), PROG (sequencing and GOTO), property lists, DEFMACRO (a facility for defining macros), and a Zetalisp-like iterative loop construct (written using the RCL DEFMACRO facility).

Accomplishments:

Various small examples have been worked, including proofs of partial correctness of various iterative programs such as an integer square root program, factorial, all-subsequences, linear-time intersection (using property lists). Small examples have also been worked to demonstrate the feasibility of reasoning about constructs which are not purely functional, such as THROW and SETQ.

Work is under way on a definition and proof of some correctness properties of an incremental development manager for a database of n-branching tree objects.

Representative published articles or reports:

The system is still under development. A prototype is documented in Computational Logic Internal Note 110, "A Verification System for a Subset of Common Lisp: A Progress Report," January 1989. The underlying proof system is pc-nqthm, Kaufmann's interactive enhancement of the Boyer-Moore prover (nqthm). A user's manual for the Boyer-Moore prover can be found in the book *A Computational Logic Handbook*, published by Academic Press, 1988. A user's manual for pc-nqthm is Computational Logic Technical Report 19, "A User's Manual for an Interactive Enhancement to the Boyer-Moore Theorem Prover," May 1988.

Current status of development:

A prototype is complete and development of the next version is well under way.

Date of project commencement:

October 1988.

Date of completion (as a research project):

The next version should be ready in a month or two, but a number of improvements are anticipated in future versions. So the "date of completion," whether as a research project or as a product or deliverable, is rather fluid.

Date of completion (as a product or deliverable):

See above.

Intended evolution:

The current prototype and anticipated next version only address partial correctness (roughly, verification of properties of programs in the sense that these properties hold under the assumption that the computations in question terminate without error). We intend to add a capability to reason about total correctness as well. The main idea is to translate Lisp definitions into definitions in the Boyer-Moore logic, possibly with extra arguments and (loosely speaking) results to deal with special variables and other parts of the state. Over time we intend to add things to the user interface so that tools other than the raw Boyer-Moore prover (even enhanced with Kaufmann's interactive enhancement pc-nqthm) are available. For example, entry and exit specs and verification condition generation might be added to the system. An assessment of goals is in progress.

Particular strengths and weaknesses:
A main strength is that the underlying proof system (pc-nqthm, Kaufmann's interactive enhancement of the Boyer-Moore prover) combines a state-of-the-art automated inference system (the Boyer-Moore prover) with a flexible and moderately pleasant interface. We believe that another strength is that the objects about which we reason (Boyer-Moore functions) will be closer in structure to the original code than current verification condition approaches.

A potential weakness of our approach is that, to develop a useful system, we intend to omit certain features of the Common Lisp language, notably destructive operations on CONS cells (like RPLACA), multiple values, readtables and other fancy I/O features, SET (which, unlike SETQ, computes the variable to be assigned to), and perhaps packages (though we may provide a rudimentary capability).

At this stage the user interface is quite primitive. We hope to make improvements along these lines, though we expect that some ability to use pc-nqthm (see above) will be necessary to make effective use of this system.

Another weakness is that ambiguities in the Common Lisp manual will be resolved in our language definition, and hence we will not necessarily be able to guarantee that all Common Lisp implementations will behave in agreement with the theorems proved. However, we hope to make our subset be in agreement with at least one implementation of Common Lisp.

Any additional users of technology (outside of development group):
None at this stage.

Additional remarks:
We believe it is important to transfer the technology that we ultimately develop. Therefore we will carefully document the final system so that it is accessible to Lisp programmers outside of Computational Logic, Inc. This documentation (some of which will be highly tutorial) together with existing documentation on NQTHM and its interactive enhancement PC-NQTHM should make formal methods more accessible to the Common Lisp community. The code will ultimately be written in RCL, in a manner such that we expect it to run correctly on any Common Lisp implementation, including of course our implementation of RCL. We should emphasize that it will probably be a couple of years or so before the system has progressed to the point where we feel comfortable about releasing it for external use.

SAFEMOS

Primary participants (project leader, group members):
Inmos, SRI, Oxford University, Cambridge University

Survey contact:
David May
Inmos plc, Bristol
or
Mike Gordon
SRI, Suite 23 Millers Yard, Cambridge CB2 1RQ
Tel: +44 223 324146
Fax: +44 223 460402
email: mjcg@computer-lab.cambridge.ac.uk

Country (or countries) of origin: UK

Level of effort (person-years, duration):
5–6 person-years, 3 years duration

Brief description:
To design and verify a system consisting of a real-time application program running via a verified compiler on a verified microprocessor. Theorem proving (hardware and software) to be done using HOL.

Accomplishments:
Not available

Representative published articles or reports:
Not available

Current status of development:
Not started

Date of project commencement:
Fall 1989

Date of completion (as a research project):
Late 1992

Date of completion (as a product or deliverable):
[Not available.]

Intended evolution:
Very simple prototype to be completed in first year, final design of hardware and software to be based on this. Result of project is hoped to be a hardware, software and verification base for building correct real-time systems.

Particular strengths and weaknesses:
To be discovered.

Any additional users of technology (outside of development group):
[None yet.]

Additional remarks:
[None.]

SPADE/SPARK

Primary participants (project leader, group members):
Bernard Carré, D.L. Clutterbuck, I.M. O'Neill.

Survey contact:
Bernard Carré
Program Validation Limited, 26 Queen's Terrace, Southampton SO1 1BQ, UK
Tel: (703) 330001

Country (or countries) of origin: UK

Level of effort (person-years, duration):
Over 20 person-years. Gradual evolution since 1980

Brief description:
A set of tools for static code analysis, path functions and verification condition generation, and proof of programs in annotated subsets of some "standard" imperative languages: Pascal, Ada, Z8002, 68000 and other assembly codes.

Accomplishments:
Being used successfully in industry, during both program development and retrospective verification.

Representative published articles or reports:
I.M. O'Neill, D.L. Clutterbuck, P.F. Farrow, P.G. Summers and W.C. Dolman. "The formal verification of safety-critical assembly code." In *Proc. IFAC SAFECOMP Conference,* 1988 ("Safety of Computer Control Systems"), Pergamon Press, pp. 115-120.

Current status of development:
Principal current developments are in proof checker and Ada (subset) support.

Date of project commencement:
c. 1980

Date of completion (as a research project):
Still evolving

Date of completion (as a product or deliverable):
First industrial product: end of 1985

Intended evolution:
The most recent tools are formally-based, but much work remains to be done on formal definition/refinement of components — this task being most substantial with the SPARK (SPADE Ada Kernel) language and support tools. Attempts are being made also to integrate the techniques with standard "design" methodologies (e.g., JSD and HOOD) and to provide support for successive refinements of designs/code from Z or VDM specifications.

Particular strengths and weaknesses:
Applicable to sequential programs only, and in particular, to annotated language subsets for which dynamic semantics can be modelled relatively simply. On the other hand, the subsets used are quite adequate for many safety-critical applications (e.g., avionics). The tools are popular in industry, where they have found many errors in systems which had been "throughly" tested, and commissioned.

Any additional users of technology (outside of development group):

Approximately 30 copies are in use in the UK, including MoD and some civil safety-critical projects. Over 300 people have been trained (a one-week course) in the use of SPADE.

Additional remarks:
None yet.

SpecBox

Primary participants (project leader, group members):
Adelard

Survey contact:
Robin Bloomfield
Adelard, 28 Rhondda Grove, London, E3 5AP, UK
Tel: (44) 1-318-7579
Fax: (44) 1-852-4738
e-mail: reb@ed.lfcs.ac.uk

Country (or countries) of origin: UK

Level of effort (person-years, duration):
[Not stated.]

Brief description:
SpecBox is a tool for supporting the construction and analysis of specification/text written in BSI/VDM. It checks for conformance to language definition as well as some semantic analyses—well-formedness rules.

Accomplishments:
It is a product, supported. PC version provides an entry level tool for VDM users. Vax and Workstation versions available for large industrial specifications

Representative published articles or reports:
P. K. D Froome, B. Q. Monahan and R. E. Bloomfield. "SpecBox - a checker for VDM specifications." *Proc. Second Int. Conf. on Software Engineering for Real Time Systems*, Cirencester, UK, September 1989.

Current status of development:
PC, Vax and Workstation available

Date of project commencement:
1988

Date of completion (as a research project):
Not available

Date of completion (as a product or deliverable):
Ongoing

Intended evolution:
Increased type checking; interface to static analysis tools; proof obligation generation.

Particular strengths and weaknesses:
Specified in BSI/VDM; command implementation; good user interface.

Any additional users of technology (outside of development group):
Yes. In use at several industrial and academic sites.

Additional remarks:
None.

Specification driven hardware design

Primary participants (project leader, group members):
Graham Birtwistle, Brian Graham, Konrad Slind.

Survey contact:
Graham Birtwistle, Dept. of Computer Science
University of Calgary, 2500 University Dr., Calgary, Alberta T2N 1N4
Tel: (403) 220-6055
Fax: (403) 284-4707
email: graham@cpsc.ucalgary.ca

Country (or countries) of origin: Canada, NSERC funding

Level of effort (person-years, duration):
3 elapsed years

Brief description:
Examination of how specification and proof can drive the design of a VLSI Chip.
The vehicle chosen was Landin's 1960s abstract SECD chip which is well known
and has fully developed semantics. The chip has been laid out (25,000 transitions,
custom, off-chip memory). The microcode was generated auotmatically from the
top level specification by transformation, given a little architectural insight. The
proof is compiled across several layers of abstraction.

Accomplishments:
- A program which takes HOL proofs into LSI net lst format for gate array
  fabrication
- SECD design proof completed (assuming that garbage collection does not
  take place) – SECD chip fabricated twice (version 1 had a layout flaw:
  the layout was not isomorphic to the specification.)
- Library of specifications and verifications of all parts in the hierarchy.

Representative published articles or reports:
B. Graham and G. Birtwistle. "The design and top level specification of an SECD
chip." In *Proc. 1989 Cornell MSI Workshop*, LNCS, Springer Verlag, 1989.

G. Birtwistle, B. Graham, T. Melham and R. Schediwy. "Hardware verification
by formal proof." *Canadian Conference on Electrical and Computer Engineering*,
Vancouver, pp. 379–384, 1988 (Invited).

K. Slind, G. Birtwistle, M. Hermann, and T. Simpson. "From logic to layout:
transforming HOL specifications into gate array netlists." *Canadian Conference
on Electrical and Computer Engineering*, Montreal, p. 352–355, 1989.

G. Birtwistle and B. Liblong. "Hierarchical Specification and Composition in
VLSI Design." *Canadian Conference on Electrical and Computer Engineering*,
Montreal, p. 363–366, 1989 (Invited.)

B. Graham and G. Birtwistle. "Verifying an SECD chip in HOL." *IFIP Workshop* on *Applied Formal Methods For Correct VLSI Design*, Leuven, Belgium, 1989.

G. Birtwistle and P. Subrahmanyam. *Hardware specification, verification, and synthesis.* Kluwer, 1988.

G. Birtwistle and P. Subrahmanyam. *Current trends in hardware verification and automated deduction.* Springer-Verlag, 1989.

B. Graham, S. Williams, G. Birtwistle, J. Joyce, and B. Liblong. *The MOSSIM specification of the SECD design.* Technical Report 89/341/03, University of Calgary. Prepared under Contract No. W2213-8-6362/ 01-SS with the Department of National Defence, 1989.

Current status of development:
90 per cent complete

Date of project commencement:
November 1, 1986

Date of completion (as a research project):
October 31, 1989

Date of completion (as a product or deliverable):
Early 1990

Intended evolution:
Originally, the proof and design were to go hand-in-hand, and there were to be two or three design iterations. This plan was destroyed when a main participant quit. It took a year to get several others up to speed. This destroyed our chances of carrying out the first part of the plan. We did the chip first.

Particular strengths and weaknesses:
Strengths: We will have a working chip which will run as a co-processor to a Sun running downloaded LispKit programs in early 1990.

Weakness: We haven't carried out the design as pushed by specs. We found out later several design features that have made the proof harder.

Any additional users of technology (outside of development group):
We have a complete documentation of the design in a Mossim notation. This is being used by three universities as a testbed for Design for Test. Cambridge, UK, will get a copy of the chip and its board. Canadian industry has expressed no interest.

Additional remarks:
The proof work has been long and hard. We will not complete a full proof in this project—although the chip has a garbage collector, we give a proof under the constraint that it is not called. A full proof will take another year. Perhaps the best result of the effort is the development of a team of four people who have now completed their apprenticeship in hardware verification.

SpecTra

Primary participants (project leader, group members):
Susan Gerhart, C. Zaniolo, K. Greene.

Survey contact:
Susan Gerhart, MCC
Software Technology Program, 3500 West Balcones Center Dr., Austin, TX 78759
email: gerhart%sw.mcc.com@mcc.com

Country (or countries) of origin: USA

Level of effort (person-years, duration):
.6 person-years to date

Brief description:
Just started. Specification development and validation shell. Theorem prover and language components to be inserted. Novel informal ⟶ formal support through issue-based methods, upon hypertext technology, also used for proof, test, and animation management. Also some components for symbolic execution based on declarative language technology. Intended base is multi-processor workstations.

Accomplishments:
Just started. Have proposal and plan. Motivation is transfer of formal methods to US commercial industry.

Representative published articles or reports:
None yet. Background: Hypertext survey, J. Conklin, Computer LDL, PAL Tech Reports MCC ACT project gIBIS, GERM TRs, MCC STD "Upstream Testing, Analysis, Verification." S. Gerhart, TAVL.

Current status of development:
Just started. LDL, gIBIS components in proprietary use.

Date of project commencement:
1989

Date of completion (as a research project):
[Not available.]

Date of completion (as a product or deliverable):
[Not available.]

Intended evolution:
Integrate language (e.g., VDM), theorem prover (e.g., EVES), language interpreter (to be done), and issue base (MCC's GERM). Apply to MCC company projects to explore use of specs for prototyping, also to critical systems developed externally.

Particular strengths and weaknesses:
Strengths: Novel support for non-formal aspects of formal methods (also safety logs); new technology for theorem proving, execution; method-oriented; integrated with other SE processes.

Weaknesses: Dependent upon external theorem provers, spec. lang.

Any additional users of technology (outside of development group):
None yet.

Additional remarks:

To be accompanied by Applied Formal Methods Testbed which will support training, tools imported from outside, experiments of industrial interest.

Tektronix

Primary participants (project leader, group members):

Software Architectures Program: Norm Delisle (Program Leader), David Garlan, Mayer Schwartz, Mike Spivey

Survey contact:

David Garlan, Computer Research Laboratory,
M/S 50-662, Tektronix, Inc., Beaverton, OR 97077
Tel: (503) 627-1847
Fax: (503) 627-5502 – include delivery station 50-662
email: garlan@crl.labs.tek.com

Country (or countries) of origin: USA

Level of effort (person-years, duration):

4–5 people, since 1987

Brief description:

The Software Architectures Program has been investigating the application of formal methods to industry for the past 3 years. Our primary emphasis has been the use of formal methods to gain insight into systems architecture, and to create formal models that can serve as reusable frameworks for a wide variety of products. In that context we are evaluating the suitability of existing formal notations for defining software architectures, and in particular we are investigating the relationship between formal specification and object-oriented design. Although our research is not dependent on particular notations, we have used CSP, Z, and Unity in our work.

Accomplishments:

We have conducted several case studies with product groups to develop formal models of instrumentation software. These have resulted in numerous formal specifications of non-toy systems, including oscilloscopes, user interface frameworks, and a hypertext reference model. We have also built two environments for developing and manipulating specifications. The first of these is a graphical environment for constructing and executing CSP programs. The second is an environment for developing Z documents—the Z Engineering Environment—which includes a WYSIWIG editor for Z, a type checker, and some rudimentary analysis tools.

Representative published articles or reports:

N. Delisle and D. Garlan. "Formally Specifying Electronic Instruments." In *Proceedings of the Fifth International Workshop on Software Specification and Design,* May 1989.

N. Delisle and D. Garlan. "A Formal Specification of an Oscilloscope." Technical Report CR-88-13, Computer Research Laboratory, Tektronix, Inc., P.O. Box 500, Beaverton, OR 97077, Oct. 1988.

N. Delisle and M. Schwartz "A Programming Environment for CSP." In *Proceed-*

ings of ACM SIGSOFT/SIGPLAN Software Engineering Symposium on Practical Software Development Environments, SIGPLAN Notices 22(1), Jan. 1987.

Current status of development:
This is an on-going research project.

Date of project commencement:
January 1987.

Date of completion (as a research project):
As an on-going research project, it has no fixed completion date.

Date of completion (as a product or deliverable):
Not applicable.

Intended evolution:
We expect the use of formal methods in industry to continue to grow. We intend to evolve our research to meet that challenge.

Particular strengths and weaknesses:
Strengths: Our work is based on solid experience with engineers building real products.

Weaknesses: Since most of our results are based on case studies, it remains to be seen if they are generally applicable outside this industrial context.

Any additional users of technology (outside of development group):
Several product groups are using the formal specifications developed through our research.

Additional remarks:
None.

Trusted Systems Development

Primary participants (project leader, group members):
George Dinolt, John McHugh, and others.

Survey contact:
George Dinolt, Ford Aerospace Corp.
email: Dinolt@WDL45.fac.ford.com
or
John McHugh
Computational Logic Inc., 3500 Westgate Dr., Suite 204, Durham, NC 27705
email: McHugh@cli.com

Country (or countries) of origin: USA

Level of effort (person-years, duration):
1–2 person-years at FAC, 6 person-months at CLI

Brief description:
Initial effort has produced a simple, trusted file server in which security is a consequence of functional correctness. System is specified as a mapping from file IDs to files where a file is status plus mapping from block ID to data block. Implementation is in terms of disk, modified as array of blocks with a block being an array of bytes. Proven Gypsy transliterated to C and runs on Sun hardware.

Accomplishments:
Successful use of history based security policy with code proof. Verified running program (albeit a small one) as a step in a planned evolution towards high performance distributed systems.

Representative published articles or reports:
G. W. Dinolt and J. C. Williams. "Formal Model of a Trusted File Server." *Proc. 1989 IEEE Symp. on Security and Privacy*, IEEE Computer Society, Washington, 1989, pp. 157-166.

Current status of development:
Continuing at FAC under IR and D

Date of project commencement:
November 1987

Date of completion (as a research project):
Ongoing

Date of completion (as a product or deliverable):
Not available

Intended evolution:
Current system operates sequentially on a request–response basis. Security policy is exact match. Performance evolution includes caching, adding pseudo parallelism (tasking) and multiprocessing. Capability evolution includes the addition of a grade server for an MLS policy and a view server for providing an O.S. (Unix, VMS, MSDOS, etc.) interface.

Particular strengths and weaknesses:
The ability to write machine proven code is a plus. The GVE is a minus. The absence of Gypsy compilation is a problem. The most difficult problem is the interlevel mapping problem, showing that the concrete disk implements the abstract file system.

Any additional users of technology (outside of development group):
Gypsy has been used for a variety of specifications and a more limited number of programs.

Additional remarks:
None.

UNISEX

Primary participants (project leader, group members):
Richard Kemmerer, Steve Eckmann, Dan Solis

Survey contact:
Richard Kemmerer
Computer Science Dept., University of California, Santa Barbara, CA 93106

Country (or countries) of origin: USA

Level of effort (person-years, duration):
5 person-years over 4 years.

Brief description:
Symbolic executer for testing and formally verifying Pascal programs. Imple-

mented in Franz Lisp. Runs on VAX and Sun workstations under Unix. Interactive.

Accomplishments:
[None given.]

Representative published articles or reports:
R.A. Kemmerer and S.T. Eckmann. "UNISEX: A UNIx-based Symbolic EXecutor for Pascal." *Software Practice and Experience* 15(5):439-458, May 1985.

S. Eckmann and R.A. Kemmerer. "A User's Manual for the UNISEX System." TRCS83-05, Dept. of Computer Science, University of California, Santa Barbara, CA, December 1983 (revised April 1985).

D.M. Solis, R.A. Kemmerer, and S.T. Eckmann. "UNISEX Pascal Language Reference Manual." TRCS83-06, Dept. of Computer Science, University of California, Santa Barbara, CA, December 1983 (revised April 1985).

Current status of development:
Minimum maintenance

Date of project commencement:
c. 1981

Date of completion (as a research project):
c. 1985

Date of completion (as a product or deliverable):
c. 1985

Intended evolution:
Maintain as needed for new Sun workstation architecture. May port to Common Lisp.

Particular strengths and weaknesses:
User friendly, free, available outside of US, good teaching tool.

Any additional users of technology (outside of development group):
Universities and limited industry in US, Italy, Japan, Germany.

Additional remarks:
[None.]

VERDI

Primary participants (project leader, group members):
Distributed Computing Group, Software Technology Program, MCC

Survey contact:
Vincent Y. Shen
MCC, 3500 W. Balcones Center Dr., Austin, TX 78759
Tel: (512) 338-3345
e-mail: shen@mcc.com

Country (or countries) of origin: USA

Level of effort (person-years, duration):
12 person-years so far

Brief description:
VERDI is a visual environment for designing distributed systems. It is based on a design language called Raddle, which includes several high-level constructs: multi-party interaction communication primitive; non-deterministic choice structure; and systematic encapsulation of concurrent processes for large systems. VERDI allows a designer to formally specify, test, and model the performance of the target system in prototype form. These tasks are made easier using the latest in interactive color graphics. Our aim is to enable the designer to evaluate alternative designs objectively before implementation.

We have integrated VERDI with a hypertext tool called Germ. The designer can store design diagrams alongside less formal information, such as design rationale and test results. This integrated environment supports visual browsing through large networks of alternative designs and refinements.

Accomplishments:
We successfully used the alpha version of VERDI to design the beta version; we also used the beta version to design performance monitors that are parts of the formal release version. VERDI is now installed at about 25 sites in MCC's shareholder companies. It is used in design applications, in training, and in marketing situations.

Representative published articles or reports:
Michael Evangelist, Vincent Shen, Ira Forman, and Mike Graf. "Using Raddle to design distributed systems." In *Proceedings of the 10th International Conference on Software Engineering*, April 1988, 102-110.

Vincent Y. Shen, Charles Richter, Michael L. Graf, and Jeffrey A. Brumfield. "VERDI: a Visual Environment for Designing Distributed Systems." *Journal of Parallel and Distributed Computing* 8(6), June 1990.

Current status of development:
Post-release maintenance; features to support designing systems with real-time constraints planned.

Date of project commencement:
Mid-1986.

Date of completion (as a research project):
[Not given.]

Date of completion (as a product or deliverable):
VERDI 3.0 released in September 1989.

Intended evolution:
[Not given.]

Particular strengths and weaknesses:
[Not given.]

Any additional users of technology (outside of development group):
[Not given.]

Additional remarks:
[None.]

VERITAS+, A broad-spectrum specification language based on dependent types

Primary participants (project leader, group members):
F.K. Hanna, Neil Daeche. Sponsored by the UK Science and Engineering Research Council.

Survey contact:
Dr. Keith Hanna, Faculty of Information Technology,
University of Kent, Canterbury, Kent CT2 7NT, UK
Tel: 0227-764000
Fax: 0227 456084
email: fkh@ukc.ac.uk

Country (or countries) of origin: UK

Level of effort (person-years, duration):
12 person-years

Brief description:
VERITAS+ is a higher-order logic designed for use as a broad-spectrum specification language and for supporting formal verification. It has a particularly expressive type structure, inherited in part from intuitionistic type theory, that allows specifications to be cast in a form that closely mirrors their intuitive content. The type constructions included dependent Pi and Sigma types, datatypes and subtypes; all function definitions are total by construction.

The logic is formally defined using the Algebraic Approach, a development of the Edinburgh LCF approach in which the logic, viewed meta-linguistically, appears as a heterogeneous partial algebra. The formal definition takes the form of a script, about 1800 lines long written and in a purely functional programming language, that defines the abstract syntax of the logic (both terms and derivations). Augmented with support tools (parsers, goal-directed proof editors, etc), this same script doubles as an efficient implementation of the logic.

Accomplishments:
The logic has been extensively used in hardware specification, verification and synthesis, in applications ranging from the verification of the detailed timing properties of complex flipflops [1] and the generic verification of a whole class of iterative arithmetic circuits (in which the dependent types were extensively exploited) [2] to the combined sythesis and verification of simple arithmetic circuits [3].

Representative published articles or reports:

1. "Specification and Verification using Higher-Order Logic: A Case Study." pp. 179-213, *Formal Aspects of VLSI Design,* ed. Milne and Subrahmanyam, North Holland, 1986.

2. "VERITAS+, A Specification Language based on Type Theory." in *Proc of Workshop on Hardware Specification, Verification and Synthesis: Mathematical Aspects,* Cornell University, 1989 (Proceedings to appear in LNCS, Springer-Verlag).

3. "Formal Synthesis of Digital Systems." pp. 532-548, *Proc. IFIP Workshop*

on Applied Formal Methods for Correct VLSI Design, North Holland, 1989.

Current status of development:
Full set of software (available under licence) for Sun-3 workstations. Released system includes infrastructure of useful theory presentations and proofs.

Date of project commencement:
1983

Date of completion (as a research project):
Ongoing.

Date of completion (as a product or deliverable):
Ongoing.

Intended evolution:
We hope to undertake large-scale formal verification of hardware and low-level software. We are presently investigating a goal-driven approach to production of high-integrity hardware that we have named Formal Synthesis. Starting from a behavioural spec, and accepting guidance from a user, one ends up with a VLSI implementation (expressed in SOLO) and a formal proof of its correctness.

Particular strengths and weaknesses:
Strengths: Rigorous definition of object logic (VERITAS+). A convincing demonstration of the benefits of dependent types for readable, natural specifications. Full mathematical notation on input and output. Proofs can be edited and stored.

Weaknesses: Documentation incomplete. Tactics (for automated proofs) not yet fully developed. Relatively slow implementation at present.

Any additional users of technology (outside of development group):
[None given.]

Additional remarks:
[None.]

VIP

Primary participants (project leader, group members):
Staff from Praxis, OCE, DNL, Maths Centrum Amsterdam

Survey contact:
Mel Jackson
Praxis, 20 Manvers Street, Bath BA1 1PX, UK
Tel: +44 (225) 444700
Fax: +44 (225) 465205
email: ...uunet!mcvax!ukc!praxis!mel

Country (or countries) of origin: UK, NL

Level of effort (person-years, duration):
Approximately 20 person-years over 3 years.

Brief description:
VIP is an ESPRIT project to describe interfaces of the Portable Common Tools Environment in VDM. PCTE can be thought of as Unix plus an object store. VDM had to be extended to handle temporal and concurrent issues.

Accomplishments:
The description was completed.

Representative published articles or reports:
There are ESPRIT technical reports. The interface definition in VDM is available.

Current status of development:
Finished.

Date of project commencement:
1986

Date of completion (as a research project):
1989

Date of completion (as a product or deliverable):
1989

Intended evolution:
We hope VIP will be used to manage PCTE evolution.

Particular strengths and weaknesses:
[None given.]

Any additional users of technology (outside of development group):
[None given.]

Additional remarks:
[None.]

Zork (Recently renamed CADiZ)

Primary participants (project leader, group members):
John McDermid, Ian Toyn

Survey contact:
John McDermid, Department of Computer Science,
University of York, Heslington, York, UK YO1 5DD
Tel: +44 904 432726
Fax: +44 904 432767
EARN e-mail: jam@minster.york.ac.uk
UUNET e-mail: ukc!minster!jam
ARPA e-mail: jam%york.minster@nss.cs.ucl.ac.uk

Country (or countries) of origin: UK

Level of effort (person-years, duration):
1 year over 12 years

Brief description:
CADiZ is a tool that performs syntax, scope and type checks on Z specifications. It also prettyprints them and arranges for them to be typeset. CADiZ supports interactive mouse-driven browsing of the resulting specifications, allowing inspection of declaration dependencies, types, signatures, and so on.

CADiZ is an effective tool both for specifiers and for readers of specifications.

Accomplishments:

CADiZ caters for the entire Z language as defined at Oxford, plus extensions such as separate checking of imported documents. Sennett's Z specification of a Z type-checker was used as the basis for implementing CADiZ's type-checker. CADiZ is implemented in C for Sun M68000-based UNIX workstations. It has been ported to a clipper-based processor, but without the interactive browsing component. These accomplishments were aided by reuse of existing UNIX tools and of code produced in previous research projects.

Representative published articles or reports:

None yet.

Current status of development:

Tidying up implementation ready for release, which will be through York Software Engineering Limited (not the Department of Computer Science, but at the same address). Also writing about work done so far. The current implementation uses AT&T's ditroff typesetting software.

Date of project commencement:

October 1988

Date of completion (as a research project):

February 1992

Date of completion (as a product or deliverable):

First release expected May 1990.

Intended evolution:

The browsing component is being ported to the X window system. The intention is to provide wider tool support for the manipulation of Z specifications.

Particular strengths and weaknesses:

Strengths: Covers whole of Z language. Optional interactive mouse-driven browsing. Integrated with existing document preparation tools. Portability through UNIX and C.

Weaknesses: Requires around 1Mbyte of memory before it willll run comfortably, and more if the optional browsing component is used.

Any additional users of technology (outside of development group):

A release of CADiZ is being tested within Plessey.

Additional remarks:

None.

F   Acronyms

AECB	Atomic Energy Control Board (of Canada)
AECL	Atomic Energy of Canada, Ltd.
BDL	Box Description Language
CAD	Computer-Aided Design
CAFR	Computer-Aided Formal Reasoning
CICS	Customer Information Control System
CLI	Computational Logic Inc.
CSP	Communicating Sequential Processes
DARPA	Defense Advanced Research Projects Agency (USA)
DBMS	Database Management System
DFD	Data Flow Diagram
DND	Department of National Defence (Canada)
DoD	Department of Defense (USA)
FFBD	Functional Flow Block Diagram
FMEA	Failure Mode Effects Analysis
HOL	Higher Order Logic
IDEF0	Integrated Definition Language 0
IEC	International Electrotechnical Commission
JSP	Jackson Structured Programming
LCF	Logic of Computable Functions
MoD	Ministry of Defence (UK)
OWR	One Way Regulator
PDL	Program Design Language
RDD	Requirements Driven Development
VDM	Vienna Development Methodology
VLSI	Very large scale integration

G Copyrights and Trademarks

The copyright to *Illustrative Risks to the Public in the Use of Computers and Related Technology* is held by Peter G. Neumann. Authorization for reproduction of the illustrative risks must be obtained from Mr. Neumann. Mr. Neumann can be contacted at the Computer Science Lab., SRI International, Menlo Park, CA 94025-3493, USA.

The following registered trademarks are proprietary to their respective organizations.

- ELLA
- Ina Jo
- Lucid
- MS-DOS
- Oracle
- OSF
- POSIX
- RAISE
- RDD
- RSL
- Spade
- Statemate
- UNIX
- VHDL
- X/OPEN

References

[AFB* 89] Alspaugh, Faulk, Britton, Parker, Parnas, Shore. *Software Requirements for the A7-E Aircraft*. NRL Report 9194, 1989.

[ALC] *The Developer* 1(1). Available from Ascent Logic Corp., Suite 200, 180 Rose Orchard Way, San Jose, CA 95134, n.d.

[Alf 85] Mack Alford. "SREM at the Age of Eight." *IEEE Computer*, April 1985.

[AW 78] T. Anderson and R.W. Witty. "Safe programming." *BIT* 18:1–8, 1978.

[AL 86] A. Avižienis and J-C Laprie. "Dependable computing: from concepts to design diversity." *Proc. of IEEE* 74(5):629–638, May 1986.

[Avi 85] Algirdas Avižienis. "The *N*-Version approach to fault-tolerant software." *IEEE Transactions on Software Engineering* SE-11(12):1491–1501, December 1985.

[Bar 89] Jon Barwise. "Mathematical proofs of computer system correctness." *Notices of the AMS*, 1989. To appear.

[BDFKN86] P.C. Baker, G.W. Dinolt, J.W. Freeman, M. Krenzin, R.B. Neely. "A1 Assurance for an Internet System: Doing the Job." *Proc. 9th NBS/NCSC National Computer Security Conference*. 15–18 September 1986, p. 130–137.

[Bev 87a] William R. Bevier. *A Verified Operating System Kernel*. Ph.D. Thesis, The University of Texas at Austin, 1987.

[Bev 87b] William R. Bevier. *A Verified Operating System Kernel*. Technical Report CLI-11, Computational Logic Inc., October 1987.

[Bev 89a] William R. Bevier, Warren A. Hunt, Jr., J Strother Moore, William D. Young. "An Approach to Systems Verification." *The Journal of Automated Reasoning* 5(4), November 1989.

[Bev 89b] William R. Bevier. "Kit and the Short Stack." *The Journal of Automated Reasoning* 5(4), November 1989.

[Boy 88] Robert S. Boyer, J.Strother Moore II. *A Computational Logic Handbook*. Academic Press, 1988.

[BP 81] Britton, Parnas. *A-7E Software Module Guide*. NRL Memorandum Report 4702, December 1981.

[But 88] Ricky W. Butler. "Fault-Tolerant Clock Synchronization Techniques for Avionics Systems." *Proc. AIAA/AHS/ASEE Aircraft Design, Systems and Operations Conference*, September 7–9, 1988.

[CDM 86] A. Currit, M. Dyer, H. Mills. "Certifying the Reliability of Software" *IEEE Transactions on Software Engineering* SE-12(1):3-11, January 1986.

[Coh 89]   Avra Cohn. "The notion of proof in hardware verification." *Journal of Automated Reasoning* 5(2):127–139, June 1989.

[CPPSB 89]   Clements, Parker, Parnas, Shore, Britton. *A Standard Organization for Specifying Abstract Interfaces.* NRL Report 8815, June, 1984.

[DLSSH 88]   D.F. Denning, T.F. Lunt, R.R. Schell, W.R. Shockley, M. Heckman. "The Seaview Security Model." *Proc. IEEE Symposium on Security and Privacy,* 1988, p. 218–233.

[DFN 88]   G.W. Dinolt, J. Freeman, R. Neely. "An Internet System Security Policy and Formal Model." *Proc. 11th NBS/NCSC National Computer Security Conference,* 17–20 October 1988, p. 10–19.

[Dij 76]   E.W. Dijkstra. *A Discipline of Programming.* Prentice-Hall, 1976.

[DLP 79]   Richard A. De Millo, Richard J. Lipton, and Alan J. Perlis. "Social processes and proofs of theorems and programs." *Communications of the ACM* 22(5):271–280, May 1979.

[DoD 85]   *Department of Defense Trusted Computer System Evaluation Criteria.* Department of Defense, December 1985. DOD 5200.28-STD (supersedes CSC-STD-001-83).

[Fet 88]   James H. Fetzer. "Program verification: the very idea." *Communications of the ACM* 31(9):1048–1063, September 1988.

[FKR 79]   L. E. Fairbanks, R. P. Kurlak, K. W. Ramby. "F-18 Flight Control Fault Tolerant (sic) Design." *Proc. Third Digital Avionics System Conference,* November 1979.

[Ger 79]   S. L. Gerhart and D. S. Wile. "Preliminary report on the Delta experiment: specification and verification of a multiple-user file updating module." *Proc. of the Conference on Specification of Reliable Software,* IEEE Computer Society, April 1979, pp. 198-211.

[Gor 87]   M.J.C. Gordon. "HOL: A Proof Generating System for Higher-Order Logic." In *VLSI Specification, Verification and Synthesis,* G. Birtwistle and P.A. Subrahmanyam (eds), Kluwer, 1987.

[Gor 89]   M.J.C. Gordon. "Mechanizing Programming Logics in Higher Order Logic." In *Current Trends in Hardware Verification and Automated Theorem Proving,* G. Birtwistle and P.A. Subrahmanyam (eds), Springer-Verlag, 1989.

[Gri 81]   D. Gries. *The Science of Computer Programming.* Springer-Verlag, 1981.

[Gut 78]   J. V. Guttag, E. Horowitz and D. R. Musser. "Abstract data types and software validation." *CACM* 21:1048-1064, December 1978.

[Hay 85]   Ian Hayes. *Specifying the CICS Application Programmer's Interface.* Oxford Programming Research Group Technical Monograph PRG-47, 1985.

[Hay 87]   Ian Hayes (ed). *Specification Case Studies.* Prentice-Hall International
           Computer Science Series, 1987.

[HS 85]   C.A.R. Hoare and J.C. Shepherdson (eds). *Mathematical Logic and Pro-
           gramming Languages.* Prentice-Hall International Series in Computer
           Science, 1985.

[Hun 85]   Warren A. Hunt Jr. *FM8501: A Verified Microprocessor.* Ph.D. Thesis,
           The University of Texas at Austin, 1985.

[Hun 87]   Warren A. Hunt Jr. *The Mechanical Verification of a Microporcessor
           Design.* Technical Report CLI-6, Computational Logic Inc., 1987.

[Hun 89]   Warren A. Hunt, Jr. "Microprocessor Design Verification." *The Journal
           of Automated Reasoning* 5(4), November 1989.

[IEC94]   *Safety Critical Software.* IEC Standard SC65A/Secretariat/94 (available
           from national standards organizations).

[IEC96]   *Safety Critical Systems.* IEC Standard SC65A/Secretariat/96 (available
           from national standards organizations).

[IEE 89]   *Software in Safety Related Systems* (ISBN 0852 963912), publ. IEE (UK)
           1989. (IEE telephone 01-240-1871)

[Jac 89]   Jonathan Jacky. "Programmed for disaster: Software errors that imperil
           lives." *The Sciences* (September/October 1989):22–27.

[JL 89]   M.S. Jaffe and N.G. Leveson. *Completeness, Robustness, and Safety in
           Real-Time Software Requirements Specification.* University of California
           at Irvine, Technical Report 89-01, 15 February 1989. (A shortened ver-
           sion is included in the *Proceedings of the 1989 International Conference
           on Software Engineering*, ICSE-11.)

[Jon 80]   Cliff B. Jones. *Software Development: A Rigorous Aproach.* Prentice-
           Hall, 1980.

[Jon 86]   Cliff B. Jones. *Systematic Software Development Using VDM.* Prentice-
           Hall, 1986.

[Kau 88]   Matt Kaufmann. *A User's Manual for an Interactive Enhancement to
           the Boyer-Moore Theorem Prover.* Technical Report 19, Computational
           Logic Inc., 1988.

[Kem 86]   Richard A. Kemmerer. *Verification Assessment Study Final Report.* C3-
           CR01-86, Library No. S-228,204, National Computer Security Center,
           Fort George Meade, MD, March 1986.

[KMU 79]   R. L. Kisslinger, W. J. Momeno, J. M. Urnes. "Design and Development
           of the Digital Flight Control System (DFCS) for the F-18." *Proc. Third
           Digital Avionics System Conference*, November 1979.

[Lala 86]   J. H. Lala. "Fault Detection, Isolation and Reconfiguration in the Fault Tolerant Multiprocessor." *Journal of Guidance, Control and Dynamics* 9(5):585-592, September-October 1986.

[Lan 83]   Carl Landwehr. "The Best Available Technologies for Computer Security." *IEEE Computer* 16(7), July 1983, p. 86–100.

[Lan 89]   Carl Landwehr. "The RS-232 Software Repeater Problem." *IEEE Security and Privacy Cipher Newsletter*, Summer 1989, p. 34–35.

[Lap 85]   J.C. Laprie. "Dependable computing and fault tolerance: Concepts and terminology." In *Digest of Papers, FTCS 15*, Ann Arbor, MI, June 1985, IEEE Computer Society, p. 2–11.

[Lev 86]   Nancy G. Leveson. "Software safety: Why, what and how." *ACM Computing Surveys* 18(2):125–163, June 1986.

[LH 83]   N.G. Leveson and P.R. Harvey. Analyzing software safety. *IEEE Transactions on Software Engineering*, SE-9(5):569–579, September 1983.

[LK 86]   J.C. Knight and N.G. Leveson. "An Experimental Evaluation of the Assumption of Independence in Multiversion Programming." *IEEE Transactions on Software Engineering* SE-12(1):96-109, January 1986.

[LM 88]   R. Linger and H. Mills. "A Case Study in Cleanroom Software Engineering: The IBM COBOL Structuring Facility." *Proc. COMPSAC '88*, IEEE, 1988.

[LSSHW 88] T. Lunt, R.R. Schell, W.R. Shockley, M. Heckman, D. Warren. "A Near-Term Design for the Sea Views Multilevel Database System." *Proc. IEEE Symposium on Security and Privacy*, 1988, p. 234–244.

[McH 74]   John McHugh. "Design and Construction Proof of a Real-time Program." Master's paper, Computer Science Dept., University of Maryland, 1974.

[Mil 80]   J. Millen and D. L. Drake. "An Experiment with *Affirm* and HDM." *Journal of Systems and Software*, December 1981.

[Mil 88]   H. Mills. "Stepwise Refinement and Verification in Box Structured Systems" *IEEE Computer*, p. 23-36, June 1988

[MIL-STD-882B] *System Safety Program Requirements.* U.S. DoD, U.S. Government Office, March 1984.

[MMS 87]   Louise Moser, Michael Melliar-Smith, Design Verification of SIFT, NASA CR-4097, September 1987.

[MoD 89a]   U.K. Ministry of Defence, *Requirements for the Procurement of Safety Critical Software in Defence Equipment.* Interim Defence Standard 00-55, May 1989.

[MoD 89b]   U.K. Ministry of Defence, *Requirements for the Analysis of Safety Critical Hazards.* Interim Defence Standard 00-56, May 1989.

[Moo 88]   J Strother Moore. *PITON: A Verified Assembly Level Language.* Technical Report CLI-22, Computational Logic Inc., June 1988.

[Moo 89]   J Strother Moore. "A Mechanically Verified Language Implementation." *The Journal of Automated Reasoning* 5(4), November 1989.

[MS 81]   P.M. Melliar-Smith and R. Schwartz. "Current Progress on the Proof of SIFT." IEEE, *Proc. FTCS-11*, June 1981.

[MS 89]   David R. Musser and Alexander A. Stepanov. *The Ada Generic Library; Linear List Processing Packages.* Springer-Verlag, 1989.

[Nau 82]   Peter Naur. "Formalization in program development." *BIT* 22:437–453, 1982.

[Neu 86]   P.G. Neumann. "On Hierarchical Design of Computer Systems for Critical Applications." *IEEE Trans. Software Engineering* SE-12(9):905-920, September 1986.

[Neu 89a] P.G. Neumann. "Risks: Cumulative index of Software Engineering Notes – Illustrative risks to the public." *ACM Software Engineering Notes*, January 1991; also in January 1987 and January 1989. (This index contains references to many cases discussed in SEN, including highlights from the on-line ACM Forum on Risks to the Public in the Use of Computers and Related Systems.)

[Neu 89b] P.G. Neumann. "Flaws in Specifications and What to Do About Them." *Proc. Fifth International Workshop on System Specification and Design,* Pittsburgh, 19-20 May 1989, In *Software Engineering Notes* 14(3):xi-xv, May 1989.

[NP 89]   P.G. Neumann and D.B. Parker. "A Summary of Techniques for Computer Misuse." *12th National Computer Security Conference*, Baltimore, MD, 10-13 October 1989.

[Oak 89]   Oakland 1989 Proceedings.

[O'Ha 87] Colin O'Halloran. *The Software Repeater (An Exercise in Z Specification).* RSRE Memo. No. 4090, MOD RSRE, Malvern, Worcs., England, October 1987.

[Par 86]   David L. Parnas. "Can Software for the Strategic Defense Initiative ever be Error-free?" *IEEE Computer* 19(11), November 1986.

[Par 88]   David L. Parnas. *Evaluation Standards for Safety Critical Software.* Techncial Report 88-220, Queen's University, Kingston, May 1988.

[Par 89]   David Parnas *Education for Computing Professionals.* Technical Report 89-247, Dept. of Computing and Information Science, Queen's University, Kingston, March 1989.

[PB 86]   Daniel L. Palumbo and Ricky W. Butler. "A Performance Evaluation of the Software-Implemented Fault-Tolerance Computer." *Journal of Guidance, Control and Dynamics* 9(2):175-180, March-April 1986.

[Pro 89]   ProCoS: Provably Correct Systems. Annex 1, Technical Annex for ES-
             PRIT Basic Research Action 3104, April 2nd, 1989.

[Pro 90]   Anders P. Ravn and Victoria Stavridou. "Specification and Development
             of Safety Critical Software: An Assessment of MoD Draft Standard 00-
             55." In Proceedings for *Industrial Experience Using Formal Methods*,
             ICSE12 Workshop, 1990.

[PS 85]   M. Paul and H. J. Siegert (eds). "Distributed Systems: Methods
             and Tools for Specification." *Lectures in Computer Science*, Vol. 190,
             Springer-Verlag, 1985.

[PWCB 83]   Parnas, Weiss, Clements, Britton. *Interface Specifications for the SCR
             (A-7E) Extended Computer Module*. NRL Memorandum Report 4843,
             January 1983 (revised 5/9/83).

[RH 89]   John Rushby and Friedrich von Henke. *Formal Verification of the In-
             teractive Convergence Clock Synchronization Algorithm using EHDM*.
             SRI-CSL-89-3, February 1989.

[Ros 81]   E. Rosen. "Vulnerabilities of Network Control Protocols." *ACM Software
             Engineering Notes* 6(1):6-8, January 1981.

[SBL 89]   O. Sami Saydjari, Joseph M. Beckman, Jeffrey R. Leaman. "LOCK Trek:
             Navigating Uncharted Space." *Proc. IEEE Symp. on Security and Pri-
             vacy*, 1-3 May 1989, p. 167–175.

[SJ 89]   Roger Shaw and Cliff Jones. *Case Studies in System Software Develop-
             ment*. Prentice-Hall International Computer Science Series, September
             1989.

[Spivey88]   J.M. Spivey. *Understanding Z*. Cambridge University Press, Cambridge,
             1988.

[Spivey89]   J.M. Spivey. *The Z Notation: A Reference Manual*. Prentice-Hall, 1989.

[Tho 81]   D. H. Thompson, S. L. Gerhart, R. W. Erickson, S. Lee and R. L.
             Bates. *The Affirm Reference Library*. USC/Information Sciences Insti-
             tute, January 1981. (Five volumes: Reference Manual, User's Guide,
             Type Library, Annotated Transcripts, and Collected Papers; 450 pages.)

[UK 87]   UK Health and Safety Executive. *Programmable Electronic Systems in
             Safety Related Applications*. Vol 1 "Introductory Guide" (ISBN 011
             8839136), Vol 2 "General Technical Guidelines" (ISBN 011 8839063),
             publ. HMSO 1987.

[Ver 80]   Verification Workshop. Proceedings in *ACM Software Engineering Notes*
             5(3), July 1980.

[Ver 81]   Verification Workshop. Proceedings in *ACM Software Engineering Notes*
             6(3), July 1981.

[Ver 85]   Verification Workshop. Proceedings in *ACM Software Engineering Notes* 10(4), August 1985.

[Wal 85]   S.T. Walker. "Network Security Overview." *Proc. IEEE Symposium on Security and Privacy*, 22–24 April 1985, p. 62–76.

[WD 89]   John C. Williams and George W. Dinolt. "Formal Model of a Trusted File Server." *Proc. IEEE Symposium on Security and Privacy*, 1–3 May 1989, p. 157–166.

[WLG 78]   J.H. Wensley, L. Lamport, J. Goldberg, M.W. Green, K.N. Levitt, P.M. Melliar-Smith, R.E. Shostak, and C.B. Weinstock. "SIFT: Design and Analysis of a Fault-tolerant Computer for Aircraft Control." *Proc. IEEE* 66(10):1240-1255, October 1978.

[WL 89]   R.A. Whitehurst and T.F. Lunt. "The SeaView Verification Effort." *Proc. 12th National Computer Security Conference,* Baltimore, MD, 10-13 October 1989.

[Win 90]   Jeannette Wing. "What is a Formal Method?"   To appear in *IEEE Computer.*

[Wor 87]   J.B. Wordsworth. "Formal Methods in the Development of CICS." *Computer Bulletin,* December 1987.

[You 88]   William D. Young. *μ-Gypsy - A Verified Code Generator for a Subset of Gypsy.* Ph.D. Thesis, The University of Texas at Austin, 1988.

[You 89]   William D. Young. "A Mechanically Verified Code Generator." *The Journal of Automated Reasoning* 5(4), November 1989.

Index